The Great and the Near Great
A Century of Sports in Virginia

Abe Goldblatt and Robert W. Wentz, Jr.

The Great and the Near Great
A Century of Sports in Virginia
Abe Goldblatt and Robert W. Wentz, Jr.

Design by: Robert Cameron

The Donning Company/Publishers, Inc.
Norfolk, Virginia Beach

Copyright© 1976 by Abe Goldblatt and
Robert W. Wentz, Jr.

All rights reserved, including the right to reproduce this book in any form whatsoever without permission in writing from the publisher, except for brief passages in connection with a review. For information, write: The Donning Company/Publishers, Inc., 253 West Bute Street, Norfolk, Virginia 23510.

Printed in the United States of America

Library of Congress Cataloging in Publication Data

Goldblatt, Abe, 1915-
    The great and the near great.

    1. Sports—Virginia—History. 2. Athletes—Virginia—History. I. Wentz, Robert W., 1932-   joint author. II. Title.
GV584.V8G64   796'.09755   76-28315
ISBN 0-915442-07-8

Contents

Introduction 6
Baseball 8
  Once Virginia Had A Team In
    The Major Leagues 10
  Eppa Rixey 18
  Dave Robertson 20
  Chuck Stobbs 21
  Virginia Professional
    Baseball Leagues 22
  The Semipros 23
  Football 26
  The Pros 28
  Bill Dudley 28
  Ace Parker 32
  Pro Football in Virginia 42
  The Super All-Americans 46
  Gene McEver 48
  Beattie Feathers 49
  Frank Emanuel 50
  Jim Breland 51
  Leroy Keyes 52
  Jake Scott 53
  Walker Gillette 54
  Ron Rusnak 55
  Steve DeLong 56
  Frank Loria 57
Basketball 58
The Consensus
  All-Americans 60
  Glenn Roberts 62
  The Virginia Squires 65
The Olympians 68
  Thompson Mann 68
  Duane Bobick 69
  Steve Riddick 69
  Bob Richards 70
  Gray Simons 71
  Melissa Belote 72
  Larry Burton 73
Golf 74
  Slammin' Sam Snead 76
  Chandler Harper 77
  Vinny Giles 79
  Bobby Cruickshank 80
  Lanny Wadkins 81
  Curtis Strange 82
Boxing 84
  College Boxing 90
Tennis 92
  Norfolk Tennis Pair Won
    1911 U. S. Title 94
  When William & Mary Won
    It All In Tennis 94
  With a South American Touch,
    Hampton Institute Won
    The Nationals 96
Stock Car Racing 98
  Joe Weatherly 107
Horse Racing 108
  Riva Ridge And Secretariat's
    Fantastic Triple Crown 110
  Norfolk Went to the Races ... 112
  The Virginia Gold Cup 114
Hockey 116
The Colleges & Universities .. 118
  The University of Virginia .. 120
  Hampden-Sydney College 128
  Virginia Military Institute .. 132
  Virginia Tech 138
  Washington & Lee University . 144
  Virginia Union 150
  College of William and Mary .. 152
  Randolph-Macon College 158
  University of Richmond 164
  Hampton Institute 172
  Norfolk State College 174
  Roanoke College 176
  Virginia State College 178
  Virginia Commonwealth
    University 182
  Emory & Henry College 184
  Ferrum College 188
  Madison College 190
  Old Dominion University 194
  Bridgewater College 198
  Lynchburg College 200
The High Schools 202
  The Longest Winning Streak .. 209
  Washington-Lee High
    School Crew 212
Extra Innings 214
  A Champion on Water 216
  Dick Shea 217
  Handball 218
  Surfing 219
  Walking and Running 220
  Fishing 221
Coliseums of Virginia 222
The Great Seal of Virginia ... 223
Statistical Index 224
Acknowledgements 232

Introduction

*Far off I hear the rolling, roaring cheers.
They come to me from many
  yesteryears,
From record deeds that cross the fading
  years,
And light the landscape with their
  brilliant plays,
Great stars that knew their days in
  fame's bright sun.
I hear them tramping into oblivion.*
  —*Grantland Rice*

This is a book about our great teams and sports heroes who have become a vital part of Virginia folklore. Our efforts to record their countless deeds into a single book have been a gigantic but fascinating experience.

We aimed to highlight the exploits of the Old Dominion's sports immortals, and the lesser lights, too, as fairly and accurately as possible. If, by chance, we failed to touch all bases, it was an oversight not intended.

It required more than a year of extensive research and considerable teamwork of many to put it all together. Therefore, we are grateful to those who helped make our task easier, particularly the sports writers and college sports information directors of Virginia. Without them, this book wouldn't have been possible. Their vast knowledge and personal on-the-scene observations at sports events through the years proved to be an invaluable source.

But the chief collaborators were those who played the game, the great and near great. After all, this is their book.

Abe Goldblatt
Robert W. Wentz, Jr.

Baseball

ONCE VIRGINIA HAD A TEAM IN THE MAJOR LEAGUES

Off and on, organized baseball has been a way of life in Virginia since before the turn of the century. But who knows when it really started? Newspaper files reveal that Union soldiers played a game called baseball during their occupation of Norfolk during the Civil War.

But it may surprise you to learn that Virginia once had a major league team. In 1884, nineteen years after Lee surrendered to Grant, Richmond represented the Old Dominion in the American Association.

The American Association was then a rival of the National League. Like so many other clubs in the infant big leagues, Richmond was unable to meet the budget on twenty-five cents admission, and the Virginia team survived only a year.

Despite an inglorious finish several years later, the American Association played a valuable role in baseball history, pioneering reforms the National League eventually adopted, like league control of umpires, Sunday baseball and the percentage system of determining winners.

Since then, there have been 42 Virginia cities and towns with pro baseball teams at one time or another. Beginning with the Virginia League in 1896, the game has met with many financial disasters, with clubs and leagues folding through the years.

In the 1920s, a blue law prohibiting the playing of pro baseball on Sunday was blamed for the Virginia League's collapse. When the Sunday ban was lifted and night baseball introduced, Richmond, Norfolk and Portsmouth revived baseball in the 1930s as members of the Piedmont League. The Piedmont was one of the few leagues in the country that survived World War II, which drained most of the manpower, leaving those unfit to fight (4-Fs) and those too old for Uncle Sam's Armed Forces to carry on the national pastime. And taking everything in consideration, they did it in fine style.

Although forced to play mostly twilight games because of blackout restrictions, attendance was good during the war years. The post-war years proved most profitable to the owners and, in 1949, every Virginia team in the Piedmont League surpassed 100,000 in attendance. But the prosperity didn't last long. Attendance declined in the 1950s when fans decided to stay home and watch a new fad—television.

But Virginia ballparks were the springboard to the major leagues for many stars. Tommy Leach, the famous third baseman of the Pittsburgh Pirates, played for Petersburg and Hampton in 1896.

Al Orth, who became known as the "Curveless Wonder," pitched for Lynchburg in 1894-95. In 15 major league seasons, the righthander won 204 games.

Christy Mathewson was a sensation for the Norfolk Tars in the Virginia League in 1900, winning 20 of 22 starts before stepping up to the New York Giants and immortality.

But Virginia League fans never knew Christy by his right name while he toiled in 1900. A Norfolk sports writer called him Mathews in the season opener. The modest and gentlemanly righthander, a Bucknell College football hero, never bothered to set the writer straight on his error, and throughout the season he was known as Mathews in the box scores and stories.

Playing for 80 dollars a month in Norfolk, Christy's contract was sold to the Giants for 1,500 dollars. It was a conditional deal. When he failed to show much in his first few games, Christy was returned to Norfolk and the Cincinnati Reds drafted him for 100 dollars and then traded him back to the Giants. Under John McGraw, Mathewson began to roll in 1902. Over a period of 12 years, starting in 1903, he never won fewer than 22 games in a season, and four times he won 30 or more. He won 373 National League games.

The rest is history. In 1936, Mathewson was one of the first five to be voted into the Hall of Fame at Cooperstown, New York.

Win Clark was the "Grand Old Man" of baseball in Virginia. His career covered more than a half century as a player, manager and executive.

Win was playing-manager of the Portsmouth Truckers when Mathewson broke in with Norfolk. Playing second base, Win laced a single through the infield off Mathewson.

"I had some remarks to say to Matty after that hit," Clark said. "Matty, very serious, turned to me and said, 'Young fellow, you'll never get another hit off me.'

"I never did either."

When Win died he was serving as secretary of the Professional Ball Players of America, an organization he helped form to give financial assistance to needy former players.

When Christy left to join the Giants, all teams but Norfolk and Portsmouth's Truckers folded because of rising financial difficulties. The twin-city rivals decided to play out the season in order to protect their players for the following years.

It turned out to be a hectic series, probably the longest in baseball history (40 games). There was so much bickering about the umpires, who feared for life and limb from the boisterous players and fans alike, that, on several occasions, John L. Sullivan and James J. Corbett, the heavyweight champions, were brought in to umpire some games. Of course, there wasn't much arguing with them.

In 1920, Portsmouth sold Pie Traynor to the Pittsburgh Pirates for 10,000 dollars, a princely sum in those days. Traynor, who played shortstop in the Virginia League, rocketed to the top as one of the greatest third basemen in baseball history. He was elected to the Hall of Fame in 1948.

In 1924, Portsmouth developed another player destined for greatness. He was Hack Wilson, a colorful and unlikely-looking outfielder whose physical build was likened to a fire plug. Owner Frank D. Lawrence invited John McGraw to Portsmouth to look over the powerful slugger. After watching the Truckers, the Giant manager said he was interested in buying Kent Greenfield, a pitcher.

"What about Wilson?" Lawrence asked, surprised at McGraw's decision.

"He doesn't look like a ballplayer,"

One of the greatest players of all time at third base, Hall of Famer Pie Traynor made the jump from Portsmouth to the Pittsburgh Pirates.

The immortal Christy Mathewson got his start with the Norfolk Tars in the Virginia League in 1900.

McGraw replied, "and besides, he ain't got no neck."

Anyway, Lawrence induced McGraw to give Wilson a chance and eventually received 10,000 dollars for him. But the Giants pulled one of the biggest blunders in baseball history. They put Hack on their triple-A list and forgot to recall him.

The Chicago Cubs quickly picked up the 5-foot-6, 195-pound outfielder for the draft price of 5,000 dollars, which turned out to be the biggest baseball bargain on record. In 1930, Hack hit 56 home runs for a National League record, and also batted in 190 runs, one of the oldest major league records to survive all assaults of the modern stars.

While Christy Mathewson's salary was only 80 dollars a month, the financial situation didn't improve appreciably for Yogi Berra 42 years later. In 1942, the New York Yankees signed Yogi, a 17-year-old catcher, for a 500 dollar bonus and 90 dollars a month, and assigned him to their Norfolk farm team in the Piedmont League.

The contract stipulated that Berra would receive the 500 dollar bonus only if he was retained until September 20, 1943. The Yankees retained him over 20 years, and his salary was eventually in excess of 60,000 dollars a year.

Yogi left his mark in Norfolk and the Piedmont League. He batted in 23 runs in two consecutive games, a rare feat in any league.

Berra was enshrined in the baseball Hall of Fame in 1972.

There have been many others who established themselves in the big leagues after playing on Virginia diamonds.

It was usually the custom every spring for some major league teams to stop off in Virginia cities, especially Norfolk and Richmond, to play exhibitions on their way home from spring training camps in Florida. These exhibitions usually drew capacity crowds, but none created the national attention that the Yankees did in a Norfolk visit.

Lou Gehrig established a remarkable playing record of 2,130 consecutive major league games from June 1, 1925, to April 30, 1939. But the streak almost ended when the New York Yankees played the Tars, their farmhands in the Piedmont League, at Norfolk on June 29, 1939.

In the second inning, Gehrig was hit in the right eye by a pitch thrown by Ray White, a young Tar righthander who, like Gehrig, was a former Columbia University star.

The "Iron Horse" slumped to the ground, unconscious. The 8,000 fans watched in silence, sensing the seriousness of the situation. Gehrig had played in 1,414 consecutive games, and it was feared the beaning would end the streak. He was helped off the field, a lump on the side of his head the size of an egg.

A worried Joe McCarthy, the Yankee manager, escorted Gehrig to the hospital, where X-rays were taken. News of the incident flashed over the wires to a stunned baseball world. Would the Iron Horse be able to return to the lineup and continue his streak?

But the next day at Washington, Gehrig was back in the lineup and smashed three consecutive triples to tie a major league record that never got into the books. The game was halted by rain in the bottom of the fifth with the Yankees leading, 4-1, wiping out all records of the contest.

The leagues that have been most significant in the state have been the Virginia League, Piedmont League, Carolina League, and International League.

In 1885-86, Richmond and Norfolk were listed as members of the Eastern League, and both cities had ill-fated experiences in this league in an attempt to revive the national pastime during the depression years of 1931-32.

Richmond has been the baseball leader in the Old Dominion. The Old Confederate capital regained admission to the International League in 1915 when Baltimore moved in after a crisis with the Federal League.

World War I brought in its wake a fresh crisis for the International League. A sharp decline in attendance forced Richmond, Providence and Montreal to drop out in favor of Jersey City, Binghamton, New York, and Syracuse.

In 1954, Richmond returned to the International League when the American League tapped Baltimore. Richmond baseball prospered that season when attendance hit 223,981. The Richmond turnstiles clicked to the merry tune of 258,861 in 1957, with a single game high of 13,395 for a contest with Jacksonville. It was the largest crowd ever to see a baseball game in the state.

Richmond was replaced by Toledo in 1965, but was back in the league in 1966, and won its first IL pennant in 1967 with Luman Harris at the helm.

Among the many stars who wore the Richmond uniform was Mel Stottlemyre, who pitched 10 consecutive victories, including six shutouts in the International League in 1964 and was named Minor League Player of the Year by *The Sporting News*. Stottlemyre later became a New York Yankee pitching ace.

In 1969, Richmond was joined by Tidewater, representing Portsmouth, Chesapeake, Norfolk and Virginia Beach, in the prestigious league. The New York Mets moved their IL franchise from Jacksonville to Tidewater, playing at Portsmouth's Lawrence Stadium and winning the pennant under Manager Clyde McCullough, who made Norfolk his home after serving in the U.S. Navy

Win Clark, called Virginia's Grand Old Man of Baseball, played against Christy Mathewson in old Virginia League as player-manager of Portsmouth. Served more than a half century as a player, manager and executive, and one of the most popular figures in the game until his death in 1959 at age 84.

Hack Wilson, who led the Virginia League in all slugging departments while playing with the Portsmouth Truckers in 1923. With Chicago Cubs in 1930 he set a National League record in homers (56) and a major league mark in runs-batted-in (190). Both records still stand.

Baseball Hall of Famer Yogi Berra started his career with the Norfolk Tars in the Piedmont League, 1943.

A Beanball Heard 'Round the Baseball World: Lou (Iron Horse) Gehrig of the New York Yankees being helped off the field after being hit in the head by a pitch during an exhibition game against the Norfolk Tars at Norfolk in 1939. The incident shook the baseball world. In jeopardy was Lou's remarkable playing streak. But Gehrig recovered and played the next day and went on to establish a major league playing record of 2,130 consecutive games.

during World War II. McCullough was voted Minor League Manager of the Year.

With a loan from the Mets, Norfolk built a new baseball stadium, which became the showcase of the International League in 1970, and in 1975 Tidewater won the pennant again with Joe Frazier in the pilot's seat. The Peninsula (Newport News-Hampton) had a fling in the IL in 1972-73.

From 1933 to 1955, the Piedmont League provided most baseball excitement for Virginia's major cities. Danville (1920-25) was the first Virginia city in the Piedmont, which was composed mostly of North Carolina cities. But in 1933, Richmond joined the league and was followed by Norfolk (1934), Portsmouth (1935), Roanoke (1943), Lynchburg (1943), and Newport News (1944). When the league collapsed in 1955, it was composed of all Virginia cities.

Herb Brett, a Portsmouth native and one of the last of the submarine pitchers, organized the Carolina League in 1945, and managed Danville to the pennant the very first season. Brett also piloted pennant-winners at Danville in

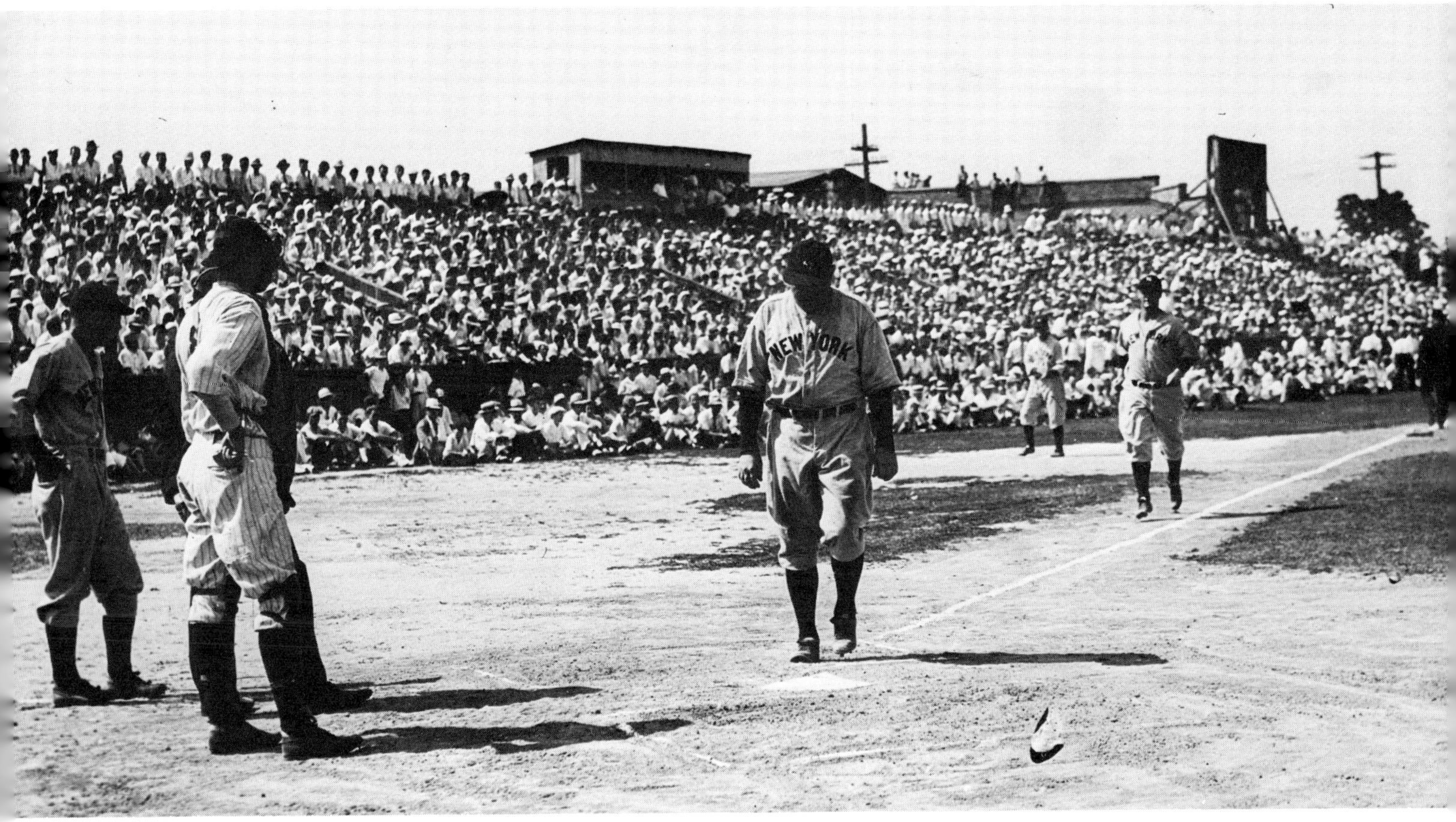

Babe Ruth and Lou Gehrig, perhaps the greatest one-two punch in baseball history, deliver runs during New York Yankees' exhibition game at Norfolk in 1930s. Gehrig, after belting a home run, is shown following Ruth to home plate. As the story goes, Ruth hit the longest home run on record at Norfolk. The ball landed on a Norfolk & Western freight train that was headed for Cincinnati.

1952 and 1953. Three times he was voted Carolina League Manager of the Year.

The Peninsula (Hampton-Newport News), Lynchburg and Salem are still members of the Carolina League.

Among the most successful and best-known baseball executives in Virginia were Frank Lawrence of Portsmouth, Eddie Mooers of Richmond and Henry P. Dawson of Norfolk. Mooers operated the Richmond franchise for many years. Dawson was general manager of the Yankees' Piedmont League operation in Norfolk, which

*Clyde McCullough managed the Tidewater Tides to pennant (1969), their first season in International League. **The Sporting News** selected McCullough, a former major league catcher who makes his home in Norfolk, Manager of the Year in the Minors.*

A pair of baseball greats, Frank D. Lawrence (left) with the immortal Connie Mack in a pre-game ceremony at Portsmouth before exhibition game with Mack's Philadelphia Athletics.

was considered one of the most successful in the minors for a dozen years.

For nearly a half century, Lawrence was known as the "Stormy Petrel of the Minors," a controversial figure who battled the rich major league operators on numerous issues. He won national acclaim in 1943 after his Portsmouth team captured the Piedmont League pennant, the city's first since 1927. *The Sporting News,* the baseball bible, named Lawrence the Minor League Executive of the Year.

The Piedmont League folded, but Lawrence, a prominent banker, didn't bow out without a fight. He sued the major leagues for $250,000, charging invasion of his territorial rights with the radio broadcasts and telecasts of big league games.

Lawrence struck out in a Supreme Court decision, and the majors sighed in relief. If Lawrence had won his case, it would have upset the entire baseball structure.

Lawrence's baseball career was marked by success and disappointments—and tragedy. On May 25, 1927 Lawrence invited Judge Kenesaw Mountain Landis, the iron-fisted commissioner of baseball, to Portsmouth as guest of honor at a Virginia League game. The High Street park, which Lawrence built in Norfolk County, on the outskirts of his city, in a fruitless effort to beat the ban on Sunday baseball, was packed with excited fans who came to get a glimpse of the commissioner.

Just before the start of the game with Petersburg, a 72-mile-per-hour squall struck, destroying the grandstand. Two persons were killed and 30 injured. Judge Landis escaped injury, but it was an experience he never forgot.

The next day, the Portsmouth players turned workers to restore the old field on Washington Street as much as possible. The game was played.

In the modern era, Hillman Lyons, Dave Rosenfield and Wallace McKenna stand out as baseball executives. Lyons, general manager of Richmond in the International League, was selected by *The Sporting News* as Minor League Executive of the Year.

Rosenfield has been on the job as general manager of the Tidewater Tides since 1963, first in the Carolina League and then in the International League. Like Lawrence, McKenna carved himself a baseball career in his home city. A Lynchburg native, McKenna has been a baseball executive since 1942, when he became business manager of Lynchburg in the Virginia League. In 1944, the St. Louis Cardinals elevated Lynchburg to the Piedmont League and McKenna became general manager and served in this capacity for ten years, including two (1952-53) as president-owner. In 1967, Lynchburg began play in the Carolina League under the Chicago White Sox and McKenna continued as general manager. He was voted Carolina League Executive of the Year in 1969, and the following year was elected league president, with league offices in Lynchburg. McKenna has served on many important baseball committees and was considered for the presidency of the National Association of Professional Baseball Leagues in December, 1975.

The ruins of the ballpark at Portsmouth following a tornado in 1927. Baseball Commissioner Landis, who cleaned up the game after the infamous Black Sox Scandal, was guest of honor at the Virginia League game and escaped without injury.

Dave Rosenfield as a young baseball executive... General Manager of Tidewater Tides since 1962... His trophy case holds two International League pennants (1969, 1975), two-time winner of Governor's Cup playoff championship (1972, 1975).

Wallace McKenna of Lynchburg, president of Carolina League, and, before taking this position, the operator of professional baseball in Lynchburg for many years.

Bob Humphreys, Hampden-Sydney's contribution to the major leagues. He pitched nine seasons in the majors, 1962-70, mostly in relief, with Detroit, St. Louis Cardinals, Chicago Cubs and the Washington Senators.

The first night baseball game in Tidewater, played at Portsmouth vs. Norfolk Tars, August 25, 1936, Piedmont League.

Richmond-born Granny Hamner, whose brother Wesley played for the Philadelphia Phillies and St. Louis Browns, was a full-fledged major leaguer, playing a major role for the famed Whiz Kids who won the National League pennant for the Phillies in 1950. An infielder playing most of the time at shortstop, Hamner batted .429 in the 1950 World Series but the Phillies lost to the New York Yankees in four games. Hamner spent 14 seasons with the Phillies. Hamner, who later managed Portsmouth in the Sally League in 1961 in a revival of organized baseball in the Tidewater area, was picked to play in three All-Star games for the National League.

H. P. Dawson, one of Virginia's baseball pioneers as executive, operated New York Yankees' Piedmont League farm in Norfolk for many years.

Hank Foiles, a Richmond native who moved to Norfolk and became a star at Granby High School before moving up to the majors. Spent a dozen years in majors as catcher with five different clubs. First major league catcher to wear contact lenses.

EPPA RIXEY
The Virginia gentleman

A fierce competitor and a hard loser, Eppa Rixey never played in the minor leagues, going directly to the majors from the University of Virginia campus. The 6-5, 210-pound southpaw won 266 games in the 21 years he spent in the National League with the Philadelphia Phillies and Cincinnati Reds while losing 251.

What makes Rixey's record even more remarkable is the fact that he pitched for a second-division team in 13 of his 21 years of service. Eppa notched four 20-win seasons (three with Cincinnati) and on two other occasions won 19 games for the Reds.

The drawling southerner, born in Culpeper on May 3, 1891, was discovered by Cy Rigley, who umpired in the National League for many seasons, and also served as baseball coach at the University of Virginia. Rixey aspired to be a chemist, graduating with honors, but Rigley persuaded him to accept an offer from the Phillies. He was 21 years of age.

Eppa never regretted his decision. The 21 years he spent on National League mounds constitutes a record for longevity.

The towering, quick-tempered Virginian didn't begin to shine until the 1916 season when he won 22 games, his best mark with the Phillies.

"All they talked about," Ep used to recall of his big year in 1916, "was a fellow named Grover Cleveland Alexander on the same team. That darned ole Pete won 33 games. The son-of-a-gun won more than 90 games in three years."

There never was a more liked and admired player by his teammates and opponents than this big, drawling Virginian.

He was named after a great aunt, Eppl Poindexter, changed to Eppa for the masculine.

Eppa was proud of his heritage, and took history as seriously as he did baseball. Word got around that you could get his goat by whistling, "Marching through Georgia"—that was one of the songs the Union soldiers sang while charging through the South.

One time Rixey was throwing batting practice and some fellow on the other bench started whistling that song at him. Eppa fired the baseball into the dugout and the players scattered.

Later on the bench, Rixey was looking down at the dugout floor and scowling.

"Eppa, why does that song make you so mad?" he was asked. After a few moments, Eppa replied:

"That song doesn't make me mad. The thing that makes me mad is that they think they're making me mad."

Eppa didn't like to lose, that's for sure. When he pitched you didn't have to ask who won the game, a teammate once recalled. All you had to do was look in the clubhouse. If he'd lost, the place would look like a tornado had gone through it, with broken chairs, tables knocked over and equipment thrown around.

The ballclub didn't like it a bit, but they said nothing because Eppa was a very big fellow and besides, he had already established himself as an institution.

In 1924, the Reds were paying Rixey a salary of 12,000 dollars, which made him the second highest paid player on the club. From 1921 to 1933, Eppa toiled for the Reds. He had one of the best moves in the majors. He hung up his glove in 1933 at the age of 42. He was still a winner, with a 6-3 record that season. He still holds several all-time Cincinnati pitching records, including most games started (356), most wins (179) and most innings pitched (2,891).

In his 21 seasons in the majors, Eppa appeared in 692 games; hurled 4,494 innings; won 266, lost 251 for a percentage of .515; fanned 1,350; walked 1,082 and allowed 4,633 hits.

In 1933, Eppa Rixey was elected to the Hall of Fame in Cooperstown, New York, the only Virginian on these hallowed rolls.

Eppa Rixey, a Virginian among baseball's immortals.

LIFETIME PITCHING RECORD OF EPPA RIXEY

Year	Club	LG	G	IP	W	L	PCT.	SO	BB	H	ERA
1912	Philadelphia	NL	23	162	10	10	.500	59	54	147	2.50
1913	Philadelphia	NL	35	156	9	5	.643	75	56	148	3.11
1914	Philadelphia	NL	24	103	2	11	.153	41	45	124	4.37
1915	Philadelphia	NL	29	177	11	12	.478	88	64	163	2.39
1916	Philadelphia	NL	38	287	22	10	.688	134	74	239	1.85
1917	Philadelphia	NL	39	281	16	21	.432	121	67	249	2.28
1918	In Military Service										
1919	Philadelphia	NL	23	154	6	12	.333	63	50	160	3.97
1920	Philadelphia	NL	41	284	11	22	.333	109	69	288	3.48
1921	Cincinnati	NL	40	301	19	18	.514	76	66	324	2.78
1922	Cincinnati	NL	40	313	25	13	.658	80	45	337	3.54
1923	Cincinnati	NL	42	309	20	15	.571	97	65	334	2.80
1924	Cincinnati	NL	35	238	15	14	.517	57	47	219	2.76
1925	Cincinnati	NL	39	287	21	11	.656	69	47	302	2.89
1926	Cincinnati	NL	37	233	14	8	.636	61	58	231	3.40
1927	Cincinnati	NL	34	220	12	10	.545	42	43	240	3.48
1928	Cincinnati	NL	43	291	19	18	.514	53	67	317	3.43
1929	Cincinnati	NL	35	201	10	13	.435	37	60	235	4.16
1930	Cincinnati	NL	32	164	9	13	.409	37	47	207	5.10
1931	Cincinnati	NL	22	127	4	7	.364	22	30	143	3.90
1932	Cincinnati	NL	25	112	5	5	.500	14	16	108	2.65
1933	Cincinnati	NL	16	94	6	3	.667	10	12	118	3.16
Total (21 Years)		NL	692	4494	266	251	.515	1350	1082	4633	3.24

WORLD SERIES RECORD

Year	Club	LG	G	IP	W	L	PCT.	SO	BB	H	ERA
1915	Philadelphia	NL	1	7	0	1	.000	2	2	4	3.86

DAVE ROBERTSON
Fined 500 dollars for hitting a home run

The New York Giants, playing the Chicago Cubs at the Polo Grounds in 1915, had a man on base. Dave Robertson was at bat and received a signal from Manager John McGraw to bunt.

A fat pitch came in.

"I couldn't resist it," said Robertson. "I slammed the ball into the rightfield bleachers and won the game, 3-2.

"I pranced to our dugout expecting to be praised for my game-winning feat. What happened? Why McGraw fined me 500 dollars for disobeying orders."

The story is part of baseball folklore.

Davis A. Robertson, born in Portsmouth, raised in Norfolk County and a resident of Norfolk most of his life, was a big leaguer in every sense.

A four-sport star at North Carolina State, baseball was Robertson's bread-and-butter. He played 10 years in the majors, seven of them under the legendary John McGraw.

He had a lifetime average of .287, hitting .307 in 1916, .300 in 1920 and .308 in 1921.

It was in the 1917 World Series that the left-handed hitting outfielder achieved his greatest success. Although the Giants lost to the Chicago White Sox, Robertson was the star of the series. He collected 11 hits in 22 times at the bat for a World Series record .500 average. It stood as a record until Billy Martin of the New York Yankees broke it 36 years later. And Robertson was the first in World Series history to get one hit or more in each of six games.

After his big league career, Robertson managed in the old Virginia League and then served as a State Game Warden for 28 years. Born June 10, 1889, he died in 1970.

Dave Robertson set a World Series record.

CHUCK STOBBS
The home run he'd rather forget

Chuck Stobbs will never forget the day he faced Mickey Mantle.

Chuck Stobbs came out of Granby High School in Norfolk and spent 12 years in the major leagues as a left-handed pitcher. His name is in the Baseball Hall of Fame in Cooperstown, New York, for a home run. Not one he hit—but one hit off him.

On April 12, 1953, Chuck was pitching for the Senators against the New York Yankees in old Griffith Stadium, in Washington. There were only 4,206 in the stands, and what they saw was an incredible blast that was unmatched until the shot to the moon. In the fifth inning, Mickey Mantle came to bat, the Yankees ahead, 2-1, Yogi Berra on first. Mantle let the first pitch go by, a ball. The next pitch by Stobbs came over the middle of the plate, thigh-high. Mantle whipped his arms around in a hissing, upper-cutting arc, throwing all his 185 pounds behind the swing.

And Wham!

The ball started its flight like a space shot and flew high over the bleacher wall 391 feet from home plate. It went 66 feet farther back and 55 feet high, caromed over a football scoreboard converted to a beer ad for the baseball season, going 50 feet farther back and 60 feet higher still.

Yankee Manager Casey Stengel was stunned. "Longest ball I've ever seen," he said.

The home run was measured at 556 feet, and the ball Mantle hit was placed in the Hall of Fame, a constant reminder to Stobbs of his famous pitch.

Chuck took the kidding of Mantle's record home run good-naturedly.

"I could hear the ball park announcer after that saying, 'Stobbs now pitching and the outfielders catching'."

VIRGINIA CITIES IN PROFESSIONAL BASEBALL LEAGUES

APPALACHIAN LEAGUE
Bristol
    1911-13, 1921-25x, 1950-55, 1969
Covington 1966
Marion 1955*, 1965
Lynchburg 1959
Narrows 1946-50
Pennington Gap 1937-40
Pulaski
    1946-50, 1952-55, 1957-58, 1969-
Salem 1955, 1957-67
Wytheville
    1953-55, 1957-65, 1967, 1969, 1971-73

BI-STATE LEAGUE
Bassett 1935-40
Danville-Schoolfield 1939-41
Danville 1934-38, 1942
Fieldale 1934-36
South Boston 1937-40
South Boston 1937-40

BLUE RIDGE LEAGUE
Abingdon 1948*
Bassett 1950*
Galax 1946-50
Martinsville 1921, 1928
Wytheville 1948-50x

CAROLINA LEAGUE
Danville 1945-58
Hampton, Newport News (Peninsula)
    1963-71, 1974
Lynchburg 1966
Martinsville 1945-49
Portsmouth, Norfolk 1963-68
Salem 1968

EASTERN SHORE LEAGUE
Cape Charles 1928
Northampton 1927
Parksley 1922-28

MOUNTAIN STATES LEAGUE
Norton 1951-53
Pennington Gap 1948-51

OLD DOMINION LEAGUE
Newport News 1930x
Petersburg 1930x
Phoebus 1930x
Suffolk 1930x

PIEDMONT LEAGUE
Colonial Heights-Petersburg 1954
Danville 1920-25
Lynchburg 1943-45
Newport News 1944-45
Norfolk 1934-55c
Portsmouth 1935-55
Richmond 1933-53
Roanoke 1943-53

VIRGINIA LEAGUE
Blackstone 1948
Colonial Heights-Petersburg 1951
Danville 1906-12x
Emporia 1948-51
Harrisonburg 1939*, 1940-41
Hopewell 1916x, 1949-50
Lawrenceville 1948
Lynchburg
    1906-12x, 1917x, 1939*, 1940-42
Newport News
    1912-17x, 1918x, 1919-28x
Portsmouth 1906-10, 1912-17x, 1919-28x
Norfolk ... 1906-17x, 1918x, 1919-28x
Petersburg
    1911-17x, 1918x, 1919-21x, 1922x, 1923-
    1911-17x, 1918x, 1919-21x, 1922x,
    1923-28x, 1941-42, 1948-50
Pulaski 1942
Richmond . 1906-14, 1918x, 1919-28x
Salem-Roanoke 1939*, 1940-42
Staunton 1939*, 1940-42
Suffolk 1915, 1919-22, 1948-51

VIRGINIA MOUNTAIN LEAGUE
Charlottesville 1914
Clifton Forge 1914
Covington 1914
Staunton 1914

VIRGINIA-NORTHCAROLINA LEAGUE
Danville 1905x

INTERNATIONAL LEAGUE
Richmond
    1884, 1915-17, 1954-64, 1966
Portsmouth/Norfolk 1969
Peninsula (Hampton-Newport News)
    1972-73

(Code: x-indicates club or league disbanded during season. *Acquired its franchise after beginning of season or for some reason began play after season opened.)

THE SEMIPROS
An award from the General

A semipro athlete is one who engages in sports for pay or gain, but does not play it regularly as his main calling or profession. When semipro baseball and football were popular in the 1920s and 1930s, games were played mostly on weekends when the athletes weren't working at their regular jobs. Former high school and college athletes, over-the-hill guys, and just plain sandlotters made up the teams. It had to be for the love of competition because there was little financial reward. If the teams had an enclosed park, admission was usually charged. If played on an open field, a collection was usually taken up among the fans. At the end of the season, the players would split the receipts—if any were left. Semipro baseball probably paid better than others. Managers would sometimes bring in pitchers with a reputation for winning from other areas for weekend games, paying them 25 to 50 dollars a game, depending on what was promised.

Perhaps the most successful of Virginia's semipro baseball teams was Craddock-Terry of Lynchburg, first known as the Cutters Club. There were other strong teams, including Roanoke, Alexandria Celtics, West Point, Crewe, Master Sales of Petersburg, Portsmouth Navy Yard, Norfolk Orioles, Charlottesville, Martinsville, Quantico Marines, Port Norfolk, Everett Waddey of Richmond and Staunton; but for most of the 1930s, Craddock-Terry enjoyed the best record.

In 1932, the Lynchburg team won 44 of 53 games, winning its first 15 games and defeating the best in Virginia, North Carolina and District of Columbia. Bruin Richardson led the way with a .401 batting average. With Specs Garbee hurling 23 victories, Craddock-Terry won 52 games and lost 19 in 1933.

And that's the way it went in the 1930s. In fact, Craddock-Terry was beating its foes with such consistency that their fans thought they were playing setups. So on Saturdays, business manager Raymond Ware would offer visiting teams a 100 dollar bonus if they beat Craddock-Terry. This would increase attendance on Sundays.

After winning the state championship in 1938, Craddock-Terry competed in National semipro baseball tournament at Wichita, Kansas, and finished fourth. Specs Garbee was one of the most outstanding players among the semipros. This indestructable righthander didn't confine his talents to the Craddock-Terry team alone. He pitched for his hometown team on weekends "and anywhere else that paid me during the week."

"I made more money pitching semipro baseball than I did at my job," Specs recalls. "My salary then was 100 dollars a month working and about 50-60 dollars a week pitching. Most of the time I pitched for four different teams during the week."

In 1934, he had an overall record of 30-11, pitching for Craddock-Terry on Saturday and Sunday and Waynesboro, Staunton and Wytheville during the week.

Garbee started playing ball in the fifth grade in Lynchburg. In 1927 at Fort Eustis, he was presented a bat autographed by Babe Ruth from Major General Douglas MacArthur as the outstanding player at the Citizens Military Training Camp.

He broke into pro ball with Greenville, North Carolina, in the Eastern Carolina League in 1929, and he didn't give up pitching until 1949. In addition to the semipros, Specs pitched and managed teams in the Virginia League, Piedmont League, Interstate League and Appalachian League. Only Beef Treakle of the Cradock A. C. in Norfolk County could rival Garbee for longevity as a semipro pitcher-manager. During World War II, Specs managed and pitched Fort Lee to the third Service Command championship in 1944-45.

An award from the General: Major General Douglas MacArthur presents a bat autographed by Babe Ruth to Specs Garbee as outstanding baseball player of the Citizens Military Training Camp at Ft. Eustis in July 1927. Garbee also won the award in 1928 as his company team won the championship both years.

1938 Virginia Champions—Fourth in National Semipro Tourney: Front row (from left): Specs Garbee, Kenner Crawley, Herman Robinson, Dave Cohen, coach; Lefty Doss, batboy; Harry Crosswhite, Tally Wood, Ted Trent and Al Cronin. Back: Judge Lucian Shrader, state director; Wayne Lugar, James St. Calirk, Billy Robertson, Nat Reasor, Henry Minnick, Peg White, Ray Ware, business manager, and Bus Fortune, manager. Garbee wasn't with team for nationals at Wichita, Kansas.

Virginia State Semipro Champions of 1932: The Cutters Club, later to be known as Craddock-Terry, which ruled the semipros in the 1930s. Front row (from left): Knots Mosby, Nathan Goff, Specs Garbee, Bruin Richardson, Kenneth Routon, Dick Dinwiddie, and Janosik. Back: Ted Trent, Bus Fortune, manager; Roscoe Sales, Earl Overman, Pat Carney, Peg White, Dedker Shaner, Carl Driskill and Raymond Ware, business manager.

Football

The Pros
They made it to the top

Ace Parker, one of the first to use the jump pass effectively in pro football.

ACE PARKER
The ace of them all

No one questions Clarence (Ace) Parker's ability to assess a football player's skill.

"We can evaluate his speed and strength. But there is something more important that we can't always evaluate," the talent scout for the San Francisco 49ers of the National Football League once said. He was pointing to his heart.

What Ace had in his playing days was heart, a competitive spirit that propelled him to football's greatest heights. Jock Sutherland, who watched a great many All-Americans when he coached the University of Pittsburgh to national prominence, was Parker's coach with the Brooklyn Dodgers of the NFL. "Ace Parker is the finest all-around back and competitor I've ever coached," said Sutherland.

Parker weighed only 168 pounds, a lightweight for NFL competition.

But at halftime of the All-Star game at Chicago's Soldier's Field on August 28, 1941, 98,000 football fans witnessed a ceremony in which Ace Parker was awarded a gold watch, symbolic of his being named the most valuable player in the NFL for 1940, beating the immortal Sammy Baugh out for the honor.

And to think that Parker was once a high school dropout. What a pity it would have been if the game had been deprived of one of its brightest stars.

"I quit Churchland High School because they dropped football," Parker recalled. Luckily, Lester Kibler and Ernie Wild, the coaches at Portsmouth's Woodrow Wilson High School, induced Parker to return to school and thus be able to play football at Wilson.

"It's the best thing that ever happened to me," Parker admits.

Actually, after playing in 1931 and 1932 and gaining wide attention as a star in five different sports, Parker didn't graduate from Wilson and he was ineligible to play another season in high school football.

Virginia Tech invited Parker to Blacksburg in the summer of 1933 to receive the credits he needed for a high school diploma. He did. Of course, Virginia Tech expected him to enroll in September.

When Parker came home to visit a few days he found Eddie Cameron, one of the assistant coaches under Wallace Wade of Duke, waiting for him.

The rest is history. Parker decided on Duke, but would not go with Cameron until he returned to Blacksburg to tell Tech officials of his decision. Parker checked in a hotel in Roanoke and there was the Duke scout waiting. He was taking no chances on Parker changing his mind.

Off to Durham Parker went, and he became a sensation at Duke. He did everything with a football. A superb kicker and passer, he wasn't exceptionally fast. But he was deceptive and in college he ran wild. Duke followers are still talking about his record 105-yard kickoff return against North Carolina at Chapel Hill in 1936. It's still the longest run in Duke history.

Picked on the 1936 All-America team and drafted No. 1 by the Brooklyn Dodgers, a team that no longer exists in the NFL, Parker never intended to play pro football.

"After I finished Duke, I signed a baseball contract with the Philadelphia Athletics. My ambition was to be a major league baseball player and I advised the Dodgers of my decision.

"After the 1937 baseball season, the Dodgers kept worrying me about finishing out the year for them. The Dodgers had already played four games. I got permission from Connie Mack (A's manager) to join the football team. I thought I'd play out the season and that would be the end of it."

Like the man who came to dinner, Parker found a new home in the NFL.

"I'll never forget my first game in Ebbets Field," recalled the Ace (he was given this name in his first game on the Duke varsity by W. N. Cox, *Virginian-Pilot* sports editor). "I reported to the Dodgers on Tuesday and played 57 minutes on Sunday. I was accustomed to friendly fans, especially when I played on the home field. But when we ran on the field the Ebbets Field fans were booing long and loud.

"I tapped the player in front of me who was Ralph Kercheval and asked, 'Who're they booing?'

"That's us they're booing," replied Kercheval, somewhat surprised that the rookie should ask such a silly question.

After all, the Dodgers were consistent losers in the NFL.

The Dodgers lost to the Philadelphia Eagles, 14-0, but Parker completed nine of 10 passes for 122 yards in his debut.

It wasn't long before the skillful Virginian became the darling of Ebbets Field and the NFL.

Parker had played 14 years of football—scholastic, collegiate and pro—and never suffered a major injury. But he broke his legs twice playing baseball. He broke his left ankle sliding into home in a game in Toronto while playing with Syracuse in 1940. But he reported to football camp right on schedule.

Although he had to wear a 36-pound brace that extended from his ankle to his knee through the first three weeks of the season, the Ace continued doing just what he had always done—running, passing, catching passes, punting, placekicking, returning punts and kickoffs and playing defense.

The Dodgers broke the Redskins' seven-game winning streak that season as Parker outdid the great Sammy

Baugh in a 16-14 upset. A week later, the 5-10 Virginian played one of his greatest games in a 29-14 rout of the Cleveland Rams. Trailing by two touchdowns, the Ace took matters in his own hands. He scored on a 68-yard pass interception, threw passes for the next two touchdowns and set up the final score with a 38-yard return of a pass interception. When Ace was injured three minutes before the end and left limping from the field, the fans stood and cheered him until he was out of sight.

He had set the stage properly for Ace Parker Day in Ebbets Field on the following Sunday. They presented Ace with a new automobile and he showed his appreciation by passing for two touchdowns and kicking both extra points in a 14-9 win over the Chicago Cardinals.

Then he led the Dodgers to their first victory over the New York Giants in 10 years. Before 55,000 in the Polo Grounds, he threw touchdown passes of 25 and 44 yards to Banks McFadden and Dick Cassiano for a 14-6 victory. He completed seven passes for 122 yards, ran for 34, kicked both extra points and got off a phenomenal 58-yard quick kick that set up a touchdown, spoiling "Mel Hein Day" the Giants had staged for their All-Pro Center.

Parker led the Dodgers to an 8-3-0 season to finish a half-game behind Washington's Eastern Division champions. He played 656 minutes in a 660-minute season. He won the coveted Joe Carr Trophy, symbolic of Most Valuable Player honors in the NFL, receiving twice as many votes as runner-up Sammy Baugh.

By this time, Parker was convinced that pro football really was his game. He had won all-NFL honors his first full season in 1938, and Brooklyn owner Dan Topping rewarded him with the "highest two-year contract in football." The contract didn't specifically stipulate that Parker had to quit baseball, but it did say that he had to agree to report to the Dodgers by August 15.

So Ace refused a baseball contract from the Pittsburgh Pirates and cancelled his plans for a big league career. The baseball hierarchy was shocked because no great athlete had ever picked pro football over baseball before. But Ace got himself in the baseball books. His first time at bat in the major leagues, he hit a home run.

Parker did request to play minor league baseball with his hometown Portsmouth team "until football practice starts." But on May 3, Parker broke his ankle again, this time the right one, sliding into base.

But came September and Ace reported to the Dodgers, and provided the one-man heroics that produced another second-place finish for Brooklyn.

The Giants won six straight games to start the 1941 campaign and then ran into the Dodgers, or rather Ace Parker. The Giants were upset, 16-13, marking the first time in 11 years the Dodgers had beaten their arch-rivals in Ebbets Field.

Parker's contributions to the victory were of a storybook nature. His crushing tackle of Len Eshmont prevented a New York touchdown in the early stages. Just before the half, he capped a 78-yard drive with a 11-yard scoring pass. In the third quarter, his passes set up a tying field goal. Finally he raced 61 yards to the New York 19 to set up the winning score.

Parker's career was interrupted by a Navy hitch in World War II, serving almost four years. He went in as a chief and came out a full lieutenant. When the war ended, the Brooklyn Dodgers had disbanded. Most ex-Dodgers were assigned to the Boston Yanks and Parker reported there in October, 1955. He was used only sparingly and was disappointed.

The next year he turned to the New York Yankees in the All-American Football Conference. The team was owned by none other than Dan Topping, who was Ace's boss with the Dodgers. Topping was reluctant to take on the 34-year-old quarterback.

"Don't pay me until you see what I can do," Parker insisted. "Then we'll talk salary." Topping agreed and it turned out to be a wise decision.

Parker was the spearhead of the Yankee surge. He played three games

Because his leg was broken playing baseball, Ace Parker had to play with a ten-pound iron brace extending from his ankle to his knee through the first three weeks of the 1940 NFL season. Despite this handicap, Parker continued to spark the Brooklyn Dodgers.

This tribute to Ace Parker by Mullin appeared in the New York World-Telegram, *November 23, 1940.*

with three dislocated vertebrae, sat out three games while the pain eased and then returned to spark the late-season rally that produced a division championship. Parker's credentials included a then-record performance of having only three of 115 passes intercepted in one season. Over a six-game span he went without an interception.

The Yankees met the powerful Cleveland Rams, who had Otto Graham at the throttle, in the championship game. The Browns won a bitter struggle, 14-9, but Parker was a star in defeat, setting up both New York scores with his pinpoint passing and field leadership.

It was his farewell to pro football as a player.

He had rushed the ball almost 500 times in a seven-year career.

Many tributes were paid Ace while he was playing, but the one that touched him most occurred in a losing cause.

"In 1939, the Dodgers played the Redskins in Washington's Griffith Stadium, which was packed to capacity," Parker recounts.

"It was a hopeless battle against the powerful Redskins. But everything went right for me. With three minutes to go, I was taken out of the game. As I walked toward the Brooklyn bench, I saw the fans stand and give me a thunderous ovation. The Washington players ran over and each shook my hand before play was resumed again."

Ace's feats were not forgotten.

In 1955, he was elected to the National Foundation Football Hall of Fame, the college shrine.

In 1972, he was inducted into the Pro Football Hall of Fame in Canton, Ohio, as one of the last and greatest of all triple-threat quarterbacks.

Giants owner Tim Mara may have said it best right after Parker had led the Dodgers' upset of the New York team in 1941: "You can kick Ace Parker on the head and you can break both his ankles, but you can never hurt his heart."

Showing the things he did best, which were about everything, this is a reproduction from the original mural of Ace Parker on display in the Pro Football Hall of Fame in Canton, Ohio.

BILL DUDLEY
The Bluefield Bullet

Bill Dudley was rather small, not particularly fast. But he had perfect control and a deceptive change of pace. He could change direction at top speed without losing momentum.

Bill Dudley was, in fact, one of the most elusive runners who ever carried a football.

In 1941—at the ripe old age of 19—he was an All-America selection at the University of Virginia. In 1946, he was the most valuable player in the National Football League, winning the Joe Carr Memorial Award. In 1966, the Bluefield Bullet was inducted into the Pro Football Hall of Fame at Canton, Ohio. He had already carved himself a niche in the college football Hall of Fame.

When Dudley attended Graham High School he tried out for the football team and was turned down. They didn't have a uniform small enough to fit him. He made the squad as a junior but never got to play. In his senior year, Bill was a star, a superb kicker, never missing an extra point.

But none of the colleges wanted to take a chance on this 5-9, 152-pound halfback until the University of Virginia was persuaded to take him on a partial scholarship (500 dollars a year).

At Virginia, the T-formation was introduced. It was right down Dudley's alley. He set a national collegiate scoring record of 134 points in 1941 when he led the Cavaliers to an 8-1-0 season, the only loss to Yale, 21-19. He ended his Virginia career with one of the greatest individual performances ever seen on the college gridiron. In the season's windup against arch-rival North Carolina, the Bluefield Bullet passed for one touchdown, scored one himself on a three-yard plunge, and then scampered 60 yards for another touchdown. But wait. For a third touchdown, he faked a punt and then zigzagged his way 89 yards. Also, he kicked three extra points and was a bruiser on defense in a 28-7 Dudley landslide. He rushed for 215 yards on 17 carries, completed seven of 11 passes for 117 more, giving him 1,824 total offensive yards for the season.

And they were still wondering whether the 170-pound Dudley was too small for pro football. But the Pittsburgh Steelers made him their No. 1 draft choice. He was 20 years old. Not only was this Virginian going to the land of giants, but there was considerable speculation as to how he would do switching from the T-formation he ran in college back to the single wing used by the Steelers.

Let Bill Explain it:

"When I first went to Virginia in 1938, we were using the single wing. In fact, Coach Frank Murray made a big-to-do with the spread formation (used at Marquette with Ray Buivd and Art Guepe) off the single wing as well as the reverse.

"He did not put the T in until the spring of 1941 and that was following the Bears beating the Redskins by such a lopsided score (73-0) in the NFL championship game. In the spring of 1941, I played under the center but due to the fact that he wanted to take more advantage of my running, he moved me back to left halfback; and I passed from that position, receiving a direct snap from the center with the quarterback going in motion as well as taking a pitchout from the quarterback, who was John Neff. (If the split-T, wishbone or other variations had been in vogue—I'd probably have stayed under the center.)

"Thus, when I went to the Steelers, I had already played the T and the single wing. In fact, in 1942, the Steelers used the 'Notre Dame Box,' which was a balance line, single wing. In 1946, when Jock Sutherland coached the Steelers, we used a single wing similar to Murray's with the unbalanced line. In 1945, when I got out of the service, Pittsburgh was using a form of the 'wing-T.' Thus, I had right much experience in playing all types of formations."

Dudley reported to the Steelers' camp and despite a bad ankle, he played the first game of the season, surprising everybody by running 55 yards for a touchdown in the opening minutes against the Philadelphia Eagles. The following week, he took the second-half kickoff and scrambled the length of the field for a touchdown against the Green Bay Packers. He led the Steelers to seven wins in their last nine games for a second-place finish in the Eastern Division, the first winning season in Steeler history. He became the darling of Pittsburgh fans, topping the league with 696 yards rushing. He was named the NFL Rookie of the Year.

During World War II, Dudley entered the Army Air Corps, served as a pilot, played football and was named All-Service halfback before being sent to the Pacific.

He returned to the pros late in 1945. Showing he lost none of his touch, he scored two touchdowns and led the Steelers to an upset over the Chicago Cardinals. Playing in only four games, Bill still managed to outscore all the

Bullet Bill Dudley

A pair of the greatest...Bill Dudley (left) sparked the Pittsburgh Steelers' single wing attack under the iron-fisted regime of Dr. Jock Sutherland. Here he chats with another famous All-American—Michigan's Tom Harmon—before a game with the Los Angeles Rams.

other Steeler backs that year.

Jock Sutherland became coach of the Steelers in 1946. Bill couldn't get along with the "dour Scot," but topped the league in rushing and pass interceptions (ten). Bill asked to be traded. He planned to return to Virginia and become backfield coach, but the Detroit Lions received permission to talk with him and signed Dudley for 25,000 dollars, the highest amount paid any player since Red Grange's percentage deal with the Chicago Bears 20 years before. The Detroit players weren't enthused by the coming of Dudley. There were rumors he'd try to run the show. Dudley soon convinced the Lions of his dedication, and they elected him captain.

Bill spent the final three seasons of his career with the Washington Redskins, and in a game against the Steelers on December 3, 1950, Bill made what many believe was his greatest run.

In his book, *Pro Football's All-Time Greats*, George Sullivan describes the run:

"It was part of Bill's playing philosophy that every punt should be caught and run back. Often he went to great extremes to achieve this. In the game in question, Joe Geri of the Steelers got off a tremendous punt. Following a diagonal course, the ball sailed downfield more than 60 yards, and appeared to be going over the goal line or, worse, out of bounds inside the Redskins' five-yard line. Dudley was right on the spot when the ball came down. To make the catch, he had to reach out of bounds, being careful his toes didn't touch the sidelines. His fingers plucked the ball from the air; then he clutched it to his chest. He faked out the first tackler who threatened to spill him, and then his blocking began to form. He clung to the sideline all the way and went 96 yards for a touchdown."

The specialists were moving in; and two-way players were on the way out. Dudley played his last game in 1953 after nine NFL seasons. He was one of the last of the two-way players—and one of the best.

Defense? This same fellow who they said was too small to play football once brought down the bone-crushing Marion Motley 13 times in an open field in a game against the Cleveland Browns.

"Under today's standards, if I had the luck, I think I would not be too small for pro football," Dudley claims. "I do not know whether I would play offense or defense, but I think all I would have needed would have been an opportunity to play. I say this not with any conceit, but the fact that football is still played today with one's head and body; and I still feel that there is room for a good football player who thinks and is thinking all the time. Also, there is room for a running back who is quick. For example, pros spread their line right far and I believe one of the qualities that I had was being able to hit a hole, break to one side or the other and read blocks. I have never felt I would outrun many people, but also I was never caught from behind very often."

Bill Dudley on one of his spectacular runs with the Steelers. Dudley, who did not have really good speed, was one of the most elusive backs who ever carried a football. This is a copy of the mural on display in the Pro Football Hall of Fame at Canton, Ohio.

Bruce Gossett played at Ferrum Junior College before going to the University of Richmond. Joined San Francisco 49ers from Los Angeles Rams in trade prior to 1970 season. In statistics up to the 1976 season, he ranks seventh among the all-time NFL scorers, with 1,031 points. He was the leader in scoring and field goals in 1966. In 1973 he had a consecutive field goal streak of 13 over a five-game period that ranks as the second longest such streak in NFL history.

*A Richmond product, Ken Willard was a starter at the University of North Carolina before being drafted in the first round by the San Francisco 49ers. Played with the 49ers 1965-73, St. Louis Cardinals in 1974. At the start of the 1976 season, NFL records showed Willard ranked ninth among the all-time rushers with 6,105 yards and 45 touchdowns on 1,622 carries in his ten-year career. Voted on NFL West Division All-Star team by **The Sporting News** in 1956. Pro Bowl 1965-66-68-69.*

George Hughes, one of William & Mary's all-time greats, All-Southern guard and co-captain in 1949, played in the offensive line four seasons with Pittsburgh Steelers. He played in the NFL Pro Bowl in 1952 and 1954, and still is active in the game as line coach with the Ottawa Rough Riders in the Canadian Football League.

Tommy Reamon played at the University of Missouri after prepping at Carver High in Newport News. With the Florida Blazers in the now defunct World Football League, he was voted co-winner of the Most Valuable Player Award in 1974. After the WFL folded, the running back signed with the NFL Pittsburgh Steelers, who drafted him in the first place.

Ed Beard, linebacker, played at Oscar Smith High School in Chesapeake, then starred for the University of Tennessee. A standout linebacker and captain of specialty teams, 1965-72, Beard (No. 50) is shown here ready to lead his group for the San Francisco 49ers.

A star at Warwick High in Newport News and then Wake Forest College, Norman Snead was the No. 1 draft choice of the Washington Redskins in 1961. He has been quarterback for several NFL clubs since then. Ranks among the top ten all-time passing leaders in pro football.

Lou Creekmur of William & Mary, All-Pro tackle with Detroit Lions, 1950-59.

Henry Jordan was a defensive tackle fo[r] Cleveland Browns (1957-58) and Green Ba[y] Packers (1959-69). Born in Emporia, at[-] tended Warwick High and the University o[f] Virginia. One of the best in NFL; elected t[o] All-Pro team three times; selected to play i[n] Pro Bowl four times and was named linema[n] of game in Pro Bowl following 1961 seaso[n;] played in seven NFL championship games[,] two Super Bowl games all with Packers.

Earl Faison, end, went to Huntington High of Newport News. He was All-Big Ten at Indiana in 1960; Rookie of the Year in AFL in 1961; San Diego Chargers, 1961-66; Miami Dolphins 1966.

Jet-fast Bosh Pritchard, one of VMI's all time greats, accelerates on this play against the Pittsburgh Steelers for the 1949 Philadelphia NFL champions. He might have gone farther but Steeler Frank Sinkovitz (57) slipped through and held him to a five-yard gain.

Tommy Thompson, All-Southern at William & Mary in 1947-48, won All-Pro honors with the Cleveland Browns in the NFL. He played center for the Browns, 1949-53, one of the best in the game.

*Carroll Dale of Wise was an All-American end at Virginia Tech. He was selected by the Los Angeles Rams in the eighth round of the 1960 NFL draft. He played five years with the Rams, eight with the Green Bay Packers before joining the Minnesota Vikings in 1973. Played in NFL championship games of 1965-66-67; the AFL-NFL championship game following the 1966-67 seasons; played in NFL All-Star game (Pro Bowl) in 1968; named to **The Sporting News** Western Conference All-Star team in 1968.*

Cornell Gordon of Norfolk moved up to pro football after playing at North Carolina A&T. A defensive back, he played with the New York Jets (AFL, 1965-69), and Denver Broncos, (AFC, 1970-72).

Chris Hanburger was one of the all-time centers and linebackers in the Atlantic Coast Conference while playing at the University of North Carolina. This Hampton athlete has been acclaimed as one of the best linebackers in the National Football League. Selected to Pro Bowl seven years, the Redskin veteran was voted NFC Defensive Player of the Year for 1972, also unanimous selection as first team linebacker in the NFC and NFL. All-Pro and All-NFC, 1973, 1974.

The Old Dominion can claim Fran Tarkenton as one of its own, too. The great Minnesota Vikings' quarterback, who holds nearly every passing record in the National Football League, was born in Richmond on February 3, 1940. His father is a native of Norfolk. He attended the University of Georgia. The all-time passing great is considered the greatest scrambling quarterback, having rushed for more yardage than any quarterback in NFL history.

J. R. Wilburn of the Pittsburgh Steelers is shown catching a pass in a 1968 game against Cleveland Browns. A product of Portsmouth's Cradock High, Wilburn gained All-Atlantic Coast Conference honors at the University of South Carolina, then spent five seasons (1966-70) with the Steelers. His NFL totals were 123 receptions for 1,834 yards.

Barty Smith of the University of Richmond was the Green Bay Packers' No. 1 draft choice in 1974. The powerful All-Southern fullback set Spider rushing records and was selected to play in four college post-season All-Star games following his graduation.

A star back at the University of Virginia, Jim Gillette played for five different clubs in the NFL—Cleveland Rams, Boston Yanks, Washington Redskins, Green Bay Packers and Detriot Lions from 1940-1948. His son is Walker Gillette, a pass receiver with the New York Giants.

PRO FOOTBALL IN VIRGINIA
The money ran out

Before the Redskins moved in, Washington had a team in the Dixie Pro Football League, which included Richmond, Alexandria, Norfolk, Portsmouth, Newport News and Baltimore. Playing their home games in Griffith Stadium, the Washington Pros won the title in 1936 by defeating the Baltimore Orioles, 3-0, on the last day of the season.

In 1937, George Preston Marshall brought the Redskins to Washington, and leased Griffith Stadium. Since there was no other enclosed field in Washington available on Sundays, the Washington team in the Dixie League changed its name from the Pros to Presidents, became the orphans of the Virginia-dominated league, playing all their games on the road.

But the Presidents won the title again in 1937.

The following season, however, the Presidents lost the final game of the season to the Portsmouth Cubs, 21-7, and threw the Dixie championship to the Norfolk Shamrocks who were coached by Dick Esleeck, a successful high school coach.

With Baltimore and Alexandria out, the league was now reduced to four teams—Washington and the three Tidewater cities (Norfolk, Portsmouth and Newport News).

Interest continued to lag in 1939 and 1940. Portsmouth, with Larry Weldon coaching and directing the attack as a triple-threat quarterback, won the title both years. At the end of the season, the team promoters by mutual consent, wrote "finis" to the Dixie League.

After World War II, in 1946, the Dixie League was revived on a higher scale. The ambitious owners figured they would cash in on the post-war boom, raising salaries and admission prices.

The league was composed of six teams—Richmond Rebels, Norfolk Shamrocks, Portsmouth Pirates, Newport News Builders, Charlotte Clippers, and Greensboro Patriots. Each supposedly had a working agreement with a National Football League club.

On paper, the Dixie League appeared to be on solid foundation. But the blunder was playing pre-season exhibition games with larger clubs. For instance, Portsmouth traveled to Scranton, Pennsylvania, and was clobbered, 52-6, by the Scranton Minors of the American League. The Washington Redskins, with the immortal Sammy Baugh at the throttle, invaded Norfolk, accompanied by their famous 110-piece marching band, and showed no mercy in scalping their Dixie League affiliates, 56-0.

The fans, naturally, became disenchanted from the start. For openers, only 1,500 fans showed up at Richmond to watch the Rebels defeat Portsmouth, 7-0; the Shamrocks repulsed the Builders, 29-7, before 3,000, and at Greensboro, the Charlotte Clippers, who went on to win the championship, topped the Patriots, 20-14, before only 2,000.

It was downhill the rest of the way and the league barely finished the season. The Richmond Rebels played in the American League in the late 1950s and did very well on the field but not at the gate.

Virginia was without organized pro football until 1965, when the Continental Football League was formed with ten teams, including Richmond and Norfolk. The other teams were Toronto, Philadelphia, Newark, Wheeling, Fort Wayne, Rhode Island, Hartford and Charleston, West Virginia.

A.B. (Happy) Chandler, former Kentucky governor and U.S. Senator and former baseball commissioner, was named the commissioner. He proclaimed the CFL as the "third major league," and insisted that the clubs seek no help from the NFL and make their way independently.

But the owners, suffering heavy financial losses after the first season, couldn't see it that way and attempted to get financial and player assistance from the NFL. In 1966, Chandler resigned as commissioner.

There were numerous shifts in 1966. The Ft. Wayne team transferred to Montreal, Newark to Orlando, Rhode Island dropped out and Brooklyn added, and in September Brooklyn withdrew.

In 1967, Richmond and Philadelphia dropped by the wayside, and Akron, Ohio, added. By the end of the season, Hartford, Toronto and Akron were out. Norfolk won the division title in 1967 and lost the playoff to Orlando, 21-17.

At the start of the 1969 season, only Norfolk and Wheeling remained from the original CFL lineup of ten teams.

On the field, the CFL presented an excellent product. The coaching was good and the sharp execution of plays provided an exciting brand of pro football. But it didn't take at the gate.

Norfolk was the bright spot. In four seasons, the Neptunes played before 400,660 fans in league games at Foreman Field, but the financial losses were staggering. In 1966, the Neptunes grossed more than 400,000 dollars but lost 60,000 dollars. The players' salaries were too steep.

In 1966 and 1967, the Virginia Sailors, a farm club of the Washington Redskins, won the championship of the Atlantic Coast Football League. The Richmond Roadrunners, affiliated with

Jim Clack, center for the Pittsburgh Steelers, is another player from the Virginia pro gridiron. He groomed for the NFL by playing with the Norfolk Neptunes.

An action photo taken during a 1926 game played in Norfolk between Red Grange's touring New York Americans and the Norfolk Blues. Grange's team won, 40-7, and collected 10,000 dollars guarantee. The local promoters took a financial beating. Tickets sold for three dollars and twenty cents and two dollars and twenty cents and critics claimed the game was priced out of range of the fans.

Jake Versprille, a triple-threat ace in amateur and semipro football in the twenties.

Otis Sistrunk is thankful he had an opportunity to play pro football in Virginia. He made the jump from the Norfolk Neptunes to the NFL and became an outstanding defensive lineman with the Oakland Raiders. Selected to AFC Pro Bowl team for first time in 1974, honored as Raiders' Lineman of the Year in 1973. In 1976, he was starting his fifth season with Oakland.

the New Orleans Saints, joined the ACFL in 1968, and the Norfolk Neptunes became a member of the league in 1970. And the Sailors were now stationed in Roanoke and known as the Buckskins.

Unfortunately, the NFL dropped all affiliations with the ACFL. The minor league, which had previously boasted of solid support from the big league, was now strapped by a financial burden too heavy to overcome.

In 1971, E. L. Gruber, a Pottstown, Pennsylvania, industrialist, whose Pottstown Firebirds ruled the ACFL, bought the Norfolk franchise and, with Ron Waller as coach, won the championship by defeating Hartford in the playoff. It was, however, a financial disaster, marking the end of another sports era in Virginia. But this type of football had its reward for a number of players like Otis Sistrunk, who moved up to the NFL.

During the 1920s and early 1930s, amateur football was popular in Virginia, especially in the Tidewater area with teams like the Clancy A. C., Norfolk Blues, Sewanee of Portsmouth, Navy Yard Marines, and Norfolk Doughboys. The players received little or no compensation but seemed to enjoy playing for the fun and glory.

Tragedy struck the amateurs when Chap Eure, a lineman for Sewanee, suffered a broken neck in a game and died from the injury.

Jack Versprille is regarded as one of Virginia's greatest amateur football players. Coming out of the Navy, Versprille burned up the sandlots with his sensational running. A triple threat, he was also a skillful dropkicker and defensive player. When his playing days were over, Jake's name was carried on by five of his sons, four of whom received college football scholarships. They were Bobby (Georgetown), Pat (Florida State), George (Howard) and Eddie (Alabama).

Coach-quarterback Larry Weldon carrying ball for Portsmouth Cubs, Dixie Pro Football League champions in 1940.

Here are the Richmond Rebels championship pro team in 1949 with coaches Tiger Walton and Keith Molesworth (back row, right), who became an outstanding executive with the Baltimore Colts.

Boom Boom Brown of the Norfolk Neptunes kicks up his heels in an Atlantic Coast Football League game against the Pottstown Firebirds in 1970.

Rebel on the loose... Tony Koszarsky picks up yardage for the Richmond Rebels against the Charleston Rockets in Continental Football League game in 1965. Koszarsky was voted the Most Valuable Rebel award.

The Super All-Americans

A consensus All-American, as compiled by the NCAA Statistics Bureau, is the combined choice of the leading selections—Football Writers Association, Football Coaches Association, Associated Press, United Press International and the Walter Camp Foundation.

According to the National Collegiate Athletic Association (NCAA) only nine native Virginians have been named to the consensus All-America team from 1925 to 1976. They are by hometowns:

Blacksburg—Jim Breland, Georgia Tech center, 1966

Bristol—Gene McEver, University of Tennessee back, 1929, and Beattie Feathers, University of Tennessee back, 1933

Newport News—Frank Emanuel, University of Tennessee linebacker, 1965 and Leroy Keyes, Purdue back, 1967-68

Portsmouth—Clarence (Ace) Parker, Duke University back, 1936

Prince George—Ron Rusnak, University of North Carolina guard, 1972

Bluefield—Bill Dudley, University of Virginia back, 1941

Capron—Walker Gillette, University of Richmond end, 1969.

All-American Bill Dudley sees daylight on one of countless long runs when he was a teenager making football history at Virginia. He was only 20 years old in 1942 when he was drafted No. 1 by the Pittsburgh Steelers. (See pro football section)

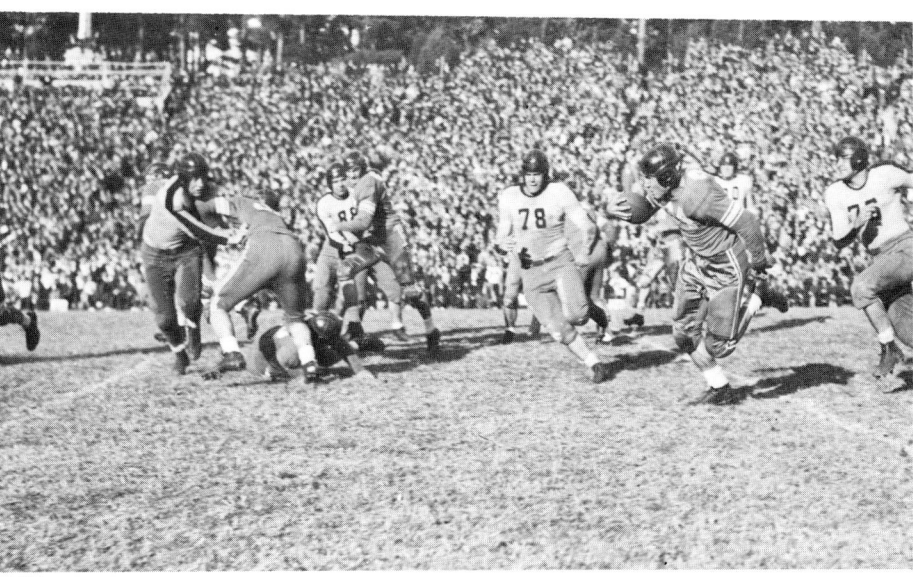

All-American Ace Parker of Duke en route to a record 105-yard kickoff return against North Carolina at Chapel Hill in 1936. (See pro football section)

GENE McEVER
The Bristol Blizzard

Gene McEver was a star at Bristol's Virginia High School. He was wooed by a number of colleges in a day when football fans thought recruiting was something the U.S. Army did. Virginia Tech, Tennessee and Alabama made the biggest pitches for the Virginian. Strangely, he had barely heard of Tennessee football.

In fact, McEver was about to enroll at Wake Forest.

"The only thing I could associate with Tennessee then was having heard of a fellow named Hatcher who could kick a football a mile," McEver recalled. (Buck Hatcher was a Tennessee kicking star in 1919-20.) "That was about all I heard about Tennessee. I was a VPI man."

Nonetheless, McEver set off for Wake Forest, out of frustration and a close friendship with a Baptist minister in Bristol.

"I was a Baptist, and this preacher kind of recruited me over to Wake Forest. Since it was a Baptist school, he had an interest in it.

"Going to Wake Forest was just one of those things. You see, I had a brother at VPI and, of course, they were trying to get me to come up there. Alabama talked to me and so did Tennessee. That's one thing I don't like about this recruiting business; they get a fellow all upset and he doesn't know what he wants to do. They finally got me to a point where I didn't really care whether I went anywhere. In fact, I started to go in the Marines. That Quantico Marines was big stuff in football then.

"I decided to go to Wake Forest and see what it looked like."

Tennessee coach Bob Neyland got wind of McEver's decision and dispatched Coach Bill Britton to Wake Forest to tell McEver that Tennessee still had a scholarship waiting for him.

The rest is history.

The Bristol Blizzard became The Volunteers' "Wild Bull."

Fast, stocky and strong, McEver symbolized the power football of the 1928-31 era. He made up one half of the Vols' famous "Hack 'n Mac" halfback combination. The other half was Buddy Hackman, who later coached at Roanoke College.

The Vols were undefeated in the McEver years (knee surgery forced him to the sidelines in 1930). Most vivid in his memory was the 1929 game with Alabama, when he returned the opening kickoff 98 yards in a jolting 15-13 upset, one of the most famous, history-making runs in football.

McEver was the nation's leading scorer in 1929 with 130 points and still is Tennessee's all-time scorer with 276 points. After a year out with a knee injury, he came back to beat Frank Thomas' first Alabama team in 1931, 25-0, scoring three touchdowns. His passing was as deadly as his smashing drives.

Small wonder that the Bristol Blizzard became Tennessee's first full-fledged All-American, and was also the first Vol to be elected to the National Football Foundation Hall of Fame. He entered the Hall in 1954.

Gene McEver, Tennessee's 1929 All-American from Bristol.

BEATTIE FEATHERS
Antelope in orange

Beattie Feathers, Tennessee's 1933 All-American from Bristol.

Beattie Feathers is a Tennessee legend. He and Gene McEver were teammates on the same Virginia High School football team at Bristol. Beattie followed the older McEver to the University of Tennessee, won All-America honors and, in 1955, was voted a niche in the National Football Foundation's Hall of Fame.

A great climax runner, Feathers led Coach Bob Neyland's fabulous Tennessee 1931-32-33 teams to 25 wins and two ties in 30 games. And he scored 33 touchdowns. He was nicknamed "The Big Chief" by his teammates, and the antelope in orange had a knack for the "big play."

Virginia Tech tried to get Feathers out of Bristol, as they did McEver—and failed again. But they got Beattie all right, right in the kisser. Beattie ran 100 yards and scored two touchdowns as Tennessee walloped the Gobblers, 27-0, in the 1933 opener.

He was a superb punter, one of the best in the Vols' history. They still tell stories about his memorable duel with Alabama's Johnny Cain in the mud at Birmingham in 1932, which ended in a stirring 7-3 victory for Tennessee.

Beattie was not a big man, 180 pounds, 5-feet-10. He had a rare combination of speed, power and balance.

He spent six seasons in the National Football League, four with the Chicago Bears, running alongside the legendary Bronco Nagurski and wearing the No. "48," which he had made famous at Tennessee. In one season he averaged 9.9 yards per carry, (101 carries, 1,004 yards), which would raise a lot of eyebrows even among today's super stars in the NFL.

Beattie would probably tell you he had a lot of help in compiling his remarkable 9.9 average. On most plays, Bronco was blocking for him. Still, it took an exceptional runner to knock off nearly ten yards a clip under any circumstances in pro football.

Feathers played his final two NFL seasons with the Brooklyn Dodgers alongside Ace Parker. But in his second season at Brooklyn he suffered a serious skull fracture, which ended his NFL career.

Beattie never ceases to marvel at what a great football player Gene McEver was. "Nobody was as good as Gene McEver. He was the greatest," Beattie praises. "It's hard to compare pro players with college players, but I'm convinced that if Gene hadn't hurt his knee after his junior season at Tennessee he would have been one of the great pro players. I played with Bronco Nagurski, and he was probably the most powerful man I ever saw. He was a tremendous football player, but he couldn't break a game open like Gene could."

If McEver is first on Tennessee's all-time list, Feathers has to be second.

In 1931, only a sophomore, he scored on 60 and 80-yard runs against Mississippi, 70 yards against Kentucky, 65 yards against NYU, and 65 yards against Duke. In 1932, he raced for a 54-yard touchdown in the North Carolina game, and for 33 yards against Ole Miss. In his senior season, he dashed 45 and 43 yards for touchdowns against Virginia Tech and 13 yards to score against Alabama.

FRANK EMANUEL
The hard way

Frank Emanuel, Tennessee 1965 All-American from Newport News.

Frank Emanuel of Newport News, a consensus All-America linebacker at Tennessee in 1965, didn't have it easy before he started disrupting the opposition in the Southeastern Conference.

He was a scrawny kid when he was growing up. He caught rheumatic fever when he was nine and later an attack of polio briefly paralyzed his left leg.

"I got awfully tired of being the smallest kid on the block," he says, "so when I was 12, I started working on a set of weights I got for Christmas."

Emanuel weighed 212 pounds when he graduated from Newport News High School, a fierce competitor who attracted many college scouts.

"Nothing gives me greater satisfaction than a head-on tackle," he once said while demolishing SEC quarterbacks and ball-carriers.

As battle souvenirs, he has several front teeth missing—two for Alabama, one for LSU and another for Ole Miss. But Emanuel's career at Tennessee almost ended in his junior year.

Doug Dickey was hired as head coach in 1964, junked the Tennessee single-wing attack and installed the T-formation. Emanuel figured strongly in his defensive plans. After the Vols lost their final game to Vanderbilt in a 4-5-1 season, Emanuel and several of his teammates went out to drown their sorrows at a local college disco. A fight resulted with another group on the way home and the police were summoned to the scene.

Dickey heard of the affair and told Emanuel he was no longer on the football squad. Frank was on a full scholarship and had no financial resources to see him through school.

"Football was my life," he says, looking back. "I didn't know which way to turn. Everything I had to look forward to was gone. I chucked it all away in five lousy minutes."

Depressed, he left school and went to Florida. He got in touch with a few semipro football clubs, but mostly he did nothing. A Knoxville businessman contacted him and advised him to return to town and get a job. He went to work for a construction firm, kept in condition at the YMCA.

Dickey was impressed with Emanuel's behavior and invited him to try out for the team in the spring. That turned out to be the making of an All-American.

"I had my chance and I was going to make it pay off," Emanuel said.

The Virginian played with so much spirit in practice that it caught on with the other players. The result was the Vols' return as a SEC power with an 8-1-2 record in 1965.

The Vols beat UCLA, 37-34, in the regular season windup and then whipped Tulsa, 27-6, in the Bluebonnet Bowl. Frank was picked as the outstanding lineman of the game. Then the Associated Press picked him on the All-America team. So did the Football Writers, *Time Magazine*, *The Sporting News*, NEA and the *Football News*. But the honor that Emanuel cherished most was his selection by teammates as the Vols' best lineman for the entire season.

Pretty good for a fellow who almost didn't get there.

JIM BRELAND
The road to stardom

Jim Breland was born in Blacksburg, the son of a Virginia Tech professor. At Blacksburg High School, he was a much sought-after fullback. He also earned three letters in basketball and one each in track and baseball.

Breland received an appointment to the Naval Academy and lettered as a sophomore on the Middies' 1963 Cotton Bowl team. Then he decided he wasn't cut out for a military career. He had his father write Georgia Tech after leaving the Naval Academy. Georgia Tech had tried hard to get him when he was in high school. Jim was happy to learn that Tech still wanted him. He had to sit out a year before becoming the Jackets' regular center in 1965. He started and finished every game at offensive center after a brief tour with the defensive unit early in September 1965.

Bobby Dodd was the Tech coach then. He had five All-American centers listed in the record books during his long reign, but said he never had one like Breland. In 1966, Dodd said, "Breland is the best blocker, the best offensive center since I've been at Georgia Tech."

Jim never made the headlines. Offensive centers seldom do. But the coaches—and opposing teams—were aware of what Breland was doing. Georgia Tech coaches figured offensive linemen had to block 60 to 70 percent to win against the class opposition the Ramblin' Wreck faced every week. The center has the toughest job because he has to get the ball back to the quarterback and then block.

Jim didn't grade out under 72 per cent on his blocking in the two years he played with Georgia Tech.

Elected co-captain of the offensive unit at the end of the 1966 season, the 6-1½, 223-pound senior didn't go unnoticed. The NCAA recognizes six of the many All-America teams. Breland made five of the six—AP, UPI, American Football Coaches, NEA and Central Press. And most of the "non-recognized" ones.

Jim Breland, Georgia Tech 1966 All-American from Blacksburg.

LEROY KEYES
A long way from home

Leroy Keyes would have liked to have stayed in Virginia to play college football so he could be close to his home in Newport News.

"I never had the chance, of course, except at an all-Negro school. They weren't taking Negroes then at Virginia or the other schools," he said before a game against the University of Virginia at Lafayette, Indiana, in his senior year.

"If I could have gone to a school close to home and been accepted not as a football player but as a student..." his voice trailed away.

Keyes, a Carver High School sensation, reached the heights at Purdue, although he confesses he nearly went to West Virginia on a basketball scholarship instead.

"When I got to Purdue I began to wonder if I had made a mistake," he said years later. "I didn't know if I could play football for a school like that."

Purdue soon found out the 6-3, 205-pound Virginian fit like a glove.

He was used as a defensive halfback in his sophomore year. He ran for 166 yards with pass interceptions, a school record, that season. People were beginning to take notice. He was put on some All-America second teams. He played on Purdue's only Rose Bowl entry, January 1, 1967, when the Boilermakers defeated Southern Cal, 14-13.

"After my freshman year I had found I could defend against guys I knew were pretty good, and I could run patterns against them. I knew then I could play. They didn't know I could run until the end of my sophomore year. I carried the ball 12 times and gained 151 yards."

That did it. In his junior year, 1967, the Newport News athlete was made an offensive halfback. There was no stopping him now.

He rewrote many of Purdue's records in rushing, receptions and touchdowns (19 in 1967, 37 career). He was a unanimous All-America selection two consecutive years (1967-68).

In 1968, he was named All-America by the AP, UPI, Kodak, Football Writers, and *The Sporting News,* among others, He was named Purdue's Most Valuable Player, an honor he cherished. He played in the Hula Bowl and East-West Shrine games.

And he was a leading candidate for the Heisman Trophy. A guy named O. J. Simpson beat him out.

"How can you beat out a guy named Orange Juice?" Leroy laughed.

Leroy Keyes, Purdue's 1967-68 All-American from Newport News.

JAKE SCOTT
A safety deluxe

Jake (The Great) Scott is listed among the NCAA consensus All-Americans and Virginia can put in a claim to him. Actually, he was born in Georgia, and his mother moved to Alexandria. Fran Tarkenton was his idol and coached him one summer at Athens in Pony League baseball.

At Bullis Prep he played flanker and tailback and was voted the outstanding prep athlete in the area.

At Georgia, Jake made the All-SEC team as a sophomore in 1967, also the All-SEC academic first team.

He played safety and in ten games of the 1968 season, Scott intercepted ten passes (a Georgia record) for 175 yards and two touchdowns. He also led the SEC in punt returns with 440 yards, on 35 returns, including a 90-yard touchdown jaunt against Tennessee.

Many experts rated Scott as the finest safety man since Charley Trippi, a super performer on Georgia's 1946 Southeastern Conference powerhouse.

Scott was voted on practically every major All-America team his junior year, including the Football Writers, NEA, *New York Daily News,* American Football Coaches, UPI, Walter Camp and *Football News.*

He passed up his senior season in 1969 to play in the Canadian Football League, and eventually wound up in the National Football League.

Scott has continued his success in pro football. A free safety, he was a five-time Pro Bowl selection with the Miami Dolphins and was picked on the All-NFL two times. He was named Most Valuable Player in Super Bowl VII. He was traded to the Washington Redskins in the final week of the 1976 pre-season training.

Jake Scott, an Alexandria resident, won All-America honors at Georgia in 1968.

WALKER GILLETTE
The Capron Comet

As the old saying goes, Walker Gillette was born to play football. His grandfather, Jim, played with the Virginia Cavaliers in 1913-14. Then Jim, Jr., played three seasons at Virginia, 1937-38-39, and was an All-State halfback and captain of the Cavaliers in his senior year. Then Jim, Jr. went to the pros and, in 1945, scored a touchdown on a pass from Bob Waterfield that helped the Cleveland Rams beat the Washington Redskins in the NFL championship game, 15-14. Jim, Jr., also played with the Green Bay Packers and Detroit Lions.

But in college, Walker went one better. He put Capron on the map. Capron, population 314, holds the distinction of being the smallest incorporated town in the country to produce a consensus All-American since 1925.

A star at Southampton High School, Walker shattered all pass-receiving records at the University of Richmond. He was a genuine All-American. In three years of college football, 1967-69, Walker caught 158 passes for 2,649 yards and 22 touchdowns, ranking him among the all-time leaders in the NCAA record book. The coach of an opposing team, watching Walker snare passes all over the field, remarked, "He's like a man among boys out there."

The pros thought so, too, because he was San Diego's No. 1 draft pick.

In a game against Mississippi State in 1969, Walker caught 16 passes for 264 yards. He caught three touchdown passes against both Furman and William and Mary in 1968.

"I don't worry about how many I catch," he said after one game, "I just worry about catching the next one."

He saw double coverage so often he sometimes wondered if he needed glasses. But the opponents just couldn't stop him from catching passes.

Walker's dad was no silent sideliner.

"Dad is like a second coach," Walker said during the 1968 season. "I think he's happy I'm doing well, but if I do something wrong, like drop a pass, he lets me know about it."

Walker played in the College All-Star game against the then-world champion Kansas City Chiefs as well as the East-West and Hula Bowl games, before joining the pros. He's playing with the New York Giants of the NFL.

Walker Gillette, Richmond 1969 All-American from Capron.

RON RUSNAK
He stole the headlines from the backs

Ron Rusnak, North Carolina 1972 All-American from Prince George.

Ron Rusnak was pleasantly surprised when he was named a consensus All-American at the University of North Carolina in 1972.

When advised he won top honors, the 6-1, 225-pound offensive guard from Prince George, remarked: "I guess my first reaction is that my teammates (they called him the Rooster) are as deserving as I am."

He was a bit modest, of course.

Rusnak's most spectacular block in his senior season came against Clemson when he hit the Tiger linebacker at the four-yard line, lifted him straight up and knocked him into the end zone. The Tar Heels scored from the 11 on the play.

"This may be the best offensive line I've seen in the ACC," Frank Howard, the former Clemson football master, said of North Carolina. "And there's no question but that Rusnak is the best one on it."

At North Carolina, he played on three bowl teams and two conference championship teams. Capping his brilliant career, he helped the Tar Heels beat Texas Tech, 32-28, in the 1973 Sun Bowl. He was one of the unsung heroes, the guys who block for the runners, who made a name for himself. Off the field, Rusnak looked pretty ordinary. Only his size distinguished him from any other college senior. On the football field, however, he was hard to ignore.

The little kids worshipped him and reporters wanted to talk to him, but they had to get the coach to point him out.

But he surpassed the quarterbacks, the tailbacks and the linebackers at their own game—publicity—although he didn't go around looking for it. His deeds told his story, putting him in the spotlight.

He always questioned his individual value. "It's everybody's job. If one guy messes up, we all look bad, even if the rest of us make our blocks. We gotta work together."

"Ron is one of the great offensive guards in college football," North Carolina coach Bill Dooley said at the time. "I doubt there has ever been a blocker like him in the ACC before."

STEVE DELONG
Tops in the nation

Steve DeLong, a Chesapeake product, played for the Tennessee Vols and became the only Virginian ever to win the Outland Award, the ultimate honor for the nation's outstanding lineman.

Steve DeLong is the only Virginian ever to win the Outland Award, which is presented annually by the Football Writers Association of America to the best interior lineman in the nation.

The Chesapeake native, a product of Oscar Smith High School, was just that when he became one of the most widely-acclaimed heroes in University of Tennessee history in 1964.

In 1962, DeLong was selected to the Associated Press All-Sophomore team in the Southeastern Conference. That merely set off a cascade of honors.

He was selected on practically every All-America team, including the Associated Press, Football Writers, *Playboy Magazine, Look Magazine,* NEA, *Time Magazine, Argosy Magazine, The Sporting News* and *Sport Magazine.*

Among other honors earned in three seasons as a Vol:
- SEC lineman of the year, 1964.
- Coaches' poll, best defensive lineman in SEC for two years.
- All-Southeastern Conference.
- Outstanding lineman in nation awards by Columbus, Ohio, Touchdown Club and Birmingham, Alabama, Touchdown Club.
- Most valuable player in the Senior Bowl.
- Captain of Tennessee and of East team in Shrine bowl.

FRANK LORIA
Pure dynamite

Frank Loria, Virginia Tech's first consensus All-American.

Frank Loria was Virginia Tech's first consensus All-American. But would you believe that Tech almost rejected him because they thought he was too small to play college football? Jerry Claiborne, who was then coach of the Hokies, was convinced to take a chance on the 5-9, 174-pound prospect from Clarksburg, West Virginia.

The calculated risk turned out to be a bonanza for the Gobblers. Loria became the best defensive back in Tech history.

He was the best running back on Tech's 1964 freshman team, but in spring practice the following year he was switched to defensive safety. An instinctive player, a rugged tackler and an excellent pass defender, Loria was one of the reasons teammates Ron Davidson and Frank Beamer did so well as sophomores in the secondary.

"He looked after them like a mother hen," said Claiborne.

In Tech's 1967 opener against Tampa, Loria repeatedly broke up Tampa's long attempts at long-bomb passes, tackled with his usual dash, especially as a linebacker on goal line defense, and several times put Tech in good field position with his punt returns.

Against Kentucky, his punt returns of 25 and 16 yards set up Tech touchdowns. In the Miami game he batted down two touchdown passes, then returned a punt 95 yards for a touchdown. In the first quarter against Kansas State, he intercepted a pass, recovered a fumble, made a last-ditch, TD-saving tackle on the next play. From his middle linebacking spot on the goal line defense he blitzed the Kansas State quarterback on first down for a nine-yard loss from the five-yard line. On the next play, he came from nowhere to deflect an apparent TD pass in the end zone and Tech won, 15-3.

"He had the knack that you don't coach," Claiborne said. "In fact, he was practically a coach on the field."

Loria ranked seventh in the nation in 1967 on punt returns. His totals included 61 punt returns for 813 yards and four touchdowns and seven pass interceptions. He started all 31 games during his career (1965-67).

As a junior, Frank was picked on two All-America teams. The honors poured in as a senior: first team Associated Press, *Look Magazine*, United Press International, NEA, American Football Coaches, *New York Daily News*, Walter Camp Football Foundation.

Loria was killed in the tragic plane crash that also claimed the Marshall University football team following a game at East Carolina in 1971. Loria was a member of the Marshall coaching staff.

Basketball

All-America Chet Giermak connects on one of his hook shots in game against W&L in William & Mary's old Blow gymnasium.

THE CONSENSUS ALL-AMERICANS

Bob Spessard, Washington & Lee, 1937.

The National Collegiate Athletic Association (NCAA) lists only six players from Virginia colleges on the consensus major college basketball All-America teams from 1925-75. They are Norman Iler (1936), Bob Spessard (1937) and Dom Flora (1958) of Washington, & Lee, Richard (Buzzy) Wilkinson (1955) and Barry Parkhill (1972) of Virginia, and Chet Giermak (1950) of William and Mary.

The format used by the NCAA in making the consensus selections for a 50-year period included (1) all consensus first team choices as compiled by the NCAA Statistics Service since 1948, using (1) the leading selections of writers, coaches, and wire services (2) consensus first and second fives in the NCAA Basketball Guides over the years and in the All-Time Basketball Record Book published in 1970, and (3) all those who were *first team* selections (on teams of ten players or less only and nationally distributed). Before 1948, most of the names came from the Converse-Chuck Taylor teams that began in 1932, and from the Helms-Bill Schroeder teams (the 1926-42 Helms teams actually were published in 1946; the annual Helms teams began with the 1943 season).

Chet Giermak, William & Mary, 1950.

Norm Iler, Washington & Lee, 1938.

Dom Flora of Washington & Lee, 1958

Buzzy Wilkinson, Virginia, 1955.

Barry Parkhill, Virginia, 1972.

Buzzy Wilkinson goes up for two points against North Carolina. He scored 2,233 career points (1953-55), one of his many records in the University of Virginia books.

GLENN ROBERTS
The Pound Pivoter

Who developed the jump shot in basketball?

Some basketball authorities claim Hank Luisetti of Stanford University now enshrined in the game's Hall of Fame at Springfield, Massachusetts, popularized the technique.

But it's a fact that a Virginian, Glenn Roberts of Pound, was the first to master the shot that revolutionized the game at Emory and Henry College several years before Luisetti's illustrious play at Stanford. Roberts received national acclaim for his basketball feats, setting a national collegiate scoring record and winning All-America honors.

Actually, Roberts never had the privilege of practicing in a gymnasium until he went to Emory and Henry. And the fact is, he developed the jump shot while he was in high school.

But let Glenn tell you about it:

"Our high school did not have an indoor basketball court when I was playing. Because of our eagerness for basketball we practiced in all kinds of weather. At times it was too muddy to dribble the ball and move effectively, especially since we practiced most of the time in our pair of all-purpose shoes.

"When we could avail ourselves of a basketball we would often congregate under our basket and practice in an unorganized way. Whoever recovered the ball after a shot was attempted was on his own to get off a shot at the basket against the combined efforts of everyone to prevent the shot from being taken.

"Because of this combination of conditions it was necessary to devise something besides an ordinary effort to even get the ball to the basket unless you got lucky. By starting to jump as high in the air as I could after recovering the ball and releasing it after jumping out of reach of the others, I started to get the

ball to the basket consistently and before long I even succeeded in making some baskets without depending on luck."

Pound was a town of only 150 people then. Glenn lived five miles from the high school and walked each way every day to classes—and practice. He was rated one of the greatest high school players ever produced in that section of the state, leading Pound to the Class C Virginia championship.

At Emory and Henry under Coach Pedie Jackson, the Pound Pivoter attracted national attention with his fantastic shot, confounding the opposition while shattering the record books.

"He'd leap into the air, grab a pass, pivot in mid-air and let the ball fly toward the hoop, connecting with amazing accuracy," is the way one writer described Glenn's shot.

"I became accurate with the jump shot in high school," Roberts recalled. "However, it was in college that I became proficient in developing multiple moves such as the forward and backward pivot and dribble to maneuver into a better shooting position. It was also in college that my timing developed to a point where I could jump and absorb the shock from the defensive effort, and then hang free in the air momentarily before releasing the ball. As a result, I could make a basket almost everytime I got the ball within the present high point distance from the basket."

It worked—and how!

Some called it the hesitation shot, looking as if he was suspended in the air. Whatever it was, Roberts was unstoppable, and his jump shot must be considered a major factor in accelerating the scoring pace of basketball as we know it today.

His credentials are proof of his

greatness.

In 80 games over a four-year period with the Wasps, 1931-35, Roberts scored 1,531 points to establish what was than an all-time national collegiate scoring record. An average of 19 points a game may not seem a lot under today's breakneck style, but in the day of low-scoring basketball and the center jump, it was incredible.

In 40 games during his four-year reign at Emory and Henry, Roberts scored more points than the entire opposition could muster. While Roberts was playing, the Wasps compiled a 72-8 record, losing only two games in his junior and senior years.

"Playing college basketball was a continual thrill," says Roberts in recounting the past, "at the time it was more thrilling to us, a team representing a school with an enrollment of 400, to beat much larger schools such as VPI, William and Mary and Richmond. It was satisfying for me to contribute to the success of the team. In retrospect, our team's success, my national scoring record and my selection to the All-America team with players from large schools stand out in my mind."

Roberts' scoring rampage was featured in Ripley's "Believe It or Not" and other syndicated articles. The Pound Pivoter was a three-time all-state selection and, in 1935, was picked to the first All-America team in Frank Menke's *All Sports Record Book,* the first Virginia native ever to receive the honor.

After Luisetti broke his record with 1,550 points at Stanford, Roberts observed: "When I was playing I didn't pay any attention to records and scores, and I never knew that I was supposed to hold the all-time collegiate record until I read it in *Collier's* magazine afterwards.

Robert's four-year record at Emory

Glen Roberts' amazing feat at Emory & Henry was immortalized in the internationally-syndicated "Believe—It-or-Not" by Ripley.

and Henry included college games only, and didn't count an additional 482 points he scored in Wasp games against independent teams. This would have given him a grand total of 2,013 points as a collegian.

After graduating from Emory and Henry with honors, Glenn coached the Norton High School girls' basketball team to two state championships. Then he played pro basketball at Akron, Ohio, in 1938 with Firestone, which won the Eastern Division championship in the National Basketball League, the only pro basketball league at the time and the forerunner of the NBA.

On one of the other teams was a fellow named Johnny Wooden, who became one of the greatest college basketball coaches of all time at UCLA.

"Johnny Wooden played his last year in the National Basketball League my first year in the league," Roberts recalls. His team, Indianapolis, used a fast break offense like he had played under Piggy Lambert at Purdue. Although he had passed his peak in physical ability, he was still an outstanding player. He played with great intensity when he was in the game. At the time his potential as a coach did not occur to me, but looking back I can see where his obvious will to win was a contributing factor in his success as a coach."

After his UCLA team defeated Kentucky for the championship in 1975, Wooden retired from coaching. His team had won the national title ten times, including seven in a row, a record not likely to be matched any time soon.

In 1942, Glenn and his brothers organized one of the most unique basketball teams in the country. Every one of the Roberts' boys followed their big brother to Pound High, won all-state honors and led their team to the state title. The Roberts' boys dominated the Akron League for five consecutive seasons, and toured the south during World War II. In one benefit game, they raised more than 50,000 dollars in War Bonds.

How would this basketball phenomenon of the early 1930s fit into the game today?

"At 6-4, I would not be a big man by today's standards," Glenn claims. "If present player competition and play conditions existed when I was playing I would have been a guard. I had adequate speed and good outside shooting ability. I would have developed necessary ball-handling, maneuverability and driving ability to supplement my jump shot to be outstanding offensively as a guard. Very little adjustment would have been required on defense because I was a good man-to-man defensive player. I accepted defense as a personal challenge."

Roberts did not play pro basketball for his livelihood.

"I played in connection with regular employment at teaching and then with Firestone. Although we were paid a salary for doing a job, Firestone was a member of the NBL, and it was a thrill to play against such teams as the New York Renaissance, but my biggest kick as a pro came in winning the championship of the National Basketball League in 1938-39."

Glenn and his brothers became successful Firestone dealers in Norton, with outlets in three states.

After his college days, Glenn Roberts organized one of the most unique pro basketball teams (above) ever. They were called the Roberts Brothers and they were really brothers. Front: (from left) Percy, Darrell and Harry. Back: Ola, Wallace and Glenn.

THE VIRGINIA SQUIRES
The debts piled up for the pros

Time ran out for Virginia's only major league franchise on May 10, 1976. That's when the Norfolk-based Virginia Squires folded in the American Basketball Association after dodging financial disaster for six years.

But the Squires gave Virginia fans that big-league feeling. There simply wasn't enough support to keep them afloat. Pro basketball is big business, big salaries, and the Squire losses amounted to several million dollars during their existence.

Earl Foreman, a Washington attorney, brought the struggling Washington Caps to Virginia in the summer of 1970 and changed their name to the Virginia Squires. He felt Virginia was a good market for a pro team, and he brought popular Al Bianchi as his coach. Bianchi was fired after winning just one game in November of the 1975-76 season, but he alone couldn't be blamed for the Squires' poor record.

In their first season in Virginia, the Squires played their home games in four different places—the Old Dominion University Fieldhouse, the old Richmond Arena, Hampton Coliseum and Salem-Roanoke Valley Civic Center.

Hampton Coliseum was the first of Virginia's super-arenas to open and it was the favorite home court of the Squires, who won 16 of 19 games before crowds totaling 105,190 on the Peninsula the first season.

From the start of his operation in Virginia, Foreman had his troubles. He was forced to sell superstar Rick Barry because Barry didn't want to play in the south. Barry never played a game with the Squires. But Coach Bianchi directed the Squires to the Eastern Division championship over Kentucky by 11 games in their first Virginia campaign.

Led by Charlie Scott, the sensational rookie from the University of North Carolina, it turned out to be the Squires' most successful season, although they lost to Kentucky, 4 games to 2, after eliminating New York, 4-2, in the ABA playoffs.

Then the Squires signed the fabulous Julius (Dr. J.) Erving, who developed into one of pro basketball's greatest, for the 1971-72 season. But even the combination of Scott and Erving and the opening of Scope in Norfolk, Richmond Coliseum and Roanoke Civic Center couldn't keep the Squires out of the red.

While the Squires created popularity, their owner continued to encounter severe financial trouble and was forced to sell star players to keep the franchise going until the end of the 1973-74 season.

Selling the stars only infuriated the public, and fan support at the end of the season came from few.

Scott jumped the franchise in March of 1972 because of a contract dispute with Foreman. A month later, the Squires' other superstar, Dr. J., disclosed he had signed a future contract with the Atlanta Hawks of the National Basketball Association. Erving tried to jump to the NBA but was brought back to the Squires by a court order. In August of 1973, Erving was sold to the New York Nets, who also purchased his obligation from Atlanta.

In the Summer of 1974, Foreman sold his interests to a group of Virginia investors who desired to keep the major league franchise alive in the Old Dominion. But losses continued to pile up and the debt-ridden Squires ran out of money and were finally folded by the ABA.

Charlie Scott goes way up in game at Hampton Coliseum. He was the super star in the Squires' drive to the ABA Eastern championship their first season in Virginia.

The sensational Juluis Erving doing what he does best—and that's scoring. But even his spectacular play couldn't keep the Squires out of the red.

The first Virginia Squires, who won the ABA regular-season Eastern Division championship in 1970-71. Kneeling (from left): Coach Al Bianchi and trainer Bob Travaglini. Standing: Roland (Fatty) Taylor, George Irvine, Doug Moe, Neil Johnson, Mike Maloy, Jim Eakins, Ray Scott, Bill Bunting, George Carter, Charlie Scott and Mike Barrett. (Note: Larry Brown also was on this team at the beginning, but an early-season hernia operation sidelined him. When he came back, Barrett had taken his starting job at guard. Brown made no bones about saying he was unhappy about the situation, and Bianchi shipped him off to Denver at the All-Star break in January.)

Earl Foreman, a Washington attorney who brought major league basketball to Virginia, selling his super stars in an effort to keep the debt-ridden franchise afloat.

This was a familiar scene on the Squires bench. Trainer Bob Travaglini (left) tries to calm down an angry Coach Al Bianchi, who often objected to the referee's call.

The Olympians

Steve Riddick, former Norfolk State star, raises his arms as he crosses the finish line to give the United States the Gold Medal in the 4 x 100 meter relay final at the 1976 Olympic Games in Montreal. Riddick ran the anchor leg.

Duane Bobick started boxing when he was in the Navy stationed in Norfolk. Won All-Navy title three times, twice captured All-Service heavyweight championship, two-time Council International Sports Military champion, 1972 Golden Gloves champion, 1971 National AAU champion, North American and Pan American Games champion 1971. Represented United States boxing team against Romania, England and Russia (3 times), winning all bouts. Had a string of 61 straight victories snapped by gold medal winner Teofilo Stevenson of Cuba in semifinals of 1972 Olympic Games. Turned pro and is ranked among the world's top heavyweights.

THOMPSON MANN
He swam his way to world acclaim

It is ironic that swimming, perhaps the least publicized sport in Virginia, should produce the Commonwealth's first Olympic Gold Medal winner.

Thompson Mann couldn't win a varsity monogram in any sport while a student at Great Bridge High School in Chesapeake, but he took to the water and swam his way to world acclaim.

Born in Norfolk, Thompson learned to swim in a Richmond community pool when he was six, launching a career that took him to world championships in Tokyo and Europe.

At the University of North Carolina, Mann was elected to the All-America swimming team 1962-63-64, and was co-captain of the Tar Heels in 1964, backstroking to the top in collegiate and National AAU competition.

Then he reached the greatest heights in the 1964 Olympic Games at Tokyo, becoming the first man in world history to swim the 100-meter backstroke in less than a minute.

In the Olympics, he streaked to the astonishing time of 59.6 seconds for a new world and Olympic mark, giving the U.S. team an unbeatable lead in winning the 400-meter medley relay championship. A year later, in world competition at Budapest, Hungary, the Chesapeake athlete had a hand in helping the United States defeat the Russians.

His 1965 conquests also included the National AAU championships for the backstroke, both indoors and outdoors.

Thompson Mann of Chesapeake, the first Virginian to capture an Olympic Gold Medal.

BOB RICHARDS
Up, up, up for a record

In the 1951 Millrose Games in Madison Square Garden, Bob Richards became the second man in history to clear 15 feet in the pole vault. Since this was before the advent of the fiberglass pole, it was considered an astounding feat of the time.

But that wasn't the only accomplishment of the Reverend Robert E. Richards, Bridgewater College's most celebrated alumnus, a minister for the Church of Brethen.

"It was the greatest thrill of my life," Bob said of his over-15 leap. "I spent thousands of hours working on it."

He went on to become a two-time Olympic pole vault champion, three-time Decathlon champion. He was voted into the Helms Foundation Hall of Fame as the outstanding athlete in North America in 1951.

Also in 1951, the Reverend Richards was voted the prestigious Sullivan Award, presented annually by American Amateur Athletic Union (AAU) to the "amateur athlete who, by performance, example and good influence, did most to advance the cause of good sportsmanship."

This champion fitted the bill. He cleared 15 feet more than 49 times, his greatest height coming in the Chicago Daily News Relays on March 17, 1951, when he went over at 15 feet, 4¾ inches.

After vaulting 15 feet, Bob started for the Decathlon, which includes ten gruelling events rolled into one. He said he did it because a guy challenged him. Within four months, he won the AAU title, setting a new record. He won the national decathlon again in 1954 and 1955.

After competing three years at Bridgewater College, Richards transferred to the University of Illinois in his native state. In 1947, he was a member of Illinois' national collegiate championship track team and was the collegiate pole vault champion.

With the U.S. Olympic team in 1948, he placed third in the games at London. He was determined to win an Olympic Gold Medal, and in 1952 at Helsinki he set an Olympic record in winning the pole vault at 14 feet, 11¼ inches.

Richards went back to the Olympic Games in 1956, winning the pole vault Gold Medal again to become the only man in history to win two Olympic gold medals in the event. In 1957, he was selected as one of the ten outstanding young men in America by the U.S. Junior Chamber of Commerce.

In his inspirational talks, the Reverend Richards says, "There's no limit what a man can do. If he believes in himself, if he works hard—the sky's the limit."

The Reverend Bob Richards, a Bridgewater College alumnus, won two Olympic Gold Medals in the pole vault. One of America's great champions.

GRAY SIMONS
The littlest Olympian

Gray Simons made two U.S. Olympic teams, both indoors and outdoors.

Who said there was no room for the little fellow among the giants of sports? Take Gray Simons, who weighs only 115 pounds but who made it to the Olympic Games. He's a product of Granby High School, which created the greatest dynasty in Virginia high school sports.

Simon was a wrestling champion, who at Lock Haven (Pa.) State made the "Granby Roll" famous in collegiate circles as he won 89 consecutive bouts—the longest string of victories in college history.

He was the first person in history to gain the Outstanding Wrestling Award in both the National Collegiate (NCAA) and NAIA (small college) championships.

He was the first person in history to gain the Outstanding Wrestling Award in the National Collegiate (NCAA) and NAIA (small college) championships.

He won a berth on the U.S. Olympic team in 1960 and 1964 and competed in the Games at Rome and Tokyo. He finished second at Rome. Although he didn't win a gold medal, Simons was undefeated in the 1964 Tokyo Games, but penalty points proved costly.

A state champion at Granby, Simon won four consecutive conference titles at Lock Haven.

As coach at Lock Haven he was voted NAIA Coach of the Year. He was elected to the Helms Wrestling Hall of Fame.

MELISSA BELOTE
The teenager who swam to gold

As an unknown 15-year-old, Melissa Belote of Springfield swam to three gold medals in the 1972 Olympic Games at Munich and won world acclaim. She was then a student at Robert E. Lee High School in Springfield, Virginia.

Melissa also set three records. She set an Olympic record of 1:05.8 in winning the 100-meter backstroke. On the final swimming day in the games, she produced a world record 200-meter backstroke in 2:19.2.

In between these two championships, Melissa was on the team that fashioned another world record when the American girls won the 400-meter medley relay in the time of 4:20.7. She swam a 4:20.5 backstroke leg, another Olympic record.

Representing the United States in international competition in 1973, Miss Belote won the world's championship in the 200-meter backstroke at Belgrade, Yugoslavia. The same year she won four national championships. She set three American records.

After her conquests in the Olympics, Melissa was given a heroine's welcome when she returned home. She was given the "keys to the city" in Springfield, and on a visit to the Virginia Legislature, the delegates stood and proudly gave this young Virginian a tremendous ovation as one of the all-time greats in Virginia sports history.

Honors poured in for Melissa. She is the only female to receive the Arch McDonald Achievement Award by the Washington Touchdown Club. In fact, they had to change the name of the award from "Local Boy Makes Good." She was inducted into the Swimming Hall of Fame at Ft. Lauderdale, Florida, and was honored at a formal dinner by New York Sports Lodge, B'Nai B'rith, New York City.

Melissa learned to swim at the age of three, entering competition at the age of eight in her neighborhood swim club. When she was ten years old, she came under the guidance of Ed Solotar of Silver Springs, Maryland. She then began to blossom as a great swimmer. But not exactly an instant success. At 12, Melissa entered her first U.S. national championship and finished 37th. In 1969, she won the 100-meter backstroke event in the National Junior Olympics. Her world conquests followed, one of the youngest athletes to reach such great heights.

Melisa Belote graduated from Robert E. Lee High School in 1975 and enrolled at Arizona State University.

In the 1976 Olympic Games at Montreal, Melissa swam the 200 backstroke in an American record of 2:17.27. But it wasn't good enough to win a medal. She finished fifth, an indication of how the world swimmers, especially the East German women, have improved since Melissa mopped up in 1972 Olympics as a 15-year-old.

Melissa Belote, a teenage swimming champion from Springfield, came home with three Olympic Medals.

LARRY BURTON
The Olympian from Melfa

Larry Burton of Melfa was probably the fastest man in Big Ten football history. When he wasn't catching passes for the Purdue Boilermakers, the former Mary N. Smith High School star was smoking on the track. He set national records in the sprints on his way to the 1972 Olympic Games in Munich. In the Olympics, he placed fourth in the 200-meter dash. In 1972, he tied the existing world record in the 300-yard dash at :30.2, and ran the 220-yard dash outdoors in :20.3 and the 100 in :09.3 in 1974, both Purdue records. Indoors he ran the 60-yard dash in :05.9 and the 300-yard dash in :30.2, also Purdue records. Once he ran a wind-aided 100 in :09.1.

So it was that Larry was a hard man to keep up with in Big Ten football. In two seasons with the Boilermakers, he caught 53 passes, for 973 yards, an average of 18.3 yards a reception, and scored seven touchdowns. In 1974, *The Sporting News* voted him All-American, first team, and in addition to being named All-Big Ten, he won a place on the Big Ten All-Academic team. He was Purdue's most valuable player in 1974, and played in the San Francisco Shrine East-West game and the Hula Bowl in Honolulu. He was on the track All-America, 1972-74, and was the New Orleans Saints' No. 1 pick in the National Football League draft.

Larry Burton, a speed demon on track and gridiron.

Golf

An excellent view of the Golden Horseshoe in Williamsburg, showing State Amateur champion Vinny Giles (1967) marking his ball.

SLAMMIN' SAM SNEAD
A record unsurpassed

There may never be another like Slammin' Sam Snead.

He is perhaps the most remarkable athlete in the world. At age 64, in 1976, he was still on the golf tour.

In his long and storied career, the Hot Springs native, born May 27, 1912, won 84 tour championships—more than any golfer in history—and dozens of other titles. His mountain drawl and dry wit, combined with spectacular play, make him an all-time favorite. He turned pro in 1933 and joined the tour in 1937. His famous smooth swing and deadly approach putting gained him three Masters Tournament crowns. Only the U.S. Open eluded him.

For almost four decades, the Virginian has stood out in a sport dominated by youth, and he still commands the respect of the top touring professionals. His Masters record alone would qualify him for greatness. He has played in more Masters than any golfer in history.

And Snead is rather proud of his Masters record.

"I won three Masters," he said, "and I could have won seven or eight if I'd putted better." His victories came in 1949, 1952 and 1954.

Snead won his first of three PGA National championships in 1942 at the Seaview Country Club, Atlantic City, by beating Jim Turnesa, 2 and 1. He won the PGA again in 1949, this time in "Snead Country." Playing at the Hermitage Country Club in Richmond, he beat Johnny Palmer, 3 and 2, to regain the title he had won seven years earlier.

In 1951, Snead became the third man in history to win the PGA Championship more than twice. At 39, Sam also became the oldest champion, up to that time. In his final with Walter Burkemo, Snead won five of the first six holes, starting with an eagle and adding two birdies and three pars. He went on to win, 7 and 6, a score second only to Paul Runyan's 8 and 7 conquest of Snead in 1938.

Snead's career earnings amounted to 611,887 dollars by 1976, but just think what his bank account would have been if the purses were as large as they are on today's tour.

He is the oldest golfer on record to win a tour championship, capturing the Greensboro Open in 1965 when he was 52 years old.

Among Snead's other achievements: Won British Open in 1946; credited with 134 victories by independent record keepers; leading money winner in 1938-49-50; Vardon Trophy winner in 1938-49-50-55; member of Ryder Cup team eight times and captain of the team five years; voted Player of the Year in 1949.

He won the Canada Cup (now World Cup) individual title in 1961, and in 1973 captured his sixth PGA Senior and World Senior titles.

In 1963, Sam Snead of Hot Springs was voted into the National PGA Hall of Fame, and there's no question but that he belongs with the game's immortals.

Sam Snead...he's done it all.

CHANDLER HARPER
A fantastic shot that cost him 100,000 dollars

Chandler Harper when he won his first Virginia State Amateur championship at 18.

Don't tell Chandler Harper about tough breaks in golf because he was the victim of the most fantastic shot in the game's history.

It was August 9, 1953, the World Golf Championship at Chicago's swank Tam O'Shanter.

The slim Portsmouth pro, a putting wizard, had satisfied a gallery of about 10,000 around the final hole that he had won the championship and the 25,000 dollars prize that went with it by planting a second shot two feet from the cup for a birdie two.

The great closing effort gave the 40-year-old Harper a 36-34-70 and a 72-hole total of 270, nine under par.

Playing right behind was Lew Worsham, the 1947 U.S. Open champion and himself a native of Alta Vista. But he was 410 yards away when Harper was being congratulated by Harry Wismer in the first national telecast of a pro golf tournament.

Worsham whipped a tremendous drive on the 410-yard final hole. As the crowd swarmed around him, Worsham drew out a wedge, looked at the hole 104 yards away, and laid into the ball. While the throng—and Harper—stood in awe—the ball sailed to the front of the long green, covered about 30 feet on three bounces and curled into the hole.

"I was dumbfounded," recalls Harper. "There has never been a more fantastic finishing shot before or since in the history of golf."

"It was the luckiest shot I ever had in my life," smiled Worsham. "I'm sorry I had to do it to my friend Harper."

Oldtimers agreed with Harper. Worsham's shot must rank with the greatest of tournament finishes. The nearest the experts could find to match it was the 220-yard double eagle 4-wood shot Gene Sarazen canned on the par 5, 485-yard 15th in the 1935 Masters to gain a tie for the championship. He beat Craig Wood in a playoff.

That one shot, which beat Harper by one stroke, was worth 15,000 dollars, the difference between the 25,000 dollars first prize and the 10,000 dollars second.

And Harper had to watch it in flight, only 10 feet off the green talking to Wismer when Worsham holed out. Jimmy Demaret was making a radio broadcast of the finish at the time and had just lauded Harper's 9-iron shot to within two feet of the cup for a three as "one of the greatest."

When the ball trickled in, Chandler was speechless, but Demaret was heard on the air to mutter just one word: "Goddam."

It wasn't Harper's first heartbreak that year. He lost by one stroke to Al Besselink in the Las Vegas Tournament of Champions, and to Tommy Bolt in the Tucson Open the same way. But the Worsham shot was the most bitter pill he had to take in a distinquished career.

"It was a bitter pill to swallow," Harper recounted, "because if I had won I was guaranteed a year's exhibition contract calling for 1,000 dollars a day plus expenses. And the way my situation was then I was in a position to play every day. So I figured Worsham's shot cost me at least 125,000 dollars."

Like Sam Snead, Harper's durability on the links has been amazing. Born in Norfolk County on March 10, 1914, captain of the first golf team at Portsmouth's Woodrow Wilson High, Chandler became at 18 the youngest ever to win the Virginia State Open (1932) and also the oldest (56) ever to win it (1968).

Chandler and his sister, Lily Harper, were perhaps the best brother-sister golf act in the country. From 1934 to 1941, Lily won seven of eight State Women's Golf Championships, including four in a row.

One year Chandler and Lily won the state championship on the very same day. Lily never turned pro, but she would have been a good one.

In all, Harper copped the Virginia State Open ten times. He turned pro in 1934.

Perhaps his greatest victory came in 1950 when he won the National PGA championship. Considered one of the game's great putters, Chandler's conquests included the International Four-Ball championship in 1955, the Tucson Open in 1950, El Paso Open in 1953, the Texas Open in 1954, and the Colonial National Open in 1955.

Harper was selected to play on the U.S. Ryder Cup team in 1955. As time rolled on, the Portsmouth pro continued to add to his conquests, winning the National Seniors Open championship in 1965, the PGA Seniors and World's Seniors championships in 1968.

He still holds the National PGA record of 189 (63-63-63) for 54 holes, and tied for 36 holes with 126.

In 1969 Harper was elected to the National PGA Hall of Fame.

Chandler Harper, elected to the National PGA Hall of Fame in 1969, includes the National PGA championship among his many trophies.

VINNY GILES
A champion who passed up the pros

Vinny Giles won both the U.S. and British Amateur golf titles.

Vinny Giles has reached the very top in amateur golf. He won both the U.S. Amateur and British Amateur, a feat accomplished by very few. As a pro, Giles may have been a super star, one of the big money winners. But he passed up a chance for fame and fortune on the pro tour.

"I wanted to go to law school," he said. "And I didn't think I wanted the gypsy life of a professional golfer. But with all the money, I don't see how I passed up the opportunity. If I had known then how much money there was to be made, I might have made another choice."

The Lynchburg native, who graduated from the University of Georgia and the University of Virginia Law School, feels he would have made it big in pro golf. So do a lot of other experts.

Now he represents young golfers. His firm, Pros, Inc., is located in Richmond. He is one of the last of the gentleman-amateur type golfers, picking five or six major tournaments a year to play.

When Giles graduated from the University of Georgia, offers poured in for him to turn pro, including one which guaranteed him 40,000 dollars a year plus expenses for three years. It took a lot of thinking for him to turn it down.

For ten years, Vinny has been regarded as one of the top amateurs in the world. He won the U.S. Amateur title in 1972 and the British Amateur in 1975. He has many other trophies, including a record six Virginia State Amateur Championships. He was once low amateur in the Masters.

He was runner-up in the U.S. Amateur three times, twice by one shot, and, in an effort to take the British Amateur for the second straight time in 1976, he went to the semifinals before being eliminated. At Georgia he was an All-American.

He is a perennial choice of the Walker Cup and World Cup amateur teams. And Vinny Giles was one of the few of the top amateurs who didn't turn pro. But he enjoys representing the young pros, which gives him a chance to stay in golf. He can also pick his time to play a round, and every now and then go out for the big trophies.

BOBBY CRUICKSHANK
Virginia claims the wee Scotsman

Bobby Cruickshank was born in Scotland in 1896 but Virginia has staked a claim to him. He excelled in various sports in Scotland before coming to America in 1921, and went on to make a name for himself in the world of golf.

They called him Wee Bobby.

He made the trip to America in the company of another Scotsman, Tommy Armour, who was eventually to win the National Open, National PGA and British Open.

Meanwhile, Bobby did okay on his own in a playing career that covered more than three decades. After winning two major tournaments in 1921 and a semi-finalist in the PGA championship in 1922, Wee Bobby tied the legendary Bobby Jones for the National Open in 1923, losing the playoff on the final hole. That same year he was again semi-finalist in the PGA Championship.

In 1932, Cruickshank was runner-up again in the USGA Open, finishing third in 1934 and 1937.

He was golf's leading money winner in 1927. His major championships that year included the Los Angeles Open, Texas Open, Hot Springs, Arkansas, Open, the North and South Open; and he teamed with Tommy Armour to win the Miami International Four-Ball title.

Wee Bobby migrated to the Old Dominion in the early 1930s when he became head pro at the Country Club of Virginia in Richmond. He became a popular and colorful figure in Virginia, staying nine years. He captured the Virginia State Open six times.

It was at the Hermitage Country Club in Richmond that Cruickshank recorded his lowest single round—a 63.

In 1967, Wee Bobby Cruickshank was elected to the PGA Hall of Fame.

"Wee Bobby" Cruickshank

LANNY WADKINS
He discovered gold

Lanny Wadkins watches as his 40-foot birdie putt on the 18th green falls into the cup on the final round of the Byron Nelson Golf Classic at Dallas, Texas, in 1973. The Virginian defeated Dan Sikes on the first hole of a sudden death to win the 150,000 dollar tournament.

In 1972, a young upstart from Richmond went on the pro tour and came home with 116,616 dollars. Now firmly established as a threat, Lanny Wadkins boosted his golf earnings to 200,455 dollars, the most money ever won by a second year player, placing him fifth among the PGA money-winners in 1973.

There's no question but that the Virginian had the makings of a superstar.

His 116,616 dollars in winnings in 1972 broke Bob Murphy's 105,595 dollars record earnings for a rookie. Lanny's big win as a rookie was the Sahara Invitational, defeating Arnold Palmer by a stroke and Jack Nicklaus by three. Entering 36 events, Wadkins also finished second in the Bob Hope Classic and lost in sudden-death to Homero Blancas in Phoenix. He finished tenth on the Exemption Point list. Not bad for a rookie.

But in his second pro year, Lanny really went to town. In 26 starts, he finished among the top ten in 13 tourneys and won twice. He won the Byron Nelson Classic in Dallas as he birdied five of the seven holes for an incoming 31 to catch Dan Sikes and beat him on the first extra hole of a sudden-death playoff. Coming from three strokes back the final day, Lanny won the USI Classic in Sutton, Massachusetts.

Then in December, 1974, Lanny underwent an operation for the removal of his appendix and a diseased gallbladder. His golf earnings dropped to 51,124 dollars that year and in 1975-76 he was fighting back in hopes of regaining his stride.

Lanny's rise in the amateur ranks was as brilliant as his early success on the pro tour. He won the National Pee Wee championship in 1963, and a series of major conquests followed. In 1970, he won the U.S. Amateur and was runner-up to Bob Goalby in the Heritage Classic.

His other amateur triumphs included the 1968 Southern Amateur, the All-Dixie Amateur, the Atlantic Coast Conference, Eastern Amateur, the Red Fox and Palmetto Invitationals. He was a member of the 1969 and 1971 Walker Cup teams and playing with Wake Forest, was voted Collegiate All-America in 1970 and 1971.

Lanny actually turned pro in 1971 after winning the Virginia State Open and pocketing 1,000 dollars. He qualified for the pro tour at the 1971 school. In the final four event of 1971, he earned 15,921 dollars, highlighted by a third-place tie in the Walt Disney World. Richer days are ahead for the young Virginian.

CURTIS STRANGE
How high is up?

Curtis Strange was the youngest golfer ever chosen to the College All-America team. He also was the youngest and only the second freshman in history to win the NCAA individual crown (Ben Crenshaw in 1971 was the other). He tied Chandler Harper and Vinny Giles as the youngest to win the Virginia Amateur at 19.

"Curtis is the best amateur in the country today," said Chandler Harper, who was grooming the Wake Forest star for the pro ranks.

He appeared ready to take the step in 1976. Curtis won his second consecutive North and South Amateur Golf Tournament at Pinehurst, North Carolina, defeating Fred Ridley, 6 and 5, in the 36-hole playoff for the title. It was revenge of sorts for Curtis, who was eliminated by Ridley in the 1975 U.S. Amateur, 2 and 1. Strange became the first North and South winner in successive years since Billy Joe Patton in 1962-63. In 1974 *Golf Magazine* named the young Virginian as the College Golfer of the Year after he won the NCAA medal and led Wake Forest to its first team title ever. Also in 1974 he won the Chris Schenkel Intercollegiate by one stroke, the Pinehurst Intercollegiate, the Western Amateur and the All-Dixie.

He won the Eastern Amateur by 10 strokes in 1975, and was picked to play on the Walker Cup team in 1975 and the U.S. World Amateur Cup team in 1974. Curtis was low amateur in the 1976 Masters.

Curtis Strange was seven years old when he started playing golf under the coaching of his late father, Tom, a pro who won the Virginia Open in 1967. Young Curtis proceeded to mop up in his own state, winning the Virginia Junior championship in 1970 and 1972. He won the State Amateur in 1973, and the Southeastern Amateur.

He was well on his way—looking for more tournaments to conquer.

On June 14, 1976, Strange announced he would forego his senior year at Wake Forest to turn pro, preventing him from becoming a four-time All-America selection.

Curtis Strange helps get a birdie putt down on the 15th hole while en route to the 1975 North and South Amateur Tournament championship at Pinehurst, North Carolina. Strange also won the tournament in 1976.

Robbye King Youel of Charlottesville, winner of six Virginia State Women's Amateur golf championships, 1963, 1966, 1969-70-71-72.

Lily Harper (now Lily Harper Martin) of Portsmouth captured the Virginia State women's amateur golf championship seven times in eight years, including four in a row, from 1934 to 1941. Lily and her brother Chandler formed perhaps the best brother-sister golf act in the United States at the time. One year, both Lily and Chandler won Virginia state championships on the very same day.

Mary Patton Janssen of Charlottesville won the Women's Virginia State Amateur golf championship six successive years, 1957-62.

Wynsol Spencer of Newport News, five times winner of the State Amateur Golf Championship, 1939, 1948, 1953, 1955, 1959.

Boxing

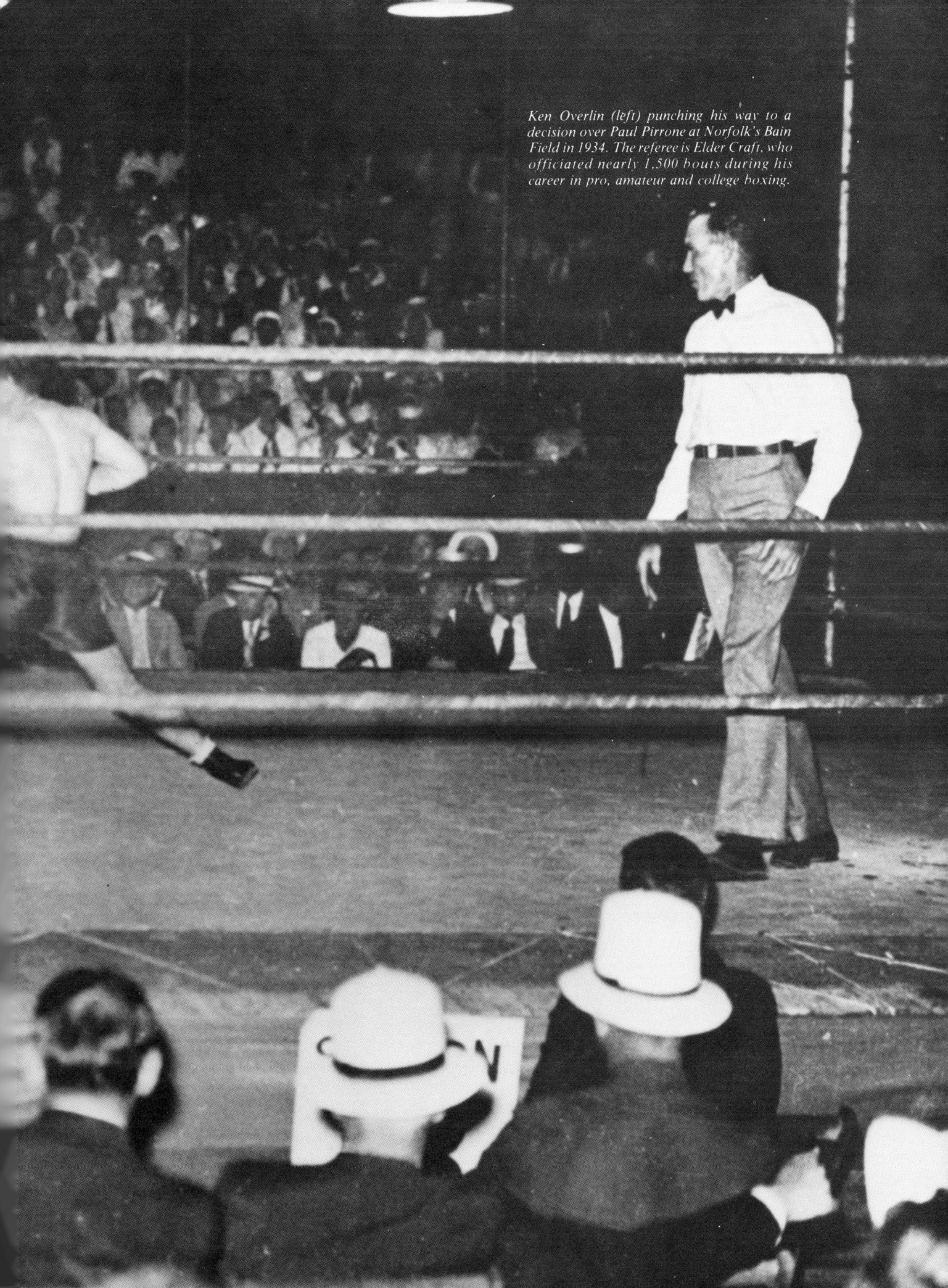

Ken Overlin (left) punching his way to a decision over Paul Pirrone at Norfolk's Bain Field in 1934. The referee is Elder Craft, who officiated nearly 1,500 bouts during his career in pro, amateur and college boxing.

Primo Carnera, the Man Mountain who later won the heavyweight title, welcomed to Portsmouth, where he fought an exhibition for matchmaker Arthur Emmerson (left) in 1934. He is shaking hands with A. Obici, president of Planters in Suffolk.

In 1932 at Portsmouth, Ken Overlin won a six-round decision over Bill Brennan. It was the first pro fight for both Navy boys. For Overlin, the bout was a stepping stone to the world middleweight championship (New York version). Brennan took another route. He boxed quite a while professionally and later coached Navy teams. In 1976, Brennan was one of the most influential men in the boxing world. Former president of the World Boxing Association, he was the WBA Championship Committee chairman. All world chamionship bouts had to be recognized by Brennan, for WBA sanction. He resigned his WBA position in September, 1976.

Brennan received no salary for his prestigious WBA position. His real job is with the Commonwealth of Virginia as executive secretary of the Virginia Athletic Commission, which controls boxing and wrestling in the state.

For a man who holds such prominence in the boxing world, Brennan actually has very little pro boxing to control in his own state. Pro boxing in Virginia, it seems, has joined the passing parade. Amateur boxing, however, is progressing and pro wrestling is mopping up at the turnstiles.

But it hasn't always been like that.

When Brennan fought Overlin in 1932, boxing was illegal in Virginia. "Bootleg boxing" thrived in Richmond, Roanoke, Newport News, Norfolk, Portsmouth, Virginia Beach and other points. The fight promoters beat the law by having fans pay their "dues" at the ticket window for admission. Usually, there was a select group sitting at ringside, including judges, police officers and city officials. Everybody, it seemed, liked to break the law and "bootleg boxing" was paying off the promoters during the Great Depression.

Then a funny thing happened.

Ralph H. Daughton, a Norfolk member of the House of Delegates, introduced a bill in 1934 that legalized boxing in Virginia.

And the fans stopped going to the fights.

Overlin was a product of "bootleg boxing" in Virginia, and perhaps the most successful. He was the "Golden Boy." The sailor from the *USS Idaho* won 25 straight bouts before losing a decision to Paul Pirrone in Philadelphia on April 30, 1934. Several months later in a return match staged in a Norfolk ballpark, Overlin gained revenge, clearly outpointing Pirrone. In 1940, New York recognized Overlin as the world middleweight champion after he defeated Cefferino Garcia in 15 rounds. Overlin lost the title to Billy Soose a year later.

Jack Levinson was a typical club fighter in those days. He had about 32 amateur bouts in Philadelphia before turning pro and coming to Virginia. He had more than 60 pro fights, mostly in Virginia rings, and has a few scars to show for his ring battles.

"I once fought three bouts in eight days," recalls the Jewish lightweight.

Levinson was managed by Chris Dundee, who also handled Ken Overlin. Dundee now operates out of Miami Beach, Florida, and is one of the most prominent promoters in the fight game today.

Among the crowd-pleasers of the late 1920s and early 30s were Tommy and Tootsie Bashara, Stumpy Jacobs, Bill Brennan, Overlin, Joe Bashara, Jake Denning, Bobby Godwin, Eric Lawson, Red Journee, Spike Hemlock, Nick Antonelli, Al Peters, Doc Conrad, Bill Bishop, George Rohanna, Joey Goodman, Lindsay Bass, Goldie Bass, Walter Kirkwood, Lew Raymond, Glenn Morgan, Midgett Wolgast, Sammie Weiss, Dick Welsh, Buddy Grimes.

"We never made much money for fighting, sometimes a hundred bucks or so," recalls Levinson. "But anything you could pick up in those depression days helped."

Jake Denning, a promising Navy light heavyweight, received 700 dollars for a fight with Sammy Weiss in Ports-

Tommy Bashara

Joey Goodman

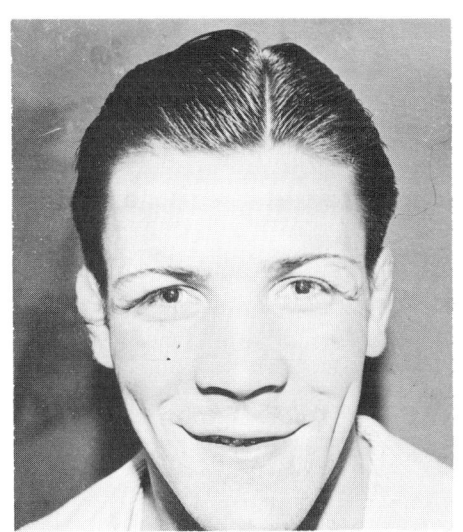
Stumpy Jacobs

Tootsie Bashara

mouth's Oasis Athletic Club. This was considered exceptional pay for a club fighter in those days, although Tootsie Bashara claims he was paid 5,000 dollars to fight Baby Miller in Richmond. Tootsie finished off Baby in 50 seconds of the first round, so it turned out to be easy money.

Levinson, who has a valuable collection of boxing mementoes, claims Stumpy Jacobs was one of the hardest punchers around. He won't get much argument there. Some of the bouts were classics, still talked about, and one of the most memorable involved Jacobs. In what was perhaps the strangest ending of a prize fight in Virginia history, the Hopewell battler fought Lou Raymond in an old converted Portsmouth movie house.

Dundee was the promoter of this bout in November, 1932, and it was supposed to be a warm-up for Raymond, who was being hailed as the next world lightweight champion. He had just defeated Harry Lenny in Philadelphia to gain No. 5 ranking. Jacobs wasn't supposed to have a ghost of a chance. In the first round, Raymond shot out of his corner and plastered Jacobs with smashing left hooks and right crosses. Stumpy just took it. He was facing a master boxer.

In round two, Raymond moved in with extreme confidence, jabbing and dancing, and befuddled the old battler from Hopewell. Midway through the round, Raymond started a right cross to Jacobs' head. Now, Stumpy was nobody's fool. He had been waiting for this opening. He slipped inside—and wham!

A terrific right hand sent Raymond to the canvas, spinning dizzily on his head. The crowd was stunned. As referee Joe Bauers reached the count of six, the bell rang. The timekeeper rushed into the ring and claimed he didn't ring the bell, pointing an accusing finger at Heine Blaustein, Raymond's manager. The arena then became a state of confusion.

It developed as Blaustein, stunned at seeing his contender being knocked out, dashed around the ring and rang the bell himself, an act certainly not acceptable in the law of the prize ring. Anyway, the underdog Hopewell battler was awarded the bout by a knockout. It took a doctor an hour to bring the boy from Baltimore to the realm of consciousness. All of which proved Jacobs could punch with the best of them.

While there's little or no pro boxing in Virginia today, the Navy maintains the interest among amateurs, turning out All-Navy champions and Olympians. The Norfolk Navy fighter making the most headway in recent years is Duane Bobick, a member of the U.S. Olympic team in 1972. The heavyweight included among his trophies the National Golden Gloves championship, the Pan-American Games championship and the National AAU title.

As a pro, Bobick won his first 36 bouts and is carefully fighting his way to the top. His goal: a shot at the heavyweight crown.

Ralph H. Daughton (right) father of legalized boxing in Virginia, and Joe Bauers, the first executive secretary of the Virginia Athletic Commission, with Max Baer when the heavyweight champion appeared as referee at Virginia Beach. The man on the left is unidentified.

Sign of the times.... During World War II many great athletes were stationed in camps throughout Virginia, and occasionally performed before the citizens to help morale on the home front. In the picture (left), sailor fred Apostoli, a former middleweight champion, points to a poster reminding one and all of one of his fights on the local scene.

Former pro boxer, now executive secretary of the Virginia Athletic Commission, Bill Brennan is the former president of the World Boxing Association and chairman of the WBA Championship Committee.

Chris Dundee of Miami Beach, Florida, one of boxing's most noted promoters and managers, got his start in Virginia. His brother, Angelo, is trainer for Muhammad Ali.

Jackie Levinson

COLLEGE BOXING
A knockout while it lasted

"When the state of Virginia went Republican, the statue of Thomas Jefferson was draped in black and similar action will probably be taken if the University of Virginia boxing team is beaten, but an untold occurrence of this kind does not seem to threaten."
  Stanley Woodard in the
  New York Herald Tribune
  in the early 1930s.

Intercollegiate boxing once enjoyed tremendous popularity in many of our colleges, surpassing basketball in spectator appeal. Boxing, as late as 1952, was still one of the youngest intercollegiate sports—and the most controversial. Despite a wave of criticism, the men behind college boxing went to extremes in an effort to create an atmosphere of respectability. Silence was requested of the spectators during a round. The proper time for applause, the fans were advised, was between rounds and at the end of bouts.

Coaches and seconds were not permitted to speak, signal, or in any way coach their participants during the progress of a round. During the NCAA boxing tournament, the referees were required to wear tuxedos. At the Naval Academy, admission to boxing matches was by invitation only. Spectators were asked to wear evening or dinner clothes.

In this elegant atmosphere of dignity, color and pugilism, the Virginia Cavaliers ruled supreme. Virginia Tech, VMI, Richmond and Washington and Lee had varsity boxing teams. The fans poured in to watch the matches. But none enjoyed the success of the Cavaliers, who always filled old Memorial Gymnasium. A two-day Southern Conference boxing tournament in Charlottesville drew 17,000 spectators in

Freddie (Bingo) Stant, a Norfolk athlete boxing for Catholic University, won the NCAA middleweight championship in 1939.

1934. There were similar crowds for two NCAA tournaments and several Eastern Collegiate championship meets on the Virginia campus.

The 1939 NCAA boxing tournament at the University of Wisconsin attracted a sellout of 42,000 fans. It was in this tournament that Frederick T. (Bingo) Stant of Norfolk, fighting for Catholic University, won the national middleweight championship, stopping defending champion Freddie McKinnon of Washington State in the finals before 17,000 spectators.

Yes, intercollegiate boxing was flying high and Virginia was one of its powers. Coach John S. LaRowe, one of the most respected men in the game, was responsible for the Cavaliers' success. He coached the first Virginia boxing team in 1922 and continued on the job 19 years. In the later years he was confined to a wheelchair. His legs were gone but not his heart. He continued coaching.

Under LaRowe's guidance, Virginia led the way for college boxing in the South and established the Charlottesville campus as one of the country's leading boxing centers in the sport.

Washington & Lee was Virginia's first dual meet opposition in 1922.

A member of the Cavaliers' first boxing team was Adolph Leftwich, undefeated as a middleweight and light heavyweight for three seasons. Leftwich was one of the few college boxers to win a first-team position on the Olympic team, representing the United States in 1924. In Virginia's first meeting with Penn State, an Eastern power, Leftwich, who captained the 1924 Cavaliers, competed in the middleweight and light heavyweight bouts the same evening, winning both. He was the first of Virginia's long line of champions. The unbeaten Cavaliers of 1933, captained by Bobby Goldstein, sent a record seven boxers to the Southern Conference tournament finals. Goldstein, a sensational lightweight who became Virginia's first NCAA champion the year before bantamweight Archie Hahn, welterweight Thomas Fisburne and light heavyweight Lewis Reiss won conference crowns.

Light heavyweight Ray Schmidt, co-captain of the 1938 Cavaliers, was undefeated in four seasons. Twice an entry in the NCAA, he won the national title both times. Also winning the national title that season was Virginia's Maynard Harlow, a skillful 145-pounder.

The 1948 Virginia team won the Eastern Intercollegiate championship as Al Hollingsworth, Bat Masterson, Buddy Shoaf and the three Marigliotta brothers triumphed.

Mortimer Caplan, who served as U.S. Commissioner of Revenue under President Kennedy, boxed for the Cavaliers and later coached the freshman team.

LaRowe, the grand old man of the only college sport that was derived from the professional field, believed that, when conducted on the right plane, boxing offered the best opportunity in the field of intercollegiate sports for development of the finest of manly traits. College boxing lost one of its greatest champions when LaRowe died in 1940 at the age of 73.

But critics of the sport finally won out. Although still enjoying great popularity, boxing was abolished as an intercollegiate activity in 1955.

Al York, a member of the 1925 Cavalier boxing team, succeeded LaRowe as coach and was in the corner when Virginia held its last boxing match (against Maryland) in 1955.

While it lasted, however, boxing held a prominent place in college athletics, especially at Virginia.

Bobby Goldstein, one of the greatest University of Virginia boxing champions.

Although confined to a wheelchair in his later years, Johnny LaRowe continued to coach the Cavalier boxers. He was college boxing's most celebrated coach.

The slender tennis veteran is the first black man to make it big in the once snobbish and exclusive game. He has won about everything in tennis worth winning, and is getting rich doing it. "Player of the Year in 1975," the Virginian enjoyed his greatest year. He won the Wimbledon title and he also won the World Championship Tennis (WCT) playoff final. His earnings for the year exceeded 315,000 dollars, the most by any tennis player in a year from tournament purses. He was ranked No. 1 nationally in 1975.

NORFOLK TENNIS PAIR WON 1911 U.S. TITLE

WHEN WILLIAM & MARY WON IT ALL IN TENNIS

Very few public tennis courts existed in Virginia prior to World War I. Tennis, however, gained popularity at country clubs, which could afford and maintain their own courts.

By 1976 tennis had become one of the leading participant sports in the state, thanks mainly to many fine courts constructed for the high schools and made available to the public. Night tennis also increased in popularity.

Tennis received considerable attention in Virginia in 1911 when Norfolk's Hugh G. Whitchead and J. Horner Winston captured the national clay courts doubles title at Omaha, Nebraska.

They entered the nationals unheralded and unseeded. Although they held the Virginia doubles crown and were regarded as among the top Southern players, they never received recognition from the national ranking committee.

Whitehead and Winston battled their way to the national double finals, where the experts figured the Virginians would certainly meet their doom. The Norfolk pair outclassed defending champions G.G. Anderso of Chicago and Walter T. Hayes of Brooklyn, New York, in the title match.

Whitehead served 62 years as an executive with the Seaboard Citizens National Bank before his retirement. He died in 1964. Winston became a prominent Chicago barrister.

William & Mary ruled the college tennis world in 1947 and 1948, capturing the National NCAA championship both seasons. Coached by Dr. Sharvey G. Umbeck, the Indians won 81 consecutive matches in a streak started in 1946. They are regarded as the greatest tennis team ever to represent a Virginia college.

The Indians not only brought home the team trophy in 1947, but Gardner Larned captured the singles championship for W&M, defeating Vic Seixas of North Carolina, 8-6, 3-6, 4-6, 6-3, 6-1, in the NCAA finals at Los Angeles.

Fred Kovaleski, one of the Tribe stars, warmed up during the previous winter. Competing in the National Indoor Tournament at New York under the W&M colors, Kovaleski upset veteran Frank Shields, 6-4, 3-6, 6-4, but later bowed out of the tourney on a loss to Bill Talbert, 12-10, 4-6, 6-1, 6-0. But he lost no prestige in the defeat.

During the summer of 1947, Fred Kovaleski won the National Public Parks tennis championship. In one of the most stunning tennis upsets of the year, Larned and Tut Bartzen defeated Jack Kramer and Ted Schroeder at an East Coast tournament. Kramer and Schroeder were regarded as the best amateur doubles team in the world at the time and won the Davis Cup championship by themselves the previous winter.

The Indians were dealt a serious blow when Larned decided to transfer to Rollins College (Fla.) prior to the 1947-48 term. But it turned out that the Indians were still the tennis masters. The Indians won their second straight NCAA championship in 1948. Not only that, but Fred Kovaleski and Tut Bartzen won the NCAA doubles title.

The 1948 William & Mary tennis team, which brought the Indians their second straight NCAA major college championship. They are Howe Atwater, Bob Doll, Bernard (Tut) Bartzen, Bill Smith, Dick Randall and Fred Kovaleski.

WITH A SOUTH AMERICAN TOUCH, HAMPTON INSTITUTE WON THE NATIONALS

Airton Silva

Twenty-nine years after William and Mary became the first and only Virginia college to win the NCAA national tennis championship, Hampton Institute became the first Old Dominion entry to capture the NCAA Division II crown.

At Maryville, Missouri, in 1976, the Pirates brought home the championship, the first predominately black school ever to win it and only the second non-California school in history to capture the tennis prize. They accomplished their mission with a junior, a sophomore and two freshmen.

And it was all because of a masterful recruiting job by Coach Dr. Robert Screen, who went to South America and came back with the very best talent. Half of the four-man team that won the championship at Maryville were from Sao Paulo, Brazil. They are junior Roger DeSantis Guedes and freshman Airton Silva. All four players were selected to the 16-man All-American tennis team.

The other two were Americans, Rodney Young, a freshman from Baltimore, and Bruce Foxworth, a sophomore from St. Louis.

In seven years under Coach Screen, the Pirates won 133 matches while losing 27. He put Hampton Institute on the tennis map.

Coach Screen wasn't satisfied that the Pirates had won eight straight Central Intercollegiate Athletic Association championships and 22 of the last 25. He wanted the National Championship. So he sacrificed an all-winning regular season record by loading the 1976 schedule with the best Division I competition.

The Pirates were 9-0 against Division II teams and 7-8 against Division I competition. But the experience paid off with a national championship.

The Pirate duo of Roger DeSantis Guedes and Foxworth also won the national doubles title.

An All-American, Guedes is perhaps HI's greatest tennis player ever. But the NCAA National Division II singles championship has escaped him after reaching the finals twice. He has another year, 1977, to achieve the goal. After finishing his college career, Guedes has ambitions of turning professional.

Coach Dr. Robert Screen. A Brazilian Connection.

Bruce Foxworth   *Rodney Young*   *Roger DeSantis Guedes.*

Stock Car Racing

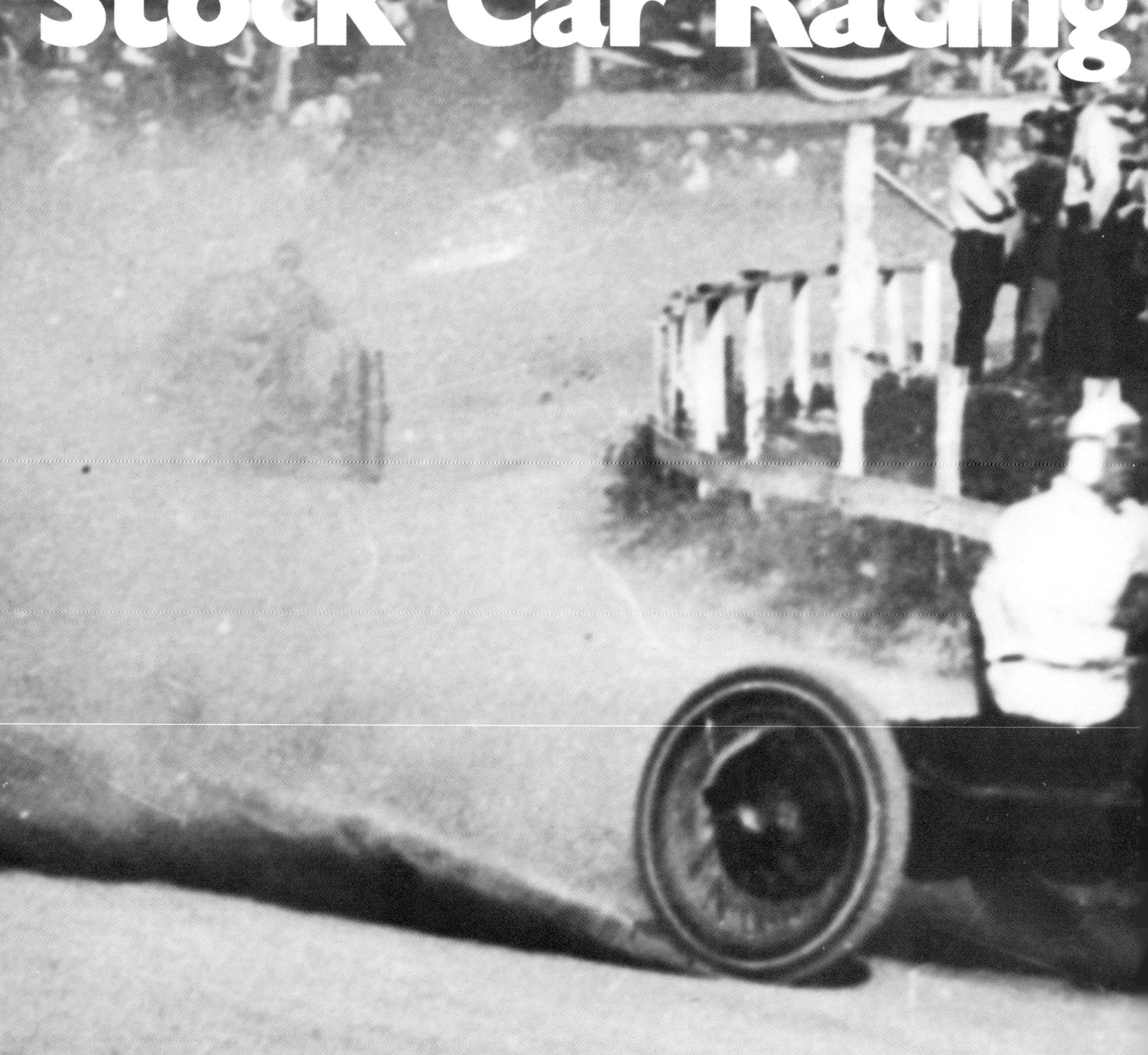

Auto racing at the old Fairgrounds in Norfolk, 1925.

Stock car racing fans in Virginia are a devoted breed. They think nothing of packing a lunch on a moment's notice and taking off for Darlington, Atlanta, Daytona and other points to see a big race. Some say the sport is an offspring from the mad chases of the bootlegging days. No matter what, this weekend drama of man and machine against time has captured the fancy of thousands of fans.

At Martinsville in 1975, a record crowd of 34,000 watched the Virginia 500 Grand National, nearly doubling the population of the city. A total of 104,000 fans watched six races during the year at the Martinsville Speedway, which is regarded as the finest half-mile track in the country.

Stock car racing is different from the Indianapolis-type racers, the sprint cars and the midgets. Body-wise, the stocks are the same as you see on the streets. And that, it seems, is where the fan appeal comes in. They like to root for the car-make they're probably driving. The difference, of course, is in the mechanical makeup, which is designed for speed.

Although there have been about 50 fatalities on the track, including deaths to seven Virginia drivers, stock car people don't like to refer to their sport as a violent one. "There are so many more violent deaths on our highways," claims Ray Melton, one of Virginia's racing authorities. "Considering the large number of races, the fatalities are extremely low."

The National Association for Stock Car Racing (NASCAR) has adopted strict safety measures for drivers, who wear helmets, shoulder and seat belts and fire-proof uniforms during races. The driver sits in a cage made up of roll bars. Gas tanks have rubberized bladders to prevent explosions.

Stock car racing is a comparative newcomer to the sports scene, originated in the South and beginning to take a foothold in the North and Canada. Its history in Virginia can be traced back to 1925, when Sam Elliott of Norfolk, driving an Oakland, won a race at Dixie Speedway, located on Granby Street in Norfolk. Sponsored by the Tighe Motor Company of Norfolk, Elliott received a trophy for his winning effort.

In 1946, the Chinese Corner Speedway, located at Virginia Beach Boulevard and Witchduck Road in what was then Princess Anne County, opened for stock car racing under the direction of Pete (Red) Mordecai, the track builder. The track, in ensuing years, was promoted by Joe Thornton, Eddie Bird and Johnny Chandler, Joe Weatherly (the track's name was changed to Joe Weatherly Speedway) and Jim Creech of the National Union for Better Auto Racing (NUBAR).

In 1947, Princess Anne Speedway, located at Kempsville and Waterworks Road in Princess Anne County, opened for stock car racing on a quarter-mile asphalt track for night racing under the promotion of Red Crise. The facility also included a half-mile dirt track, later utilized for racing on Sunday afternoons. Through the years, promoters for the track included Johnny Tadlock, Nelson Royall, Bill Rose, George Carter and Weatherly.

The famed Martinsville Speedway opened on September 7, 1947, and ran its first NASCAR-sanctioned race in 1948. NASCAR is the major league of stock car racing.

Richmond's first stock car race was run at the old fairgrounds track (now Parker Field) over a half-mile dirt track. Bill France, Sr., and Jack Kochman organized the race, which was promoted by Bob Sall.

One of the top cars entered in the first Richmond race was built by Bill Hubbard and Bill Moffitt of Norfolk. The car was sponsored by the College of William and Mary's automotive shop and, according to Hubbard, was driven by Bill France, Sr., who later became NASCAR president.

In 1949, Nelson Royall and Bill Rose opened Royall Speedway, eight miles west of Richmond, and the Richmond Speedway, north of the city, opened shortly afterwards.

Other tracks were opened, including Old Dominion Speedway in Manassas, Starkey Speedway in Roanoke, Fairgrounds Raceway (Strawberry Hill) in Richmond, and South Boston Speedway. In later years, the stock cars competed at Fredericksburg and Petersburg fairgrounds, Dude Ranch in Hampton, Chestnut Avenue track in Newport News, Brunswick Speedway in Lawrenceville, Dinwiddie Speedway near Petersburg, Hilltop near Charlottesville, at Galax and the four-counties fairgrounds track in Suffolk.

During the early years of stock car racing in the Commonwealth, local associations were formed as governing bodies. In the Tidewater area, there were two such groups: The Tidewater Stock Car Racing Association and the Virginia Beach Straight Stock Car Racing Association. In the Richmond area, it was the Richmond Stock Car Racing Association. Johnny Tadlock, Bob Lambert, Sr., C.V. Whittemore and Paul Sawyer served as presidents of the Tidewater group. Buck Latham was president of the Virginia Beach association.

NASCAR was officially organized in December, 1947, and with the start of the 1948 season, the Modified Division went into action, making it the oldest racing category in NASCAR.

In answer to a long-standing demand for less expensive racing equipment, NASCAR's busiest division was developed in 1949. The cost of constructing a first-class Modified Division car had become prohibitive because of the advancing skill of racing mechanics and engineers. So the "mostly stock" Sportsman Division was born.

NASCAR's Grand National Circuit was founded in 1949. Nine Grand National races were staged that year, one at Martinsville Speedway. Robert (Red) Byron of Atlanta won the Martinsville race, emerging as champion of the newly-formed National Division.

Joe Weatherly opened the 1952 season at Princess Anne Speedway under the NASCAR banner, won 49 of 83 races that year and finished as runner-up to National Modified champion Franie Schneider. In 1953, Weatherly won the National Modified.

Monk Tadlock, of the famed Norfolk racing family, was appointed NASCAR Chief Steward for the Princess Anne track.

The first NASCAR-sanctioned race in

The famed Martinsville Speedway in Martinsville, showing a record crowd of 34,000 fans that attended the 1975 running of the Virginia 500 Grand National Championship race.

Stock car racing at the old Princess Anne track in Norfolk in 1952.

The late Gene Lovelace of Newport News, one of the top Modified and Late Model Sportsman drivers in Virginia's stock car racing history, died of a heart attack at Southside Speedway, located eight miles west of Richmond.

the Richmond area was held at the Richmond Speedway in 1952, with Gunnie Cousins and Garnie Allen the promoters and Mike Poston the Chief Steward. Mike Poston headed a group that operated stock car races at the Strawberry Hill State Fairgrounds in 1952. When Poston stepped aside, Royall and Rose took over the promotion of the facility.

Paul Sawyer and Weatherly promoted the Fairgrounds Raceway in Richmond, the Joe Weatherly Speedway at Chinese Corner, and the Wilson, North Carolina, Fairgrounds track in 1955. Sawyer bought Weatherly out in 1956 and paved the way for the Fairgrounds Raceway in August, 1968, at which time Sawyer inaugurated the 500-lap events for the elite Grand National Division cars.

The Fairgrounds Raceway is now one of only two tracks in Virginia (the other is Martinsville) that presents the Winston Cup Grand National Division races. Sawyer's partner is Ken Campbell of Richmond. The Grand National Richmond 500 is run each season on the Sunday following the Daytona 500 in February. The Capital City 500 is run at the Fairgrounds annually on the Sunday after the Southern 500, the Labor Day spectacular, at Darlington, South Carolina.

In 1959, Jim Creech, Johnny Stokes and Harold Hunley promoted a Grand Prix race at the old Joe Weatherly Speedway in Princess Anne County. Ray Platte was the winner of the 60-mile event and collected 984 dollars as his purse.

In 1960, NUBAR was organized by Creech, Stokes and Hunley, headquartered at Chinese Speedway. NUBAR-sanctioned races were held at the Dude Ranch Track in Hampton, the Dinwiddie track near Petersburg, the Four Counties Fairgrounds track in Suffolk, Wilson, North Carolina, and the Keller Fair on Virginia's Eastern Shore.

Clay Earles, Sam Rice and Henry Lawrence were builders of the Martinsville Speedway, which opened for its first race on September 7, 1947, with only 750 seats and 10 acres for parking.

Today the track covers 200 acres and has permanent seating for 30,000 fans, plus the infield area. France, Sr., of Daytona Beach, Florida, helped promote the first Martinsville race and, in 1949, became Earles' only partner.

The first Grand National race at Martinsville was run in 1949 in a storm of dust. The track was paved in 1955, with the first Virginia 500 in the spring of 1956. Richard P. (Dick) Thompson of Roanoke joined the Martinsville staff in 1956 and is now vice president and assistant general manager. He is generally recognized as one of the best public relations directors in the business.

The Martinsville schedule now includes the Dogwood 500, a doubleheader of 250-lap NASCAR National Championship race and a 250-lap National Championship Late Model Sports event run each March. The Modifieds return for a 150-lap National championship race a week prior to the Spring running of the Winston Cup Virginia 500 in April. There are three similar events in the Fall.

The Virginia 500 in 1975 paid a purse of 75,000 dollars—a NASCAR record for a half-mile track.

Since its inception in Virginia, many stock car tracks have closed down. In addition to Martinsville and Richmond, the only Virginia tracks now operating include Southside Speedway near Richmond, Old Dominion Speedway in Manassas, East Side Speedway in Waynesboro, Langley Speedway in Hampton, Winchester Speedway in Hillsville, Natural Bridge Speedway, Coeburn Speedway, Virginia Raceway, eight miles north of Saluda, and Franklin County Speedway in Calloway. Rumors of the construction of super speedways in Virginia have flourished for many years, but none has developed. Paul Sawyer or Clay Earles may be the prime movers for a super speedway if one is ever built.

Through the years, Virginians have received national acclaim through their stock car activities. Curtis Turner of Roanoke, in the opinion of many racing authorities, was one of the greatest drivers of all time. Winner of more than 350 races in his spectacular racing career,

The late Ray Platte of Norfolk, one of the top Modified drivers in the history of Virginia stock car racing shown in his famed #58 at the Chinese Corner Speedway back in the early 1950s. Platte was fatally injured in a racing accident at the South Boston Speedway in South Boston, Virginia during the 1963 race reason.

The late Earl Bryant of Portsmouth, shown with the Arnold McCoy's Modified Chevrolet #27. Bryant, a consistent winner on tracks throughout the Southeast, was fatally injured in a racing accident at Concord, North Carolina, in 1961.

The late Curtis Turner of Roanoke, winner of more than 350 races in his career. Turner was fatally injured in an airplane crash in Pennsylvania in 1970.

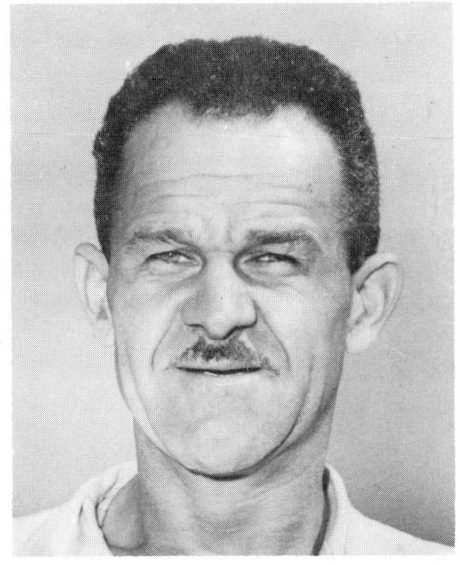

Wendell Scott of Danville, the first Negro driver in stock car racing in Virginia. Scott, a top competitor for many years in the Modified and Sportsman divisions, moved up to the Grand National division of NASCAR and won one Grand National race at Jacksonville, Florida, now retired.

Bill Champion of Norfolk, top star for many years in the Modified and Sportsman division of NASCAR. Now a veteran competitor in the Grand National division of NASCAR. Champion, winner of more than 250 races in the Modified and Sportsman divisions was a top midget and motorcycle racer in the early days of his racing career.

Ray Hendrick of Richmond, one of the all-time greats in the history of stock car racing. He has won more than 500 races in his career in the Modified and Late Model Sportsman divisions. Still active.

Turner died in a plane crash in Pennsylvania in 1970.

Weatherly was one of the all-time great driving champions in NASCAR, winner of the 1953 National Modified championship and the Grand National championship in 1962-63. He was only in his prime when he was fatally injured in a race at Riverside, California, in 1964. Bill Dennis of Glen Allen was three-time winner of the Permatex 300 late model sportsman championship race at Daytona Beach. He also won the NASCAR Grand National Rookie of the Year award in 1970. Eddie Crouse of Glen Allen won the National Modified championship (NASCAR) in 1962-63. And Joe Thurman of Rocky Mount won the 1967 National Late Model Sportsman championship of NASCAR. Lennie Pond of Ettrick, a top late model sportsman driver who moved up to the Grand National Division of NASCAR won Rookie of the Year honors in 1973. Ray Hendrick of Richmond, driver in NASCAR's modified and Late Model Sportsman divisions, was the winner of more than 500 races in his career.

Bill Champion of Norfolk, winner of more than 250 races in the modified and late model sportsman divisions, was a Grand National competitor.

Shields Parsons of Norfolk, an early co-owner of a race car, was appointed by President Eisenhower as Federal Attorney for Eastern District of Virginia.

Ray Melton of Virginia Beach is generally conceded to be the all-time great stock car race announcer, a 20-year veteran chief announcer for the prestigious Darlington Raceway. Dean of stock car race announcers, Melton has been featured in motion pictures, raceway documentaries and in national publications.

The honor roll of Virginia stock car racers who were killed:

Eldredge Tadlock of Norfolk, at High Point, North Carolina, in 1941; Joe Jernigan of Norfolk, at Richmond in 1951; Melvin Forehand of St. Brides, at Suffolk in 1951; Earl Bryant of Portsmouth, at Concord, North Carolina, 1961; Ray Platte of Norfolk, at South Boston, 1953; Gip Gibson of Charlottesville, at Saluda in 1974, and Weatherly.

In the pioneering of stock racing in Virginia credit must go to many—drivers, mechanics, car owners and officials. And no stock car story would be complete without the listing of the following:

From the greater Tidewater area (Norfolk, Virginia Beach and Chesapeake)—Joe Jernigan, Johnnie Rhodes, J.A. Falk, Johnny Tadlock, Eldredge Tadlock, Mont Tadlock, Roscoe Stallings, Sam Elliott, Mac Peels, Shields Parsons, Charlie Whittemore, Slick Boyd, Marvin Sawyer, Barney Ballance, Duke Young, Eddie Byrd, Bill Hubbard, Bill Moffitt, Bill Hyatt, Ray Platte, Bill Sawyer, Frank Haddock, George Swain, Harold Hunley, Sam Satterfield, Greek Koscos, Rusty Russ, Frank Roman.

And Al Rudd, C.C. White, Paul Sawyer, Bud Ralph, Eddie Tarpley, Homer Shook, Wes Morgan, Eddie Pitts, Dale Ore, Duke Chambers, Pepper Martin, C. Martin, Marty Martin, Bob Lambert, Sr., Willie Wilson, Jim Creech, Johnny Stokes, Jimmy Eley, Frankie Leland, Chester Foreman, Pete Bogg, Clarence Humphreys, Frank Hall, Jay Shreves, Pete Babb.

And Bob Koolidge, Bus Barnette, Junie Nelson, Joe McIver, Shorty Bowers, Red Sewell, Jimmy Yates, Mooney Williamson, Jimmy Cox, Ace Adams, Arnold McCoy, Bill Champion, Earl Bryant, Pete Mordecai, Jack Thornton, Blackie Sims, Bill Yow, Rudy Hires, Gene Lovelace, Curtis Estes, George McChesney, Bob Jennings, Ralph Rose, Oliver Dail, Archie Poyner, Junie Hudgins.

And Bernard Spivey, Buck Lethma, P. Williams, Red Bland, Early Pangle, Jimmy Williamson, Earl Davenport, Bobby Clark, Bob Pierce, Hurricane Harry Jennings, Bill Lorah, Mel Oldham, George Salas, George Richley, Snuffy Smith, Dick Girvin, Ernie Hill, Melvin Foreman, Leo Russ, Ralph Steed, Harry Theobold, David Byrd, Tommy Dixon, Don Crouch, Pete Love.

And Preston Nesbitt, J.S. McCracken, William R. Senters, Lester

Bill Dennis of Glen Allen, three time winner of the Permatex 300 for Late Model Sportsman cars at the Daytona International Speedway in Daytona Beach, Florida. Dennis was also winner of the NASCAR Grand National Rookie of the Year award in 1970.

Runt Harris of Richmond, one of the real pioneer drivers in stock car racing in Virginia, also one of the greatest, won 33 races in one season and was Virginia State Sportsman Champion in 1960. Now semi-retired.

Pepper Martin of South Norfolk, the first NASCAR Sportsman Champion of Virginia in 1952.

F. Shattuck, Robert Nesbitt, Robert G. Scott, Jack H. Horner, Harold Newell, Andy Scott, Robert Ingram, Milton M. Stegall, Henry L. Yon, Walter Sawyer, Jimmy Revell, James H. Wood, Joe Weatherly, Red Neighbors, Bruce Warren and Ray Melton.

From the Richmond area—Nelson Royall, Bill Rose, Runt Harris, Junie Donleavy, Hank Stanley, Ray Hendrick, Emanuel Zervakis, Ted Harfield, Sonny Hutchins, Buck Masons, Mike Poston, Hal Kemp, Bob Apperson, Bart Stark, Dean Max, Leslie Herman, Eddie Crouse, Al Fleming, Jack Schulte, John Harris, Kenneth Campbell, Gunnie Cousins, Garnie Allen and Tim Sullivan.

Roanoke—Curtis Turner, Hank Rivet and Buddy Wilson.

Smithfield—Bob Powell.

Hampton—Jack Mulligan, Charlie Crane, Bill Lowery, Butch Torrie, and Joe Hendrick.

Newport News—James Tyre and Randy Hutchison.

Marion—Gayle Warren.

Keysville—Homer Shook.

Stuart—Glen Wood, Leonard Wood and Leonard Martin.

Bassett—Pee Wee Martin and Otis Martin.

Colonial Heights—Bud Wamsley.

Danville—Wendell Scott.

Fredericksburg—Al Grinnan.

Alexandria—Wes Morgan.

Collinsville—Gifford Wood.

Martinsville—Clay Earles, Clyde Minter, Coleman Lawrence, and Fred Dove.

Suffolk—Earl Briggs.

Ray Melton of Virginia Beach, veteran chief announcer of the famed Darlington Raceway in Darlington, South Carolina, interviews Grand National driving star, Cale Yarborough of Timmonsville, South Carolina, on his second win of the Southern 500 in 1973.

Dick Thompson of Roanoke, Virginia, vice-president and assistant general manager of the Martinsville Speedway, one of the best public relations men in all of racing.

H. Clay Earles, president of the Martinsville Speedway in Martinsville, one of the most successful of all the NASCAR-sanctioned track promoters.

Joe Weatherly Stock Car Memorial Museum in Darlington, South Carolina, built in honor of the late great stock car race driver from Norfolk.

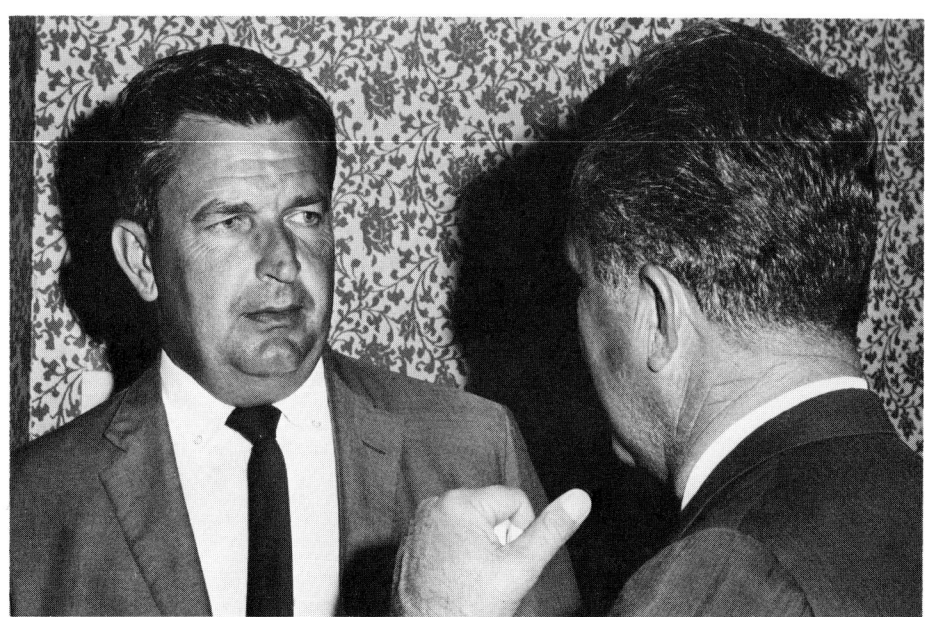

Ken Cambell (facing camera) and Paul Sawyer, operators of the Richmond Speedway.

Joe Weatherly shown in his famous Rhodes Special Ford No. 9, in which he won the 1953 National Modified Championship of NASCAR. The Rhodes Special was engineered by race car builder Johnny Rhodes of Norfolk.

JOE WEATHERLY
Auto racing's clown prince

Joe Weatherly.

A legend in stock car racing.

A cut-up, too, anything for a laugh—and a victory. He was aptly named "The Clown Prince of Stock Car Racing."

A real practical joker, he lived up to the name en route to glory—and an untimely death.

Norfolk-bred and perhaps Virginia's greatest contribution to the National Association of Sports Car Automobile Racing, Weatherly oddly enough started his colorful career as a motorcycle jockey in 1946, later becoming a pioneer in stock racing and one of its first heroes.

Off the track, he'd do most anything for a laugh.

Once, before a race, he and his buddy put a horse in their hotel room. They happily paid the damages.

"It was worth it," he laughed.

On another occasion, he proudly rode a mule in the Darlington 500 parade—to pay off a bet.

"What was your greatest thrill?" a writer once asked him.

"Getting paid after a race," the flamboyant Weatherly replied.

Behind the wheel, though, it was all serious business for Little Joe, a champion of the first order. He had several narrow escapes, but a scar on his face was a memento of a non-racing collision. He first won fame as a motorcycle racer, winning national championships in 1948 and 1949. He had one serious mishap in motorcycle competition, but survived with scratches.

Then he turned his attention to stock-car racing, where the risk of life and limb was even more dangerous, but the purses fatter. Several years later he won the championship of modified track division of NASCAR, becoming a favorite with the fans.

Joe was a frequent winner of the famed Daytona Beach races. Within the space of five days in 1961, he won the 100-mile Grand National stock car race and the race of champions on the Florida track. In 1962, he won the 100-mile twin stock car race on the same track.

It was in 1961 at Daytona Beach that little Joe escaped serious injury. He overturned his compact car, but emerged unhurt. In 1962, he won the race of champions, a 25-mile sprint for late model cars.

For two consecutive years, 1962-63, he was the top-ranking driver in the NASCAR Grand National Circuit. His winnings in 1963 amounted to 58,110 dollars, a lot of money for a fellow who not so many years before collected parking lot fees at the old Princess Anne track in Norfolk when the circus played there.

Joe was wheeling his way to fans and fortune. His earnings were piling up. From 1959 to 1964, he won 103,445 dollars in NASCAR events on four major Southern tracks alone. But Joe's luck ran its course. At Riverside, California on January 19, 1964, Joe's Mercury, bearing the familiar No. 8, hit a retaining wall during a 500-mile road race. Joe was killed. He was 41.

But NASCAR kept his name and a legend alive. The Joe Weatherly Stock Car Museum, a project valued at more than 50,000 dollars, stands at the prestigious Darlington Raceway.

A memorial to Norfolk's happy-go-lucky racing champion.

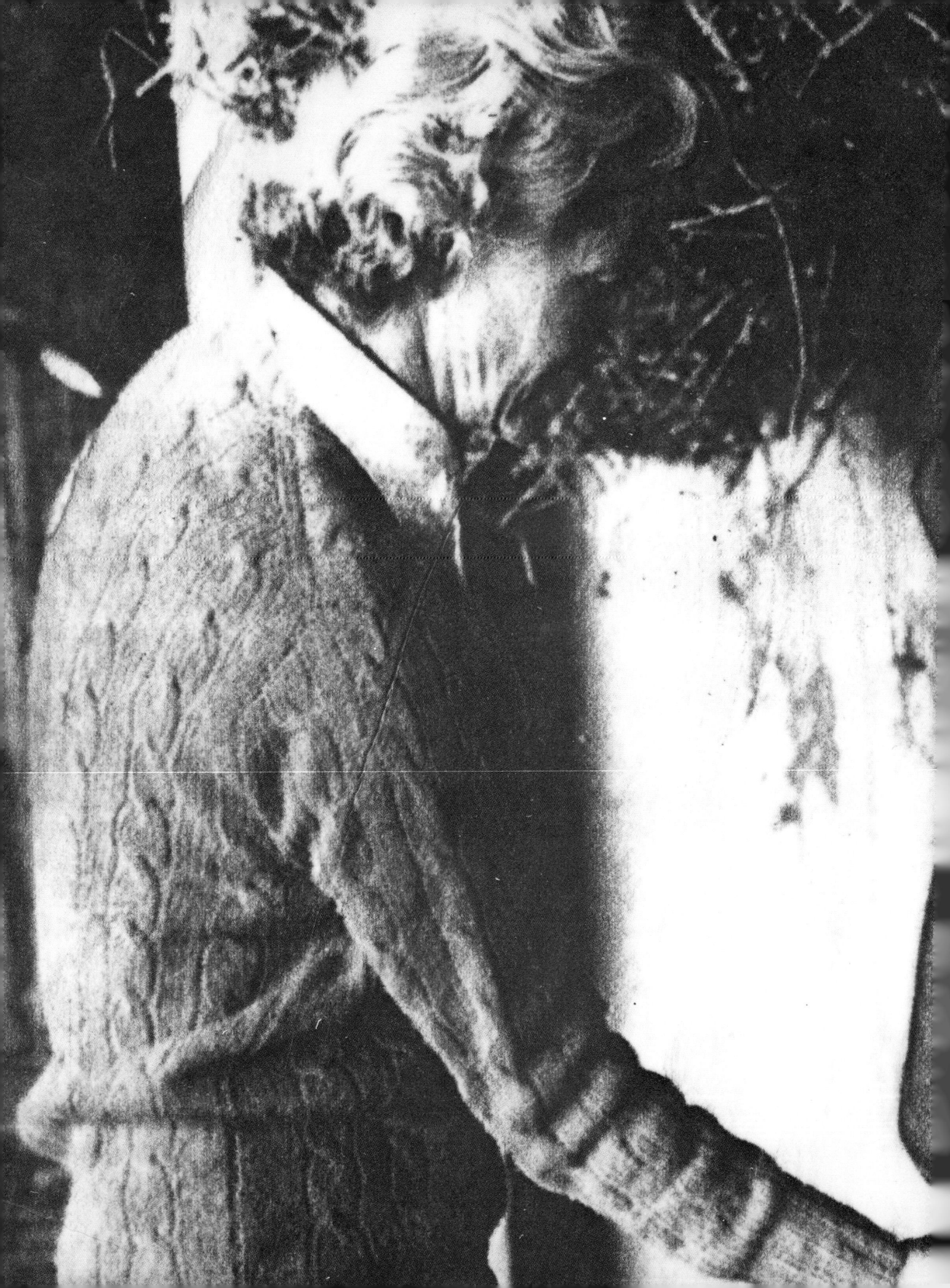

Horse Racing

Mrs. Penny Tweedy and Secretariat, the famed Triple Crown winner.

Riva Ridge and Secretariat's fantastic Triple Crown

Exercise boy Jim Gaffney holds Secretariat shortly before the Virginia entry won the Belmont Stakes in 1973 and became the first Triple Crown winner since Citation in 1948.

One of the greatest thoroughbreds in history, Virginia-bred Secretariat became the first horse since Citation in 1948 to win the Triple Crown. The great horse carried the colors of Mrs. Helen Chenery (Penny) Tweedy, owner of Meadow Stables at Doswell in Caroline County. Secretariat was foaled at the Meadow on January 30, 1970. In 1972, Mrs. Tweedy's Riva Ridge won the Kentucky Derby and the Belmont Stakes, but his chances of capturing the Triple Crown were washed away at the muddy Preakness in Baltimore. But in 1973, Secretariat won it all, the Kentucky Derby, Preakness and Belmont. Secretariat was a super-horse and won the Belmont by 31 lengths after romping to victory in the Kentucky Derby in record time.

Mrs. Tweedy took over the responsibilities of operating the Virginia stable in 1967, when her 85-year-old father was hospitalized and her mother died. Her father, Christopher Chenery, established the 3,000-acre estate in the mid-1930s as a farm for horses. He made his Meadow Stable a formidable force in American racing. Hill Prince, First Landing, Sir Gaylord and the grand filly and mare Cicada carried his blue and white colors to many stakes victories. Hill Prince won the Preakness in 1950 and was named "Horse of the Year."

Had it not been for Penny Tweedy's love for horses and her devotion to her father, there might never have been a Riva Ridge or Secretariat. Riva Ridge ended his career as a four-year-old in the fall of 1973 with winnings of 1,111,497 dollars and 17 victories in 30 starts. He set a world record of 1:52 2/5 for a mile and three-sixteenths in the Brooklyn Handicap.

In his meteoric career, Secretariat won 16 of 21 starts and 1,316,808 dollars, placing him fourth—behind Kelso at 1,977,896 dollars—among all-time money winners. His most spectacular victory came in the Belmont Stakes when he set an American record of 2:24 for one and a half miles, shaving the Belmont record by two and three-fifths seconds.

About 600 thoroughbreds bred in Virginia get to the races every year. Yet, pari-mutuel betting in the Old Dominion has never been legalized. This is a puzzling fact because Virginia is one of the leading breeding states in the country.

R. B. (Dick) Keeley, one of the state's foremost authorities on horses, points out that Virginia is outranked only by Kentucky and Maryland in the breeding field.

"There are approximately 150 breeding farms in Virginia," says Keeley, a Virginia Beach hotel executive, horseman, breeder, owner and a judge in the American Horse Show Association. He's a strong advocate of pari-mutuel betting.

"We're not taking full advantage of our resources," he claims. "Virginians travel to other states to attend races, spending millions—money that could be kept in our state. Horse racing would be a boom to the economy of the state."

Meanwhile, Virginia continues to breed champions. There have been a number of Virginia-bred champions, including Sword Dancer, Shuvee, Cida, Sun Beau, Hill Prince, First Landing and Sir Gaylord. Kentucky Derby Winners Reigh Count and the great Secretariat were foaled in Virginia. The largest and perhaps the best breeding farm in Virginia, according to the experts, is Rokeby Stables in Upperville, owned by Paul Mellon of Pittsburgh.

One of the world's greatest standard bred farms for trotters and pacers is the Curles Neck Farm in Henrico County, owned by G. C. K. Billings. Billings' Ulhan was a world champion pacer and Lou Forester was a world champion trotter.

Curles Neck Farm's The Harvester won the Hambletonian. Billy Direct was one of the great sires. Billings also had the first imported horse—Omar Khayyam in 1917—to win the Kentucky Derby.

There are three major race events held in Virginia—the Deep Run Hunt, Virginia Gold Cup and the Camp Town Races in Hanover County.

The Deep Run Hunt Club was formed in 1887, when fox hunting was traditional in Virginia. The Hunt Club progressed rapidly and in 1896 moved to Rosedale Lodge near the Hill Monument in Ginter Park, Richmond. There were stalls for 40 horses, a mile race track, a shed for bicycles and a nine-hole golf course, one of the first in Virginia.

In a history of the Deep Run Hunt Club, Oliver Jackson Sands, Jr., writes that race meetings were usually a combination of races and show events, held both spring and fall beginning in 1895.

In 1910, the races were held at the Country Club at Virginia until disrupted by World War I. They were revived in 1923 at an old farm on Broad Street. In the 1920s, the races were held at Curles Neck, attracting the best steeplechasers in America, then Strawberry Hill.

In 1974, the Deep Run Hunt Club was forced to give up sponsorship of the races, and the event has continued as the Strawberry Hill Races under the direction of the Atlantic Rural Exposition.

Among the great jumpers competing at Curles Neck were Marion DuPont Summerville's Battleship, the first American-bred and owned horse to win the English Grand National (1937), Troublemaker and Drinkmore Lad. Battleship was the greatest steeplechase sire in history.

The Camp Town Races, featuring western-style flat racing, was started in 1951. Dick Keeley was there, riding to victory in the relay and mile. Attracting the young people, the Camp Town Races draw crowds up to 35,000 fans to Bleinheim Farm.

Jean McLean Davis of Portsmouth has won 65 world's championships in the country's most prestigious horse shows. Here she is shown in 1963 with The Tempest, which won the world's amateur five-gaited gelding and amateur five-gaited stake championships. Edith Fable in 1943 was Jean's first world champion.

NORFOLK WENT TO THE RACES
Until the governor's raid

Once there was a first-class horse racing track in Norfolk...with betting—until Governor Harry Stuart ordered 20 armed detectives to swoop down on the bookmakers.

The Jamestown Race Track, sometimes known as the Country Club Track, flourished from 1910 to April, 1914. It was located off Hampton Boulevard near the Naval Base. The track was a mile long and wide enough to accommodate a large number of entries.

When the track opened the management forgot to get the sanction of the powerful New York Jockey Club, which controlled nearly all the tracks. And all horses, owners, trainers, and jockeys participating in the Norfolk meeting were barred from racing at any track under the jurisdiction of the New York Jockey Club. But the following year the Jockey Club gave its sanction, and many of the country's finest horses and outstanding owners, including August Belmont, president of the New York Jockey Club, poured in for the Norfolk racing.

The city went for the horses in a big way. On opening day merchants closed a half day so employees could attend. Featured races were named for various Norfolk hotels and business establishments.

In 1911, the state sought to annul the track's charter on grounds of gambling. The case went to court and was declared a mistrial. The jury was hopelessly divided.

Then on April 8, 1914, Governor Stuart made his move. After the second race, 20 men hired by the governor from the Baldwin Detective Agency of Roanoke swooped down on the track armed with pistols and rifles. At first the spectators thought it was a movie company making a picture at the track. The detectives caught everybody by surprise. Fourteen people were arrested and charged with making book, but the detectives had a devil of a time getting their prisoners behind bars. They attempted to get a waiting street car of the Atlantic Terminal Line to take them and their prisoners directly to Ocean View. The motorman refused on the grounds that it was not his run. The detectives threatened to run the car themselves, but the motorman would have none of that. He jumped off the car carrying the control with him. Then the detectives commandeered an auto which, according to the press, broke down conveniently. Finally, the prisoners were taken to the county jail in Portsmouth.

The racing program was called off after the raid but resumed the next day with no purses and the winners dividing the gate receipts. It didn't work.

The men arrested and charged with bookmaking were fined 100 dollars and jailed six months. Although they noted an appeal, the management of Jamestown Track issued a statement saying the track was being closed down. The last day of racing was April 10, 1914.

It was royal entertainment while it lasted.

Horse racing and betting were front page news in 1910. Four years later the track, located in Norfolk, was raided by 20 detectives on orders by the Virginia Governor.

Virginian-Pilot.

14 PAGES.

NORFOLK, VA., WEDNESDAY, NOVEMBER 2, 1910, FOURTEEN PAGES.

THREE CENTS PER COPY.

SNAPSHOTS AT JAMESTOWN ON OPENING DAY

Guy Fisher, Winner Of The Norfolk Handicap, With Jockey Lang Up.

Finish Of The Handicap, Guy Fisher Leading High Private.

PERFECT START OF NORFOLK HANDICAP.

The Oval Illustration Shows Dr. Heard Leading Lizzie Flat Over The Sixth Jump. The Lower Picture shows A Section Of The Grandstand Watching The Second Race.

STRIKING GARMENT WORKERS AIDED BY SOCIETY LEADERS OF WINDY CITY

Garbed As Sewing Girls They Participate In Riotous Scenes —Police Dumbfounded On Identifying Number Arrested

ROUGH TREATMENT BY COPPERS AROUSE LEADERS

Chicago, Nov. 1—Mounted police today charged threatening mobs of striking garment workers and made numerous arrests in the cloak quarters of the city, only to be dumbfounded when met by obdurate groups of club women and society leaders who, when taken into custody produced engraved calling cards at police stations in lieu of bail bonds.

It was a new experience for the police, and it plainly confused them. A score of these women champions of the garment workers were taken into custody, but they were immediately released when their identity became known.

One woman was struck by a policeman's club, but her name did not become known, as she was hurriedly placed in an automobile and taken home. Most of the club women involved in today's demonstration were garbed as working girls and police could not distinguish them from strikers until after arrests were made.

Riotous, Spectacular Scenes.

Riotous and spectacular scenes developed downtown, on the north side and on the west side. More than five hundred men and women engaged in the downtown demonstration, which was broken up by the police after considerable trouble. As they left their headquarters in LaSalle street, the strikers and their sympathizers clanged bells, blew whistles and tooted horns. The line of march proceeded into the wholesale quarter near the Chicago river, passing large tailoring establishments, whose employes were beckoned to join the strikers. More than 5,000 took part in one of several incipient riots on the West Side. In each instance women led the strikers and their cause.

"I would take oath that we are doing absolutely nothing wrong in law," said Miss Ellen Starr, a club woman. "The only persons who are violating the law were the policemen who treated us roughly and so dreadfully with their clubs some of the club women were leading peacefully past the shops."

Rough Treatment By Police Arouses Indignation

Miss S. M. Franklin, another volunteer picket, was indignant because of the manner in which she had been treated by the police.

"I know they would not have let me go if I had not presented my card," said Miss Franklin. "They seemed to think that I was a particularly dangerous character. Perhaps it would have been a good plan to let them take me to jail and that would have shown how little legal foundation they have to stand on."

Prominent women wealthy women to open their houses to qualitative striking girls, offers of picket service from women, social and club leaders and pledges of assistance came from many places. Letters were received today by Mrs. Raymond Robins, president of the Women's Trade Union League, from those to volunteer were Mrs. Agnes Hopkins and Mrs. G. Perce, Deputy Factory Inspector Edgar L. Watson today addressed a mass meeting of striking cloakmakers. Chicago girls on the strike. Mrs. ..., who ...

COMPETING ROADS AGREE ON ALL ADVANCES IN RATES

Admitting This Stanley Johnson Denies To I. C. C. That Present Rates Are Too High

Chicago, Nov 1—Presentation of evidence in the rate hearing before the Interstate Commerce Commission was concluded this afternoon. Arguments on the evidence will be heard by the Commission at Washington on December 1 and after due deliberations the Commission will announce what it is generally considered will be the most important decision ever emanating from it.

The hearing was instituted at the instance of shippers who arose in protest when Western railroads announced that rates of fifty different commodities would be advanced.

In a general way the argument presented by the railroads was that the increased rates were necessary for the following reasons:

1. Increased wages to employes.
2. Increased cost of maintenance and operation.
3. Public demand for increased efficiency and expansion of transportation facilities.

The position taken by the shippers was that the railroads at present are receiving a generous return on their actual investment, and among other things sought to show in their examination that the low rate of earnings shown in the statistics presented was due more to over capitalization than to low rates.

During the examination today of Stanley H. Johnson, Assistant Freight Traffic Manager of the Rock Island road, Commissioner Lane asked some pointed questions.

"I have found in my experience," he said, "that railroads find very little difficulty in raising rates without much justification, and at any time they may see fit. If there were no restraint placed on the roads could not the roads advance the rates without end?"

"Of course if the railroads were utterly indifferent to public opinion and were not absolutely fairminded men, the rates might be raised ordinarily, but this would not be done as the roads only ask a fair profit," replied Mr. Johnson.

"Is it not a fact," asked Commissioner Lane, "that deep down in the mind of the traffic manager he knows that even the present rate is too high?"

This brought a laugh from the crowd during which the witness replied in the negative.

Mr. Johnson admitted that no general advances in rates were made by the roads without agreement with the competitors.

"Why they do," he added, "it would mean going out of business."

TWENTY AEROPLANES NEEDED IN U. S. GOVERNMENT SERVICE

Is Estimate Of General General Allen, Chief Signal Officer, In His Annual Report

Washington, D. C., Nov. 1—Twenty aeroplanes at least are needed by the United States government service, says General Allen, chief signal officer of the army in his annual report made public tonight.

Three aeroplanes seemed to be regular objects of different branches of the country throughout the summer. Major General Allen, of the signal corps, be present in groups of three for the ... of signal corps officers and men for the air ... necessary training demanded in this country.

General Allen contains the oft-repeated assertion that the United States is going to be isolated position is not likely to prove involved in war, and that therefore the true conservative procedure is to adopt a moderate system for aerial equipment along such line as other nations have determined upon the trials have rested in military purposes, thus admitting the development of experimental aeroplanes.

General Allen, called attention to the fact that he has been able to buy only one Wright aeroplane and three signal ... aeroplanes are being ...

REPUBLICANS ALSO MAKING APPEALS FOR FUNDS

And Judge Parker Shows Their Circular Contains Names Of Wall Street Financiers Thought To Have Influence

Plattsburg, N. Y., Nov. 1—Judge Alton B. Parker, the Democratic candidate for President in 1904, spoke here tonight for the Democratic State ticket. Five special trains brought big crowds from all parts of the country to ...

MARRIED 2 WEEKS, IN SUICIDE PACT

Young Groom Dead And Bride In Serious Condition When Room Was Entered

---

NEWARK DRIVERS JOIN THE STRIKE

Scheduled Conference Looking To Settlement In New York Didn't Materialize

---

FATE OF GRACE | **FATALLY INJURED**

THE VIRGINIA GOLD CUP
For the glory of a trophy

On April 3, 1922, eight Fauquier County sportsmen met and established a four-mile race to be called the Virginia Gold Cup. Today, the steeplechase over 22 timber fences is one of the most unique horse races of its kind in America. It is the only race of this type still run for the glory of a trophy. There is no money purse.

The Gold Cup has become a Virginia tradition, run annually on the First Saturday in May, the largest sporting event in Northern Virginia. The spectacle attracts crowds of 20,000 to Warrenton to witness a card of thoroughbred races featuring the Virginia Gold Cup.

The trophy is kept by its winner for one year, then must be returned to be put up for competition. Except for a miniature souvenir replica which the recipient keeps permanently, there is no other prize to the winner. This derives from the tradition of strict amateur philosophy in which the race had its beginnings. Until 1940, only amateur riders were permitted to ride for the Gold Cup. Today they must be acceptable to the committee.

The trophy can be retired by three victories by the same owner, not necessarily with the same horse or consecutively. It is interesting to note that since the race was originated the Gold Cup has been retired only five times. David L. Ferguson's Leeds Don, in 1965-66-67, is the only horse to win the race three consecutive years. The first race in 1922 was run at Fauquier Springs and Mrs. William Hitt of Middleburg won three of the first four Gold Cup races to retire the trophy. Mrs. Sumner Pingree of Boston won the race four times, but not in succession.

Only five mares have won the Virginia Gold Cup—Mrs. C. E. Perkins' Parana in 1924, T. M. Bowen's Dum Dum in 1927, Mrs. C. C. Rumsey's Tiguca in 1928, Thomas Stokes' Never Worry in 1947, and Gilliam, owned by Captain J. L. B. Benley of Orlean, in 1956. At 17, Never Worry is the oldest contender to win the race.

In 1924, the race was run at Broadview. The race was run over the Clovelly-Clovercroft course on Springs Road from 1927 to 1935 due to fire that started during races at Broadview. But Broadview is really the home of this famous race.

Mrs. Frank Gould won the cup in 1937 and 1938 with her Ostend, but it was not until 1940 when Black Sweep, ridden by Johnny Harrison, retired the trophy for Mrs. Gould.

Christopher Creer was the next owner to retire the Gold Cup, but it took him a number of years to turn the trick. He first won it in 1941 with Goldun, ridden by Jackie Bosley III, followed by Houseman, ridden by Mike Smithwick, in 1946, and in 1953, Greer finally retired the trophy when Smithwick rode Rayquick to victory.

Joseph Aitcheson has ridden more winners than any jockey in Gold Cup history. He won with Alfred H. Smith's Grand Chal in 1957, Randolph D. Rouse's Ricacho in 1960, William L. Schlusemeyer's Mainstay in 1961, and Mrs. Paul R. Fout's Moon Rock in 1964.

A Three-Time Winner, Mr. and Mrs. David Ferguson's Leeds Don, the only horse to win the Virginia Gold Cup three consecutive years.

VIRGINIA GOLD CUP WINNERS

1922—Mrs. K. E. Hitt's "Irish Laddie"
1923—Mrs. K. E. Hitt's "Oddity"
1924—Mrs. C. E. Perkins' "Parana"
1925—Mrs. K. E. Hitt's "John Bunny"
1926—Howard Bruce's "Billy Barton"
1927—Mrs. T. M. Bowen's "Dum Dum"
1928—Mrs. C. C. Rumsey's "Tijuca"
1929—Mrs. Walter J. Salmon's "Dunks Green"
1930—Sumner Pingree's "Soissons"
1931—Mrs. John Hay Whitney's "Seraglio"
1932—Sumner Pingree's "Melita II"
1933—Sumner Pingree's "The Prophet"
1934—Sumner Pingree's "Melita II"
1935—John Schiff's "Indigo"
1936—Carlton H. Palmer's "Ghost Dancer"
1937—Mrs. Frank M. Gould's "Ostend"
1938—Mrs. Frank M. Gould's "Ostend"
1939—W. F. Cochran, Jr.'s "Or Else"
1940—Mrs. Frank M. Gould's "Black Sweep"
1941—C. M. Greer, Jr.'s "Goldun"
1942—Mrs. A. S. Carhart's "Sir Romeo"
1946—C. M. Greer, Jr.'s "Houseman"
1947—Thomas Stokes' "Never Worry"
1949—Thomas Stokes' "Never Worry"
1950—Alvin Untermyer's "Done Sleeping"
1951—Mrs. A. S. Carhart's "Mister Mars"
1952—Mrs. Simon T. Patterson's "Gift of Gold"
1953—C. M. Greer, Jr.'s "Rayquick"
1954—Hugh J. O'Donovan's "Lancrel"
1955—Cyrus Manierre's "Uncle Pierre"
1956—Capt. J. L. B. Bentley's "Gillian"
1957—Alfred H. Smith's "Grand Chal"
1958—Mrs. Henry Obre's "Coup-de-Vite"
1959—Mrs. George P. Greenhalgh, Jr.'s "Judge Beacon"
1960—Randolph D. Rouse's "Ricacho"
1961—Wm. E. Schlusemeyer's "Mainstay"
1962—Mrs. June H. McKnight's "Hill Tie"
1963—Mrs. June H. McKnight's "Hill Tie"
1964—Mrs. Paul R. Fout's "Moon Rock"
1965—David L. Ferguson's "Leeds Don"
1966—David L. Ferguson's "Leeds Don"
1967—David L. Ferguson's "Leeds Don"
1968—Mrs. A. C. Randolph's "Walrus"
1969—John W. Warner's "Annual Meeting"
1970—Thomas H. McKoy, Jr.'s "King of Spades"
1971—The Hon. John W. Warner's "Annual Meeting"
1972—Dr. J. M. Rogers' "King of Spades"
1973—Bella Vista Farm's "Portobelo"
1974—Rokeby Stables' "Mongogo"
1975—Paul Mellon's "Chapel Street"
1976—William Lanahan, Jr.'s "Semington"

Paul Mellon's Chapel Street (middle), ridden by Padfy Neilson, takes an early lead in the 1975 Virginia Gold Cup, and held the pace to triumph.

Trailing Randolph D. Rouse's Ricacho (#3) at this point, Grand Chal (#6), owned by Alfred H. Smith and ridden by J. Aitcheson, Jr., came on to win the 1957 Gold Cup. Ricacho was ridden by Patty Smithwick.

Hockey
The ice man cometh

The ice age came to Virginia with the sprouting of multi-million dollar coliseums across the state.

It was 1971 when the Richmond Coliseum, Norfolk Scope and Roanoke Civic Center opened for business. That same year Richmond became the home of the Robins in the American Hockey League, and the Detroit Red Wings based a team in Norfolk, using both Scope and Hampton Coliseum for home games in the AHL, which was a spectacular development in an area where people had previously confined their ice activities to high balls and popsicles.

Youngsters who were brought up in a football and basketball atmosphere started carrying around hockey sticks and skates, looking for ice. But there weren't enough public rinks to accommodate them, hindering a well-planned youth program on ice. The big arenas were reserved most of the time for the pro hockey teams.

Salem, which constructed the first of the handsome new arenas in the state, introduced ice hockey to Virginians in 1966. Later, Salem shared the Roanoke Valley Rebels of the Eastern Hockey League with the newer Roanoke Civic Center.

The Rebels drew a crowd of 8,191 for a playoff game at Roanoke, second largest in modern Eastern Hockey League history. In 1972-73, the Rebels played before a total attendance of 109,000 customers, second only to Syracuse in EHL attendance that season. Ice hockey appeared to be catching on as a spectator sport in the Old Dominion.

The Richmond Robins, working with the Philadelphia Flyers of the National Hockey League, drew a total of 224,000 to their new coliseum in their first season and 188,878 the second season.

It took longer for the Norfolk team to catch on. Playing 26 games in Scope and 11 in Hampton Coliseum, the Wings' attendance in 1972-73, when they made it to the AHL playoff semifinals, was 127,564, an increase of 8,164 over 1971-72.

But it wasn't enough, although attendance increased gradually each season. After winning the Southern Division championship in 1974-75, the Detroit Red Wings announced they were folding their operation in Tidewater. Meanwhile, with operational costs soaring, attendance was on the decline in Richmond and the Robins folded operations in the AHL in 1976-77.

The Eastern Hockey League broke up after the 1973-74 season, and in 1974-75 Roanoke and Hampton played in the new Southern Hockey League. Norfolk joined the league in 1975-76. But all teams struggled to finish the season, taking a bath in red ink. Richmond collapsed in the AHL and joined the SHL for the 1976-77 season.

The ice man was beginning to melt.

Like a Man from Mars, this is the goalie.

The Virginia Wings raised their championship flag but closed shop after the season because of heavy financial losses in the AHL. The Tidewater Sharks of the Southern Hockey League then moved into Scope. Coach Doug Barkley (right) and Norfolk Mayor Irvine Hill watch the flag-raising.

A sellout crowd for an American Hockey League game in Norfolk Scope during the 1973-74 season. It wasn't enough. The Virginia Wings folded after the following season.

In hockey, sometimes the situation gets out of hand like this episode in front of the Virginia Wings' bench during an American Hockey League game in Norfolk's Scope.

The Colleges & Universities

THE UNIVERSITY OF VIRGINIA
Mayer, then Dudley
—and a basketball team that performed a miracle

About a quarter century before Bill Dudley arrived on the scene, Gene (Buck) Mayer was making football history at the University of Virginia. In fact, this skillful, all-purpose halfback was the Cavaliers' first All-American, selected by Walter Camp on the first team in 1915, after he led Virginia to an 8-1 season.

Some football historians maintain the 1915 team, beaten only by Harvard, 9-0, was the Cavaliers' best, and not even the great Dudley was able to match some of Mayer's records; nor, for that matter, any other back in the first 88 years of intercollegiate football at the University.

Mayer's records still standing in the Cavaliers' record books include:

Most points game (36 vs. Richmond, 1915); most points season (142 in 1914); most points career (312); most touchdowns career (48).

In the four years Mayer played (1912-15), the Cavaliers went 6-3, 7-1, 8-1, and 8-1, for a 29-5 record. Defeats to Georgetown, 8-7, in 1913, Yale, 21-0, in 1914, and Harvard in 1915, kept the Cavaliers from going unbeaten. Mayer captained the 1915 team, which defeated Randolph-Macon, 20-0; Yale, 10-0; Richmond, 74-0; Georgia, 9-7; VMI, 44-0, Vanderbilt, 35-10, South Carolina, 13-0, and North Carolina, 14-0.

And it wasn't until 1941 that Virginia was able to produce another true All-American—a young man named Dudley. They called him Bullet Bill, and the name fit.

Coach Bill Murray installed the T-formation in the spring of 1941. That fall, the Cavaliers lost only to Yale (21-8) and Do-Everything Dudley wrapped up a fantastic career by scoring all the points in a 28-8 triumph over North Carolina, which was certainly one of the greatest performances by a player in Virginia college football history. (There is more on Dudley's career in the pro football section.)

Since Coach Murray's departure in 1945, Virginia football has had its ups and downs. But the Cavaliers were up quite a while when Art Guepe, Murray's successor, was coaching. Guepe's teams enjoyed six straight winning seasons (1947-52). In the third game of the 1951 season, the Cavaliers went on a scoring spree, averaging 35.1 points a game in knocking off their last six opponents.

After Guepe left following an 8-0-2 season in 1952, the Cavaliers' football fortunes took a turn for the worst. But in 1958, the first season for Coach Dick Voris, the Cavaliers shocked Duke 15-12, after dropping a 20-15 thriller to Clemson in the opener. Cavalier supporters gained new hope. Not for long, however. The Cavaliers lost 28 straight games for a record they would rather forget. It wasn't broken until the opening game of 1961 when the Cavaliers defeated William & Mary, 21-6, at Norfolk.

The largest Scott Stadium crowd was 34,000 for the Duke game in 1952, Guepe's last season as Cavalier coach. The Cavaliers went into the contest, with four straight victories, having blanked Vanderbilt, Virginia Tech and George Washington in succession and defeated VMI, 33-14. Duke spoiled the occasion before a record crowd, 21-7. Largest away crowd for the Cavaliers—81,391 against Michigan at Michigan Stadium in 1971. Virginia's biggest rampage? Well, in 1890, two weeks after losing to Princeton, 115-0, the Cavaliers routed Randolph-Macon, 136-0.

After Mayer and Dudley, only Palumbo (1951), Tom Scott (1952), John Papit (1949) and Jim Bakhtiar (1957) received prominent All-American recognition.

While football has held the center of

President Calvin Coolidge and Mrs. Coolidge attend a football game at the University of Virginia.

Joe Palumbo (1949-51), Virginia defensive guard, AP and NEA first team All-America, 1951.

interest at Virginia, no team in University history has created as much national excitement as the 1975-76 basketball team. Nobody gave Coach Terry Holland's Cavaliers a ghost of a chance to get past the opening game of the Atlantic Coast Conference tournament at Landover, Maryland, much less to win it all.

But Virginia upset North Carolina State, 75-63, in the first round. In the semifinals, the Cavaliers toppled Maryland, 73-65. And saving their best for the last, the Cavaliers stunned regular-season champion North Carolina, 67-62, before 19,600 disbelieving fans.

In three days, Virginia succeeded in bumping off one member of the Top 10 and two of the Top 20. It was a miracle they said couldn't happen. But it did. Wally Walker was the tourney's most valuable player, and nobody could possibly dispute his selection.

The fact that the Cavaliers lost to DePaul in the first round of the NCAA East Regional, took none of the glitter away from their first ACC basketball championship. The way they accomplished it will long be remembered.

Richard D. Anderson, who is regarded as the father of athletics at the University of Virginia. It is believed Anderson was the first businessman to direct the administration of college athletics anywhere. He was treasurer, beginning in 1888, and served for many years. He expanded the Virginia athletic program, especially in football, and was largely responsible for the Cavalier baseball team going to the World's Fair in Chicago in 1892. After beating the West, the Cavaliers were finally halted by Yale. Anderson died in 1899.

The amazing Mr. Buck Mayer, who scored 144 points for the Cavaliers in 1914 and, in 1915, became the state's first full-fledged All-American.

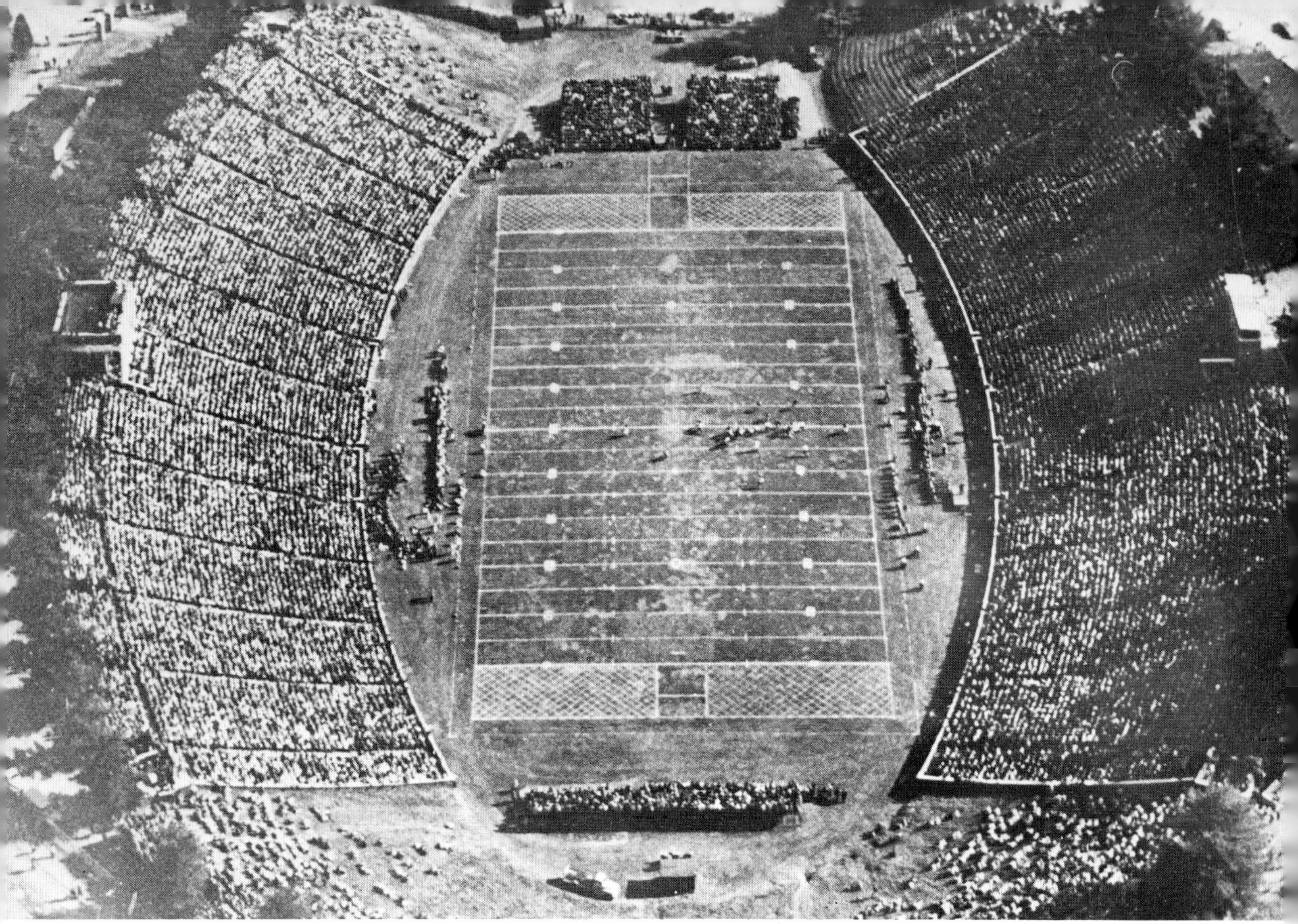

They packed 'em into Scott Stadium in Charlottesville in early 1950s.

John Papit, holder of Cavaliers' career rushing record and others, is shown getting off one of his gains (circa 1949).

Rapid Johnny Papit, a Philadelphia star who went south, scored one touchdown in unbeaten Virginia's 26-14 upset of Penn on November 5, 1949. Papit, the nation's leading rusher, was held to 54 yards, but 160-pound quarterback Dick (Whitey) Michels was 9-for-12 passing, sufficient statistics to give the Cavaliers their first victory over Penn. Papit is the Cavaliers' all-time rushing leader, with 3,237 yards (career). He was selected to the NEA first team All-America in 1949.

Thomas C. Scott was named a first-team end on the AP and NEA All-America Football teams in 1952. Only two-sport All-American in U. Va. history, Scott was an All-American defenseman in lacrosse in 1953. In 1952, he played on Virginia's national champion lacrosse team.

Some of the Cavaliers' most fruitful years in football came under the regime of Art Guepe, who coached from 1946 through 1952.

All-American Bill Dudley as he looked when he was a teenager making football history at Virginia. He was 20 years old in 1942 when he was drafted by Pittsburgh Steelers. (See story in pro football section)

Coach Frank Murray introduced the T-formation at Virginia and turned loose a young man named Bill Dudley.

W. H. Baumberger of Navy makes a leaping interception of a Virginia pass in a play that led the Middies to a 13-7 victory over the Cavaliers in 1933.

James Abol Hassen Bakhtiar (1955-56-57) was called "The Persian Prince" and he gave a royal performance for the Cavaliers. He was the Cavaliers' all-time leader in rushing attempts with 555 carries. He rushed for 2,434 yards in his three varsity seasons. Picked on Football Writers Association first team All-America, 1957.

Virginia's Billy Langloh drives past Phil Ford and Walter Davis of North Carolina to score two points during the final game of the 1976 ACC tournament at Landover, Maryland. The Cavaliers won in one of the greatest upsets in basketball history.

Happy Virginia basketball players Dave Koesters (24) and Billy Langloh (21) are surrounded by delirious fans after the Cavaliers upset top-seeded North Carolina for the ACC tournament championship, 67-62, at Capital Centre in Landover, Maryland, March 6, 1976.

Virginia's Wally Walker accepts the trophy as the most valuable player of the 1976 ACC tournament after leading the Cavaliers to the championship, defeating North Carolina, 67-62, in the final. The basketball net, cut down by the conquering Cavaliers, is over Wally's shoulders.

HAMPDEN-SYDNEY COLLEGE
Death Valley

Hampden-Sydney opponents speak of it with reverence. To Tiger athletes, past and present, it is a tradition, a symbol of pride; a battleground.

"Death Valley" is the intriguing name they call Hampden-Sydney's athletic fields, constructed on what was a frog-pond—in a magnificent setting on the campus in the heart of Virginia's historic southside, seven miles below Farmville.

As tradition has it, so frequent were defeats of invading teams in this natural amphitheater that the name "Death Valley" was once given by a member of a defeated Richmond College baseball team. The name stuck.

Frank Howard, who coached Clemson football from 1940-1969, did borrow the name, calling Clemson Memorial Stadium "Death Valley" in an effort to throw fear into opponents. But Hampden-Sydney alumni rose up in protest, and the Clemson coach was soon set straight that "Death Valley" was a Hampden-Sydney legend.

In the complex is "Yank's Corner," a memorial to World War II dead and a tribute to the immortal Charles A. (Yank) Bernier, who served the Tigers so many years as athlete, coach and athletic director. He won the respect of "his boys" as well as the college sports world.

Hampden-Sydney is older than the nation itself (chartered in 1775) and its series with Randolph-Macon is the oldest college football rivalry in the south and the sixteenth oldest in the country.

(In 1970, the largest crowd (9,000), including Vice President Nguyen Cao Ky of South Vietnam, saw the Tigers beat the Yellow Jackets, 14-0, to wrap up an unbeaten season, and clinch a bid to the Knute Rockne Bowl.)

William Ford Bull of Norfolk is regarded as the father of intercollegiate athletics at Hampden-Sydney, serving as captain of the first four Tiger football teams, 1892-95. One of the smaller schools in enrollment (790 in 1975), the Tigers through the years managed to hold their own against the big ones.

In 1901, the Tigers rolled over Richmond, 70-0, in their most lopsided win ever, but in 1920 the unbeaten VMI Keydets clobbered Hampden-Sydney, 136-0, one of the largest scores ever produced by a Virginia college team. But the Tigers didn't play dead. After this humiliating defeat, they regrouped for successive victories over Lynchburg, Randolph-Macon, Guilford and William and Mary to win the Eastern Virginia Athletic Association championship.

The Tigers of 1926 gained recognition by tying Virginia, Florida and Marshall, all 0-0. But they were the scoreless wonders in 1947, failing to register a point in six consecutive games. In 1948 a fullback named Lynn Chewning, out of St. Christopher's prep, became Hampden-Sydney's first Little All-American. Chewning, later to gain football fame at the Naval Academy, scored 78 points in pacing a 6-2-1 season.

Other Hampden-Sydney first-team

10	Long, D.	B
12	Lawler, Bill	B
13	Harris	B
14	Long, B.	QB
15	Nelson	QB
16	Bertram	QB
17	Apperson	B
18	Penhale	B
19	Overstreet	B
20	Bryant	B
21	Page	B
22	Lawler, B.	B
23	Holland	E
24	Richmond	B
27	Shelly	B
28	Coghill	B
29	Junes	E
30	Hartman	B
33	Blackburn	E
34	Blandford	B
35	Thompson	E
36	Offterdinger	B
37	Atkinson	B
38	Tucker	B
39	Hentz	E
40	Powers	B
41	Payne, K.	B
42	Shreckhise	B
43	Tyler	B
44	Beverly	B
45	Burgess	B
48	Owens	B
50	Roberts	C
52	Stanley	C
53	Henderson, C.	C
54	Webb	G
55	Bounds, M.	C
56	Carson	G

The 1971 Tigers season games. Sydney's greatest Bridgeport, 17-12 thriller.

Lynn Chewning, Fullback, 1948.

Hampden-Sydney First Team All-Americans

Stokely Fulton, Center, 1954.

Lewis Everette, Fullback, 1962.

in 10 regular as Hampden-m, they lost to Rockne Bowl

57 Saul C	66 Cox .... G	75 Van de Castle .... T	84 Houck .... E
58 Keefer .... G	67 Stovall .... G	76 Abels .... T	85 Allen .... E
59 McGlothlin C	68 Whitley .... T	77 Drumwright .... T	86 Winston .... E
60 Overton .... G	69 Kincaid .... G	78 Lowry .... G	87 Harper .... E
61 Payne, J. .... G	70 Martin .... T	79 Richardson .... B	88 Leidy .... E
62 Taylor, B. .... G	71 Mapp .... T	80 Eads .... E	90 Graham .... E
63 Taylor, Bob .... G	72 Thomas .... T	81 Shelor .... E	91 Baldwin .... T
64 Bounds, R. .... T	73 Kirk, B. .... T	82 Morton .... E	93 Henderson, G. .... G
65 Funderburk .... T	74 Parsley .... T	83 Capehart .... E	98 Kirstein .... T

All-American Lewis Everette shown picking up yardage for Hampden-Sydney in 1962.

Mike Leidy, All-Mason Dixon and All-VCAA linebacker, 1972, voted berth on All-America third team.

Defensive end Ed Kelley, 1974-75, Kodak Division II All-American.

Stokeley Fulton turned out to be an outstanding coach after winning All-America honors at Hampden-Sydney. Taking over as head coach in 1960, his Tigers have won four conference championships, and two trips to the Knute Rockne Bowl. His 1971 team compiled a 10-0 record. He was voted NCAA College Division Coach of the Year.

All-Americans to follow Chewning were center Stokeley Fulton (1954), halfback Bill Benson (1958), fullback Lewis Everette (1962).

The Tigers compiled an 8-1 record in 1955 and Jim Hickey was named Virginia's Coach of the Year. And under Coach Bob Thalman in 1956-57, Hampden-Sydney won 13 straight. The 1957 team lost only one of nine games. Hickey compiled a 23-8-2 coaching record at Hampden-Sydney, and Thalman was 26-9-1.

Fulton really never left Hampden-Sydney, joining the football staff in 1957 and becoming head football coach and athletic director in 1960. Then things began to happen. Fulton's Tigers won conference championships four times. The 1970 football team enjoyed a 9-1 season, losing to Montclair State, 7-6, in the Knute Rockne Bowl. The Tigers led all NCAA colleges and universities in scoring defense, allowing opponents but 2.8 points a game.

Then the following season Fulton produced Hampden-Sydney's greatest football team in history. The undefeated Tigers won all ten games, leading the NCAA College Division in scoring and total defense (3.4 points and 115.6 yards per game). The Tigers, captained by Baughn Stanley and Dave Shelor, dropped a heart-breaking 17-12 decision to Bridgeport University in the Knute Rockne Bowl.

Fulton was voted NCAA College Division Coach of the Year.

Hampden-Sydney produced its winningest basketball team in 1948-49 as the Tigers, captained by Bill Bales and Amby Vulgan, won 23 of 26 games to capture the Virginia state championship. The team was coached by George (Gummy) Proctor, who was an outstanding official for many years.

Proctor officiated many bigtime college football and basketball games. He served as Hampden-Sydney athletic director in addition to his other duties, and the Tigers list him in their Athletic Hall of Fame along with Yank Bernier and the late Hank Crisp of the University of Alabama, the late Deke Brackett of Arkansas, UCLA and Marshall, who died in the tragic plane crash carrying the Marshall football team in 1970, Bob Thalman, a winner as VMI football coach, and Jim Hickey, who was a former University of North Carolina football coach.

Hampden-Sydney's first basketball team, 1908.

Bill Hardin, Hampden-Sydney's all-time scoring leader (2,070 points), and 1963 Little All-American.

Bill Hardin (left), Coach Bill Pegram and Dave Trickler accept trophy after Tigers captured the 1963 Fort Eustis Basketball Tournament championship.

VMI
...and the Institute was heard from, definitely

W. H. Taylor (Class of 1892), VMI's first football captain.

The Battle of New Market... Stonewall Jackson... the Legend of Jimmy Leech and the Flying Squadron 1920... and the Miracle Keydets of basketball... This is VMI.

The historic Institute has won acclaim in athletics through the years, but not since the Battle of New Market, when the Corps of Cadets marched into battle and defeated a unit of Union soldiers in the Civil War, has VMI created such an explosion on the national scene as their basketball team did in 1976.

Nobody in their right mind would have bet a penny on the Keydets winning the opening round game in the NCAA East Regional in 1976, much less reaching the final eight in the entire country. After all, basketball hasn't been VMI's cup of tea as football has been through the ages. In fact, going into the 1975-76 campaign, the Keydets had been without a winning basketball season for 45 long years. In five previous seasons, they had won just 33 games and just one in 1970-71.

In 1963-64, VMI managed to win the Southern Conference tournament championship although they had won but 12 games during the season. The Keydets upset Davidson in the semifinals and defeated George Washington in the championship game. But in the opening round of the NCAA East Regional they were outclassed by Princeton, 86-80. But two of the players were to be heard from 12 years later—as Keydet coaches.

Bill Blair was a star of the 1964 tournament champions and, assisted by former teammate Charlie Schmaus, he coached the Keydets to the conference title in 1976. But everybody thought that was the end and VMI would merely show up for the East Regional.

VMI was one of three Virginia teams that made it to the 1976 NCAA Regionals, something that never happened before. Virginia and Virginia Tech were eliminated in the opening round, but the Keydets upset nationally ranked Tennessee.

Then in the semifinals, the Keydets did it again, this time surprising DePaul 71-66 in overtime, moving into the East finals against unbeaten Rutgers. The Keydets, a long shot, had shattered all odds and were one of eight teams left in NCAA tournament play, a development that startled the experts.

Against Rutgers (30-0), the Keydets stayed in the game until they ran into foul trouble. At the half, VMI had four players with three or more fouls. That doomed them. Rutgers won, 81-75, but many wondered how the Keydets might have fared if they hadn't been hampered by fouls.

Millions watched them on national television, a far cry from the comparatively few who were in the stands 56 years before that watching the mighty VMI Flying Squadron, led by the immortal Jimmy Leech, equal the record for highest score in the history of Old Dominion college football. The Keydets swamped Hampden-Sydney, 136-0!

The Keydets of 1920 are regarded as one of the greatest football teams ever produced in the state. And Jimmy Leech was something else again. The unbeaten Flying Squadron crushed nine opponents, including Virginia, Pennsylvania, North Carolina State and Catholic University, piling up 431 points to 20 for the opposition.

Leech was a complete football player. Offensively and defensively, there was nothing he couldn't do. He scored 210 points in 1920, a VMI record. And he had a hand in many other touchdowns.

In a 96-0 romp over Catholic U., Leech ran wild. The triple-threat scored eight touchdowns, passed for one and

Jimmy Leech...210 points in one season, 66 points in one game.

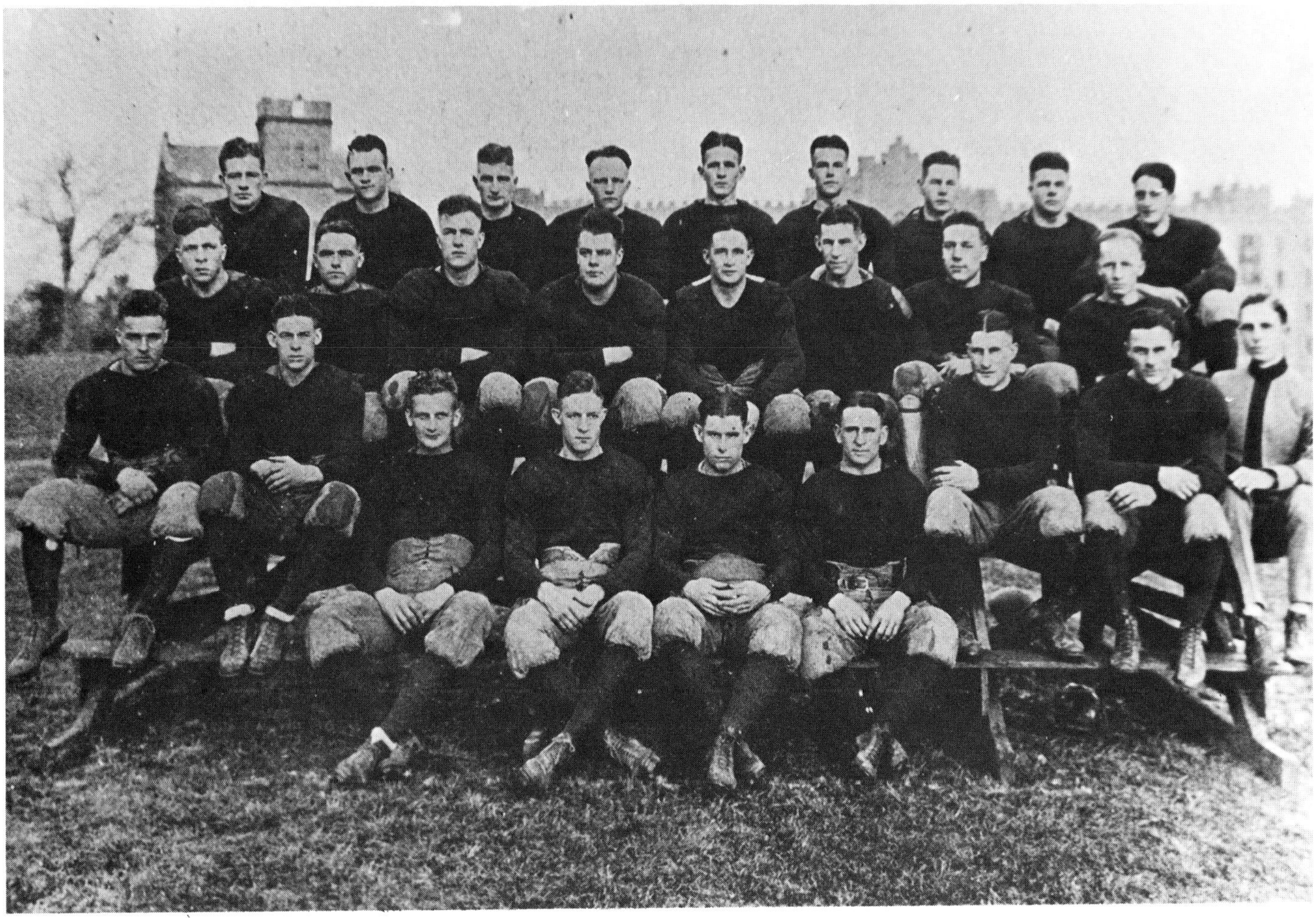

The famed VMI Flying Squadron of 1920.

Joe Muha, All-Southern from VMI, led the National Football League in punting in 1948 with a 42.7 average while playing with the Philadelphia Eagles.

Al Hawkins, minus helmet, scoring touchdown for Flying Squadron against Clemson in game played in Norfolk, November 9, 1929. VMI won, 12-0. The other touchdown was scored by Tommy Scott, who is in the VMI Hall of Fame.

kicked 12 points-after-touchdowns, giving him credit for 66 points in a single game. It's still a record.

Leech was a super star of the first order, but he was overlooked in the 1920 All-America backfield, which included George Gipp of Notre Dame, Donald Lourie of Princeton, Gaylord Stinchcomb of Ohio State and Charles Way of Penn State. A Lexington native, Leech died on August 18, 1951. His name is enshrined in the National College Football Hall of Fame. After Leech, VMI wasn't able to produce another undefeated football team until 1957.

Through the years VMI football has been identified with many stars, especially backs like Paul Shu, Bosh Pritchard, Joe Muha, Lynn Chewning, Bill Brehaney, Johnny Mapp, Sam Woolwine, Bobby Jordan, Sam Horner, Howard Dyer, Don Kern, Bob Habasevich and Ronnie Norman. They were among the many All-Southern players the Keydets have produced. Pritchard, a broken-field stylist from Hopewell, led the nation in punt returns in 1939. He became an outstanding pro player with the Philadelphia Eagles in the NFL.

In 1951, Tom Nugent coached the Keydets to a 7-3 record and a share of the Southern Conference championship with Maryland, each with 5-0 league marks.

The Keydets enjoyed their greatest football success under Coach John McKenna, who produced VMI's first undefeated seaon since the famed Flying Squadron of 1920. McKenna's 1957 Keydets went 9-0-1, and only a 21-21 tie with Holy Cross in the second game of the season kept VMI from a perfect record.

Woolwine and Lou Farmer, an All-Southern guard, were co-captains of the 1957 Southern Conference championship team, which also included All-Southerners Jim McFall, a tackle; and back Bobby Jordan. Woolwine was major college football's national champion in kickoff returns for two seasons —1955 and 1956.

Coach McKenna's Keydets also won Southern Conference titles in 1959 and 1960. The Keydets, led by Horner and Dyer, lost only one game in 1959 (to Penn State). After 13 years at VMI, McKenna departed following the 1965 season. Some lean years on the gridiron followed and it was left to Coach Bob Thalman to turn VMI around. In a surprising turn of events, the Keydets captured the Southern Conference championship in 1974 as Ronnie Norman paved the way by rushing for 1,045 yards. Thalman, who brought the Keydets back after winning only three games the previous season, was voted Coach of the Year in the Southern Conference. He was only the second VMI coach to win the award, McKenna having gained the honor three times.

Bosh Pritchard, VMI's All-Southern back, was the 1941 national champion in punt returns in the major college division. Played 11 years in the NFL, including the Philadelphia Eagles' championship teams in 1948-49.

Fullback Sam Horner (1956-59) scored 13 touchdowns; averaged 41.8 yards on 65 punts; scored career total of 102 punts; two-time All-Southern.

VMI's Curt Reppart leaps to pass ball in back of Tennessee guard Johnny Darden to Ron Carter as Keydets upset Tennessee in first round of NCAA East Regional playoffs at Charlotte, North Carolina, in 1976.

The scoreboard tells the story of VMI's stunning upset over nationally-ranked Tennessee in the 1976 NCAA East Regional Tournament. The clock shows 13 seconds left and the situation pretty well in hand as John Krovic takes a foul shot.

Guard Lou Farmer (left) and back Sam Woolwine, both All-Southern selections, were co-captains of VMI's last undefeated football team in 1957. Woolwine established himself as one of VMI's all-time runners. He led the nation in kickoff returns two seasons, gaining 1,147 yards in this category for career (1955-57). In all-purpose running, he gained 2,787 yards.

Tight end John Hince made the big catch for the Keydets in 1967, catching this pass from Russ Quay that gave VMI a 12-10 victory over Virginia Tech.

Quarterback Howard Dyer and center Lee Badgett, 1960 VMI co captains. Dyer was called the "Mississippi Gambler" because of his daring ways and gained a career total of 2,879 yards (rushing and passing combined) for a VMI record; had a 52.1 percent pass-completion mark; scored 17 touchdowns and 104 points, including 27 two-point conversions; named All-Southern two years. Badgett was named to the Pop Warner All-American team for scholar-athletes, and studied at Oxford on a Rhodes Scholarship.

Halfback John Traynham, named co-captain of the 1961 Pop Warner All-America team for scholar-athletes, receives his award from Coach John McKenna. One of the Keydets' tri-captains in 1961, Traynham was the highest ranking Pre-Med Cadet in his class. In 1960, he ranked second in the nation with a punt return average of 24.6.

VIRGINIA TECH
One victory away from national glory

Roscoe Coles, Virginia Tech vs. Richmond, 1974

Virginia Tech football received very little national attention until 1932. That year the Gobblers made such an impression that the college football experts began studying the maps trying to find out where Blacksburg was located.

Henry (Puss) Redd was in his first year as head coach. And what his Gobblers did to the surprise of a lot of outsiders was knock off six straight opponents, including Georgia (7-6) and Kentucky (7-0). And when you go around beating teams in such high position in the football world, then people have to take notice.

Now the stage was set to meet the mighty Alabama Crimson Tide of Rose Bowl fame at Tuscaloosa, Alabama. The Gobblers were dreaming of an undefeated, untied season. The odds were stacked heavily against them. Alabama featured All-American fullback John (Hurry) Cain, and he was enough to throw fear in the hearts of those who dared to oppose the Crimson Tide, especially on their home ground. But Redd's men had no fear and took the game to Alabama, and before long it was Alabama on the short end and fighting for life.

The Gobblers, captained by Bill Grinus, scored in the second quarter. Heinie Groth caught a pass from Ray Mills and raced 45 yards to the Alabama 20. Then Al Casey, outrunning Dixie Howell, grabbed Mills' pass on the goal line to score.

In an effort to protect their lead, the Gobblers gave the Tide a safety in the third period when Casey intentionally ran out of the end zone. They succeeded in stopping Hurry Cain but not Dixie Howell, who finally slipped through for ten yards late in the game for a 9-6 victory.

But the Gobblers came so close to national glory and this team is still regarded as one of the best ever in Tech football history. It was their only defeat as they closed out the season by blanking Virginia, 13-0, and VMI, 26-0, in the old Thanksgiving Day Classic played annually in Roanoke.

Tech has produced many fine football teams. In the so-called modern era, the 1954 Techmen, under Coach Frank Moseley, went undefeated (8-0-1). The 1963 team (8-2), under Coach Jerry Claiborne, won Tech's only Southern Conference football title; the 1966 and 1968 Tech teams, other Claiborne productions, played in the Liberty Bowl, and in 1975 Jimmy Sharpe's team, after losing its first two games, wound up 8-3.

The greatest Virginia Tech players?

Mel Jefferies, who served as sports information director for a number of years and was an authority on VPI football, came up with an all-time Gobbler football team covering the years 1920-29:

All-Time Tech Team, 1920-29:

	Pos.	Wt.	Ht.	Class
Harry Hardwick	LE	175	5-10	'23
Tex Wilson	LT	200	6-2	'23
Harry Stark	LG	202	5-11	'32
Joe Moran	C	205	6-2	'25
Henry Crisp	RG	192	5-11	'21
Bob Baker	RT	230	6-4	'25
George Parrish	RE	185	6-4	'21
Rip Wallace	QB	185	5-11	'23
Bird Hooper	LH	185	6-0	'31
Frank Peake	RH	175	6-1	'29
Pasco Gettle	FB	200	5-11	'25

Tech has had many great players before or since but perhaps the greatest of them all was the legendary Hunter Carpenter, who played from 1900 to 1905. He is the only Tech player in the National Football Hall of Fame.

In 1904, Carpenter transferred to the University of North Carolina. "I want to help Carolina beat Virginia," was his explanation for making the switch. For three years Carpenter and the Tech team had lost to Virginia by narrow margins. He thought Carolina had an excellent chance of doing it in 1904 and he actually led the Tar Heels to victory over the Cavaliers.

Carpenter was elected captain of the 1905 Carolina team but decided to return to Virginia Tech. He led the Gobblers to nine victories in 10 games, including a 16-6 conquest of Army at West Point. Tech was the first Southern team ever to beat an Army eleven. Virginia also was beaten by Tech for the first time. The only loss in 1905 was to Navy, 12-6.

As a runner and defensive player, Carpenter could do it all. But he was ignored on Walter Camp's All-America team, as Camp always loaded his all-stars with players from Princeton, Yale and Harvard. But those who saw Carpenter were convinced the Tech star had no equal.

Tech can point with pride to many fine football players since the thirties. Tackle George (Greek) Maskas was a standout in the mid-forties. Tackle George Preas, running back Dickie Beard and end Carroll Dale were stars of the fifties. Dale, later to become a pro star, was Tech's first solid All-American.

Standouts in the sixties included quarterback Bob Schweickert, fullback Sonny Utz, Frank Loria, defensive end George Foussekis and linebacker Mike Widger, in the seventies, quarterback Don Strock, receiver Ricky Scales, and backs Phil Rogers and Roscoe Coles.

Hall of Fame—Virginia Tech's Hunter Carpenter—a legend of the early days of VPI football—has been inducted into College Football's Hall of Fame—the only football player from the school even to win that honor. The career of Carpenter (at the right) drew widespread attention to football, then a new sport on the campus. Player at left is unidentified.

A classic picture of what appears to be a perfect play for Virginia Tech in a 1929 game against Pennsylvania in Philadelphia. Tech halfback Phil Spear finds a big hole as Harry Stark (left) takes out his man and Mitt Owens does his job at the right. Tech forced heavily-favored Penn to come from behind for a 14-8 victory.

E. H. Lane, Sr. of Altavista, for whom Virginia Tech's new stadium was named, was one of the early arrivals for the first game played in the magnificent facility on October 2, 1965.

Tech's Tommy Francisco receives award as the outstanding player in the 1965 Harvest Bowl game at Roanoke.

Quarterback Bobby Owens in the end zone after a 13-yard run with just 13 seconds remaining that gave the Gobblers a 9-7 victory over William and Mary in the first game played in the new Lane Stadium on October 2, 1965.

Virginia Tech's split end Gene Fisher holds on after making a catch in 1966.

Jon Utin kicking one of his ten field goals for the Gobblers in 1967.

George Foussekis and Frank Loria lead Virginia Tech team on charter flight to Liberty Bowl game in Memphis in 1967.

Coach Jerry Claiborne directed the Virginia Tech football team to two bowl games.

Ken Edwards on the loose for Virginia Tech in 1967.

As a sophomore in 1976, Roscoe Coles rushed for 1,045 yards on 194 carries for a new Virginia Tech rusing record for a season. He teamed with Paul Adams (768 yards) and Phil Rogers (762) for a combined 2,575 yards for the season, leading Tech to an 8-3 record, the Gobblers' best since 1966.

Phil Rogers, getting some superb assistance from his teammates in clearing the way, steams ahead in 1973 game against VMI. Rogers went on to become Tech's all-time career rushing leader with 2,461 points.

Bobby Steven's historic shot drops through the net at Madison Square Garden as Virginia Tech defeated Notre Dame, 92-91, in overtime to win the NIT championship in 1973.

Steven's shot, recorded at the same instant from another angle.

Keith Neff of Virginia Tech, first Virginian ever to pole vault 17 feet, winning first place in the 1976 Pitt Invitational Indoor Track Meet by clearing a height of 17 feet even. A product of West Springfield High School in Northern Virginia, Neff is the first Tech trackman named to the University Division All-America track and field team by the United States Track Coaches Association. He was born in Portsmouth, Virginia.

Coach Jimmy Sharpe's Gobblers lost their first two games of the 1975 season and then bounced back to finish with an 8-3 record.

WASHINGTON & LEE UNIVERSITY
Onetime bigtime

Washington & Lee's football team, coached by George Barclay and led by quarterback Gil Bocetti, won eight of 10 games in 1950, capturing the Southern Conference championship and accepting a bid to play in the Gator Bowl at Jacksonville, Florida.

It was to be the General's last hurrah in bigtime college athletics.

The old school in Lexington, which started playing intercollegiate football in 1873, announced in 1954 that it was abolishing subsidized athletics. The college sports world was stunned. Rich in tradition, the Generals had produced many fine teams and athletes through the years.

Following two successive 8-1 seasons, the Generals won all nine football games in 1914 and captured the South Atlantic championship under Coach Walter B. (Jogger) Elcock. The Generals followed with a 7-1-1 season in 1915. Those were the years of the immortal Cy Young (not to be confused with the baseball pitcher of the same name).

Warren E. (Tex) Tilson coached W&L football for most of the 1930s, his Generals winning the Southern Conference championship in 1934 with a 7-3 record. It wasn't until 1950, with George Barclay coaching, that the Generals won another Southern Conference crown. The Generals lost to Wyoming, 20-7, in the 1951 Gator Bowl.

After the athletic program was de-emphasized, life went on at W&L and with some fantastic results in football that gained the Generals national recognition. Frank A. Parsons best described it in an article written in the *Magazine of Washington and Lee University* in the summer of 1969:

"...One footnote is appropriate here in acknowledgement of the contribution the members of the football squads of 1959 through 1962 and their head coach, the late Lee M. McLaughlin, made to the quieting of those who disassociated amateur football with good football. Throughout those seasons, this dedicated group of young men—all playing for the love of the game, compiled a record of 28 victories, five losses and two ties. They sang the 'Swing' in their dressing rooms before the game and at halftime, and there were some Phi Beta Kappas among them. In 1961 they were unbeaten in nine games. *Sports Illustrated* featured them in a mid-season lead story, and at season's end the Washington Touchdown Club selected them as the outstanding small college team in the nation. They demonstrated emphatically that football did not die at W&L, nor did they bury a way of life in Lexington on July 23, 1954."

Perhaps the greatest all-around athletes in W&L history were Cy Young and Leigh Williams, a gifted athlete from Norfolk's Maury High. Young was the Generals' leading scorer in football, basketball, baseball and track, serving as captain of three varsity sports. He was elected to the National Football Hall of Fame in 1958.

Williams, who died of leukemia in 1940, a day short of his 32nd birthday, also was a four-sports star, winning 16 monograms at W&L in the "Roarin' Twenties."

"In my mind, he's the greatest athlete ever to come to this school, and I've seen them all the past 53 years," the former W&L coach and athletic director Cy Twombly once said of Williams.

In basketball, the Generals won the Southern Conference championship in 1934, and again in 1937 with Bob Spessard playing the key role. Indeed, the last subsidized athletes to appear at W&L were 1957-58 basketball players Dom Flora, Frank Hoss, Gary McPherson and Dave Nichols. Flora was a consensus All-American, as were Norman Iler and Spessard before him.

The Generals won the College Athletic Conference basketball championships in 1967, 1970 and 1972.

There is nothing minor about the W&L lacrosse team. The Generals, who fielded their first lacrosse team on a club basis in 1938 and joined the United States Intercollegiate Lacrosse Association in 1947, rank among the nation's best.

The Generals were undefeated in 1973 and 1974 and participated in the NCAA Tournament three straight years, reaching the semifinals in 1973 and 1974.

Gil Bocetti led W&L to the 1951 Gator Bowl after winning the Southern Conference championship. It was the Generals' great moment but their last hurrah in bigtime college football.

Leigh Williams, a W&L immortal, was a star in four sports—football, basketball, track and baseball.

The late Lee McLaughlin coached the Generals to an unbeaten, untied season in 1961. They were recognized as the best small college team in the nation. In 1962, his Generals compiled an 8-1 record and won the College Athletic Conference championship. McLaughlin made W&L's de-emphasized athletic program work.

W&L's super star in four sports. The immortal Cy Young in football, basketball, baseball and track gear. He excelled in each.

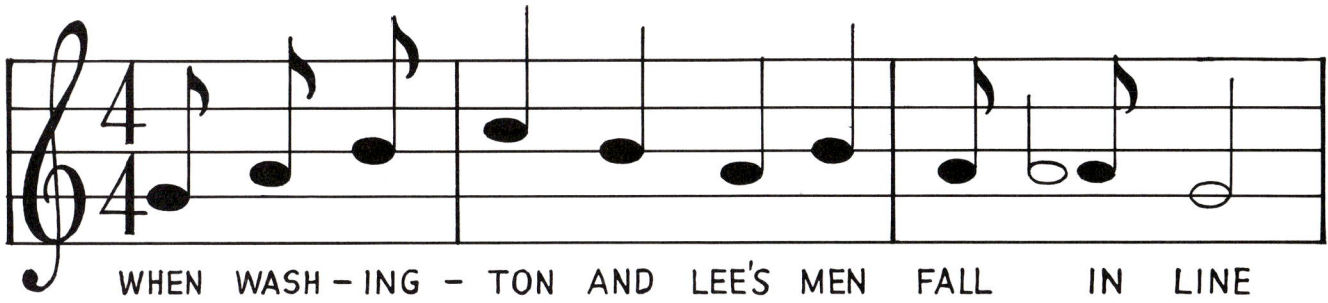

WHEN WASH-ING-TON AND LEE'S MEN FALL IN LINE

They won four straight South Atlantic Division championships (1971-74), and have placed over 50 men on All-American lacrosse teams.

W&L Coach Jack Emmer has been named National Coach of the Year three straight times, an unprecedented record in lacrosse.

The Generals are very much alive and kicking in all sports in this stronghold of amateurs.

But while the Generals compete in the college division in most sports, they're definitely in the middle of things in the University Division in lacrosse. The Generals finished unbeaten in regular-season play in 1974 and were ranked as high as No. 2 nationally. Their only loss came in a one-goal decision to eventual champion Johns Hopkins in the NCAA semifinals.

In 1975, however, with most of the stars graduated, Emmer produced the biggest surprise in the country. The Generals had a mediocre 7-6 record when they finally started moving.

In four straight games in the space of two weeks, W & L beat Roanoke, Rutgers, Virginia and Johns Hopkins. The Generals defeated No. 1 Johns Hopkins, 11-7, on Hopkins' Home Field, where the Blue Jays had not lost in three years, a 27-game streak.

The upset came in the NCAA Championship Tournament, where the Generals lost to Maryland in the semifinals.

At the end, W & L was ranked fifth in the nation, a remarkable achievement considering its slow start.

So it can be said, the swinging Generals are very much alive and kicking in all sports in one of the nation's great strongholds of amateurs.

* * *

In 1954, Washington and Lee University stunned the sports world by announcing it was abolishing subsidized athletics.

But the Generals are still swinging on the hit parade.

There are hundreds of college fight songs.

The Irish conquered while they sang, "Cheer, Cheer for Old Notre Dame." The Yellow Jackets rallied to the tune of "I'm A Ramblin' Wreck from Georgia Tech."

"On Wisconsin" fired the Badgers to victory. At Yale, it was "Boola Boola." At Cornell, "Far Above Cauga's Waters," and at Princeton, "Old Nassau."

But few stirred the imagination as did the "Washington and Lee Swing."

Composed in the early 1900s, the "Washington and Lee Swing" is the most popular football song ever written, still played more than any other. The song has done more to bring the Lexington institution national identity than the Generals' greatest teams. While the Generals are playing athletics at the small college level, their fight song continues in the bigtime.

Three undergraduates are credited with the origin of "The Swing," Mark Sheafe ('06) strummed out the melody for the song on a guitar, but never wrote it down because he couldn't read music. Thornton W. Allen ('13) put it down on paper in 1909, presumably from Shaefe's unwritten melody, and had it copyrighted. The words were written by C.A. (Tod) Robbins ('12).

Published in 1910, "The Swing" has had an intriguing history loaded with controversy over the song's actual ownership. Tulane played it during a Rose Bowl game, and referred to it as the "Tulane Song." In 1931, during the

W&L fan in New Orleans reported. In 1930, the Alabama band called it the "Alabama Swing," playing it at games over the radio. In the same year, Rudy Valee sang it over radio as the "Tulane Swing."

Thornton Allen, who was the one who plugged the song into national popularity, undertook a national investigation regarding the question of copyright infringement. Allen won his fight. Both Tulane and Alabama and others were convinced the song was W&L's prize musical possession.

During World War I, the song was used as the official marching song of Camp Sherman. The W&L men in camp were, needless to say, delighted. When W&L alumnus John W. Davis ran for President in 1924, the "Washington and Lee Swing" was adopted as the Democrats' campaign song. At their final weekend dance in 1935, an aroused group of W&L students ran Glen Gray and his Casa Loma band out of town because he refused to play "The Swing."

There was nothing like it since "Dixie."

No other college song has been recorded more than the W&L piece. Big name bands in the 1930s and 1940s recorded it on practically every major label—Hal Kemp and Tex Beneke (Victor), Louis Armstrong with the Dukes of Dixieland (Audio Fidelity), Johnny Long (Signature) Dean Hudson (Bluebird), Kay Kyser (Columbia), Jan Garber (Capitol), Alvino Ray (Capitol) and Bob Crosby (Decca).

Kyser, the University of North Carolina graduate who became a famous band leader, elaborated on his version, playing it in symphonic style, as a fox trot, a waltz, march and even hillbilly. When Kyser went on television with his "College of Musical Knowledge," he opened his first program with the "Washington and Lee Swing."

Nearly every high school band in the country has "The Swing" in its repertoire, the words changed to fit their own school. Often a student entering the freshman class at W&L hears "The Swing" played, and remarks, "They're playing my high school song." He's soon set straight on the song's rightful ownership.

"The Washington and Lee Swing" is a perennial, a best seller among college songs," according to Robbins Music Corp. of New York City.

"... And for the university I yell, I yell like hell...."

Coach Jack Emmer put W & L on the lacrosse map. He was voted National Coach of the Year for an unprecedented three straight years (1972 at Courtland, 1973 in College Division at W & L and 1974 in University Division at W & L). His 1974 Generals were undefeated in regular season play (14-0) and ranked No. 3 nationally.

Defenseman John Strock ('31) and midfielder Charlie Stieff congratulate attackman Bob Morgan on one of his four goals in 9-5 victory over Virginia.

Playing on muddy Wilson Field, the W&L Generals defeated Sewanee, 8-0, a victory that led them to the College Athletic Conference football championship in 1962.

VIRGINIA UNION
"The Dream Team"

One of the greatest college basketball teams in the Commonwealth was the Virginia Union Panthers of 1938-39 and 1939-40, which swept to two successive Colored (since changed to Central) Intercollegiate Athletic Association championships.

The Panthers were called the "Dream Team." An all-black school, the Panthers were getting little attention from the white population. But soon the word got around about this amazing basketball team and the Panthers became a source of pride for all Virginians.

Coached by Henry Hucles, the Panthers were fantastic shooters, especially from long range. Recalling the exploits of the Panthers, one of the players recently pointed out, without batting an eye, that "we had an 80 per cent shooting average" which certainly makes them a "Dream Team."

In 1939, Dick Williamson wrote in the *Richmond Times-Dispatch:*

"The best basketball team in the state of Virginia, in case you haven't heard, is located right here in Richmond. Not only the best in Virginia, but quite possibly the best in the East, as far as putting the ball through the basket goes. This team is the Virginia Union Panthers.

"The Panthers played a game against Morgan College of Baltimore Friday night. In 60 seconds by the clock seven goals from the field were made. The action was so swift the scorer couldn't keep up the pace."

The Panthers were led by Wiley (Soup) Campbell, their great scorer and captain, and the team included Melvin Glover, their second top scorer, Orbert Knighton, Gilbert Fraser, Kavonzo Hyde, Floyd (Les) Atkins, Leroy Kennedy, John Hayes, Robert Daughtry, Wilmotte Burton, Robert Harris. The team was so well balanced it made little difference who Coach Hucles put in the game.

They won 40 of 44 games in two seasons (always defeating the team that beat them in the return match); the Panthers prospered under adverse conditions. They had no gym on campus. They practiced and played most of their games in the cramped little gym at the Community Center on West Charlotte Street in Richmond. Sometimes they played games on the stage at the Richmond Mosque, which could accommodate more fans. No matter where they played, the Panthers turned 'em away.

Despite its success, Virginia Union was ignored in post-season invitations. They challenged Long Island University for a regular-season game but were rejected. In 1939 Long Island's famed blackbirds, coached by Clair Bee, went undefeated, captured the National Invitational Tournament in Madison Square Garden and claimed the mythical national championship.

At the end of the season, the Long Island seniors invited Virginia Union to New York to play them.

Sports Editor Jimmie Jones of the *Richmond Times-Dispatch* wrote: "Local sportsmen, regardless of creed, class or color, have greeted with justifiable pride the somewhat startling feat of the Virginia Union University basketball team, which last week journeyed to New York and there defeated Long Island U's celebrated Blackbirds by the score, 36-28.

"While it's true this was not the official LIU team and the game was not an officially recognized one, it is true that the team which was beaten by the Panthers was made up of the regular Long Island lineup, including five seniors who have started most of the team's games this season—Bromberg, Torgoff, Kaplowitz, etc. It was also virtually the same team which had just finished winning the National Inter-Collegiate Invitational Tournament.

"The Long Island authorities have a perfect right to disclaim any responsibility for or sanction of the game, and probably will do so on the grounds their regular season during which the Blackbirds were undefeated in 25 scheduled games had ended.

"But this does not alter the fact that Virginia Union defeated the team that won most of LIU's games this year and last, including four starting regulars off that team and one first-line substitute. And that was something no other team was able to do."

The famed Harlem Globetrotters, who in 1940 defeated the Chicago Bruins for the world professional basketball championship, stopped off in Richmond. In those days, the Trotters would play a local team and clown around. The Panthers would have none of it. Abe Saperstein's Globetrotters then got down to serious business and just did beat the Panthers in the final minute.

Honors are still piling up for the "Dream Team." Campbell and Glover have been elected to the Black Hall of Fame.

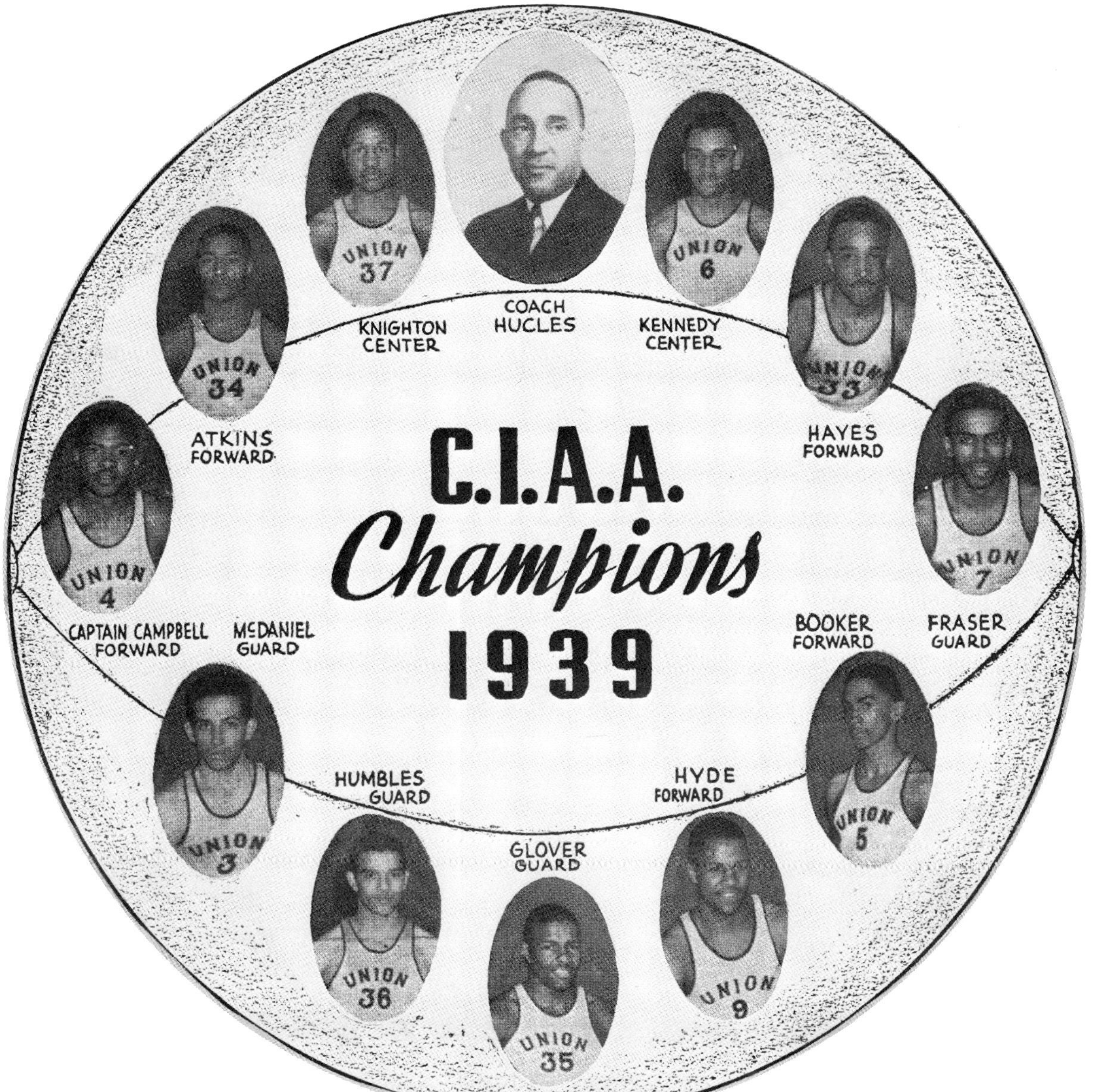
COACH
HUCLES
KNIGHTON
CENTER
KENNEDY
CENTER
ATKINS
FORWARD
HAYES
FORWARD
C.I.A.A.
Champions
1939
CAPTAIN CAMPBELL
FORWARD
McDANIEL
GUARD
BOOKER
FORWARD
FRASER
GUARD
HUMBLES
GUARD
HYDE
FORWARD
GLOVER
GUARD
UNION 37
UNION 6
UNION 34
UNION 33
UNION 4
UNION 7
UNION 3
UNION 5
UNION 36
UNION 35
UNION 9

UNION
32

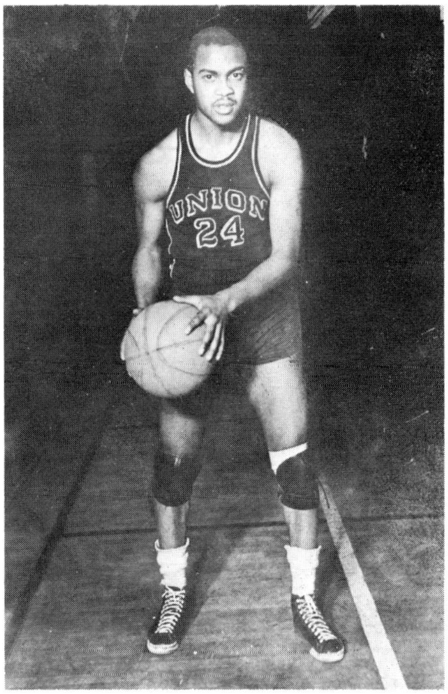
UNION
24

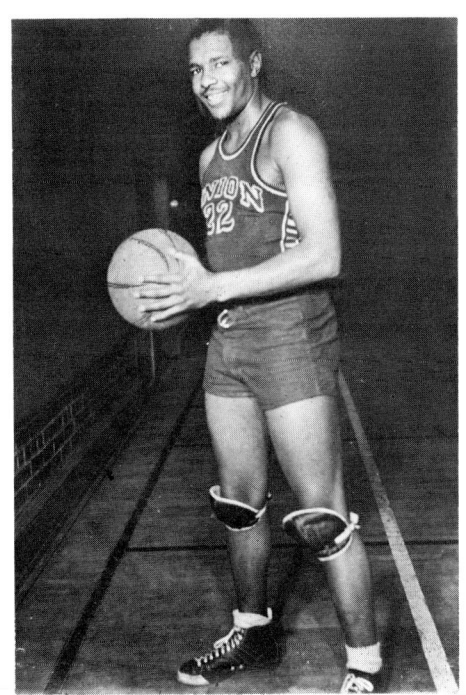

Wiley (Soup) Campbell and Melvin Glover, of Virginia Union's famed "Dream Team." Both have been elected to the Black Hall of Fame.

COLLEGE OF WILLIAM & MARY
A Japanese quarterback, upsets, the Voyles-McCray years

It was an unusual combination—a Japanese quarterback in command of the Indians. His name was Art Matsu, and he was very good, too. Under Coach J. W. Tasker, Matsu was a star in 1925 when the Tribe won seven of 11 games and outscored the opposition, 236 points to 86. The following season, Matsu was team captain and sparked the Indians to a 6-4 season.

Matsu became the first W & M player to move into the pro ranks, playing quarterback for the Dayton Triangles in the National Football League in 1928. While the Triangles failed to win a single game that season, Matsu paved the way for many other W & M stars to follow him to the NFL.

Among them were, Gerrard (Buster) Ramsey, Knox Ramsey, John Kreamcheck, Lou Creekmur, Harvey Johnson and Tommy Thompson, each of whom distinguished himself in pro football by being picked on the All-NFL first team.

George Hughes, who was co-captain of the Indians in 1949 and captained the Pittsburgh Steelers; Ralph Sazio, another former W & M co-captain, and former coach Marv Levy are still alive in the game in the Canadian Football League. Sazio, highly successful as a coach in the CFL, is general manager of the Hamilton Tiger-Cats; Levy is coach of the Montreal Alouettes and Hughes is line coach of the Ottawa Roughriders.

Many upsets have been recorded by W & M football teams, the 27-16 upset over Navy with Levy coaching being one of the greatest. But a tie game with mighty Harvard in 1930 astounded the football experts just as much, bringing the unheralded Indians national recognition they never enjoyed before.

Coached by Branch Bocock, the Indians invaded Harvard Stadium after bombing Bridgewater, 81-0, the week

Ralph Sazio, co-captain of 1947 Indians who lost only one game. Played tackle for Hamilton Tiger-Cats and later coached the team in the Canadian Football League.

Art Matsu, W & M's outstanding Japanese quarterback in the twenties. First W & M player to play in the NFL.

before. Harvard wasn't impressed. The Ivy Leaguers, a national power then, scheduled W & M as a midseason breather.

In fact, Harvard was more concerned about the following week's game with Michigan, and regarded the Virginians so lightly that Coach Arnold Horween ordered his aides to start his substitutes before he fled the scene to scout Yale against Dartmouth in the Yale Bowl.

Outweighed from five to 35 pounds in every position, the Indians overwhelmed the Crimson starting substitutes with their amazing speed and then outplayed the regulars.

"The gallant little football band from ancient William and Mary outfought and outsmarted all Harvard's mighty army," said the report from Cambridge, Massachusetts. Playing with cold and deadly fury, the Indians blasted their way to a 13-6 lead. Harvard scored first and then Happy Halligan pounced on a Harvard fumble, caught a pass from Mitch Mozeleski and raced to Harvard's 20-yard line. Halligan, an end, then swapped positions with Mozeleski and fed halfback Red Maxey a touchdown pass. Mozeleski drop kicked the extra point for a 7-6 lead.

In the second period, W & M stopped Harvard's running attack. With the regulars now in the game, the Crimson switched to laterals. The fast-charging Halligan intercepted one, feinting and dodging his way 30 yards to put the Indians ahead. The Harvard cheering section, awed by the gallant lightweights from Virginia, voiced its disappointment when Mozeleski missed his try for the extra point.

The Crimson finally tied the score in the last period, W & M held for three downs on its three and Harvard just did make it across the goal line on the fourth try. The game is still rated as one of the greatest spectacles ever staged in old Harvard Stadium.

The Indians went on to hold their last four opponents scoreless for a 7-2-1 record. In his five years as head coach, Bocock's record was 26-20-3. The Indians averaged 23.1 points a game, a rather explosive attack for football in that era. Halligan and Maxey rank among the all-time greats in Virginia college football.

Monk Little (left), regarded as the greatest William & Mary track star with his coach, Scrap Chandler, and as they appeared at a get together in 1975. In three years for the Indians in the early 1930s, the 138-pound Little scored more than 600 points. He was a one-man track team, running the 100-yard dash in 9.6, the 220 in 21.2, the 400 in 48.6. He broadjumped 25-7, a W & M record that held for many years, and threw the javelin 207-11. He was outstanding in the Penn Relays in the javelin and broadjump.

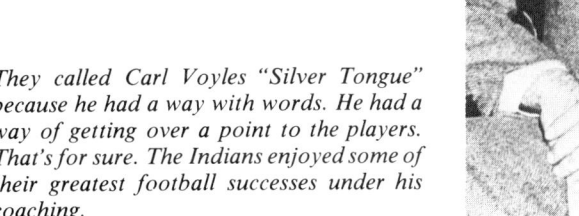

They called Carl Voyles "Silver Tongue" because he had a way with words. He had a way of getting over a point to the players. That's for sure. The Indians enjoyed some of their greatest football successes under his coaching.

After Bocock, W & M played a winning hand under Coach John Kellison and leaders like Otis Douglas and Gerry Quirk.

Then the Indian football fortunes skidded until Carl M. Voyles, plucked from Wallace Wade's staff at Duke, came on the scene and lifted W & M to its greatest heights. The Indians launched a domination of college football in Virginia that lasted ten years. It was the fruitful Voyles-McCray era.

In the seventh game of Voyles' first season in 1939, the Indians lost to Virginia, 26-6. They didn't lose to a state opponent again until the opening game of 1950, when VMI prevailed, 25-19. The unbeaten streak against state opposition included 41 victories and one tie, a record unmatched before or since in Old Dominion college football.

After Voyles left, Rube McCray stepped up as head coach, which meant more glory for the Indians. This time they took the bowl route. There's room for argument as to which was W & M's finest team. Receiving strong support is McCray's team, led by co-captains Ralph Sazio and Bob Steckroth and such all-time W & M greats as Knox Ramsey, Tommy Thompson and Jack Cloud. They won nine of ten games, losing only to North Carolina and Charlie (Choo Choo) Justice, 14-7.

After routing Richmond, 35-0, in the season's finale, the Indians were offered several bowl bids, accepting the Dixie Bowl in Birmingham. Cloud scored two touchdowns and had one called back as the Southern Conference champions outgained their foes but lost a 21-19 thriller to Arkansas.

In 1948, George Hughes, Vito Ragazzo, Buddy Lex, Cloud and Thompson sparked the Tribe to another successful season. The Indians, losing only two games, tied mighty North Carolina with Justice, 7-7, and Boston College, 14-14. They capped the season by beating North Carolina State, 26-6, and Arkansas, 9-0, avenging the Dixie Bowl defeat. In the Delta Bowl, the Indians clobbered Oklahoma, 20-0.

No history of W & M football would be complete without the mention of the "Iron Indians" of 1953. This was perhaps the most fascinating of all Indian teams. Coached by Jackie Freeman, the "Iron Indians" had only 23 players, including a 135-pound kicking specialist named "Hadacol" Hines. Despite the lack of manpower, they captured the admiration of college football as they tied powerful Navy and whipped Wake Forest, Virginia Tech, George Washington, North Carolina State and Richmond in a 5-4-1 season.

One of the most popular figures in college athletics, Bill (Pappy) Gooch served in nearly every capacity—coach, athletic director and business manager— in his nearly four decades at W & M. He died in 1964.

Rated as one of William & Mary's greatest teams, coached by Carl Voyles and captained by Marvin Bass, these Indians captured the Southern Conference championship in 1942, winning nine games, tying Navy and losing only to the powerful North Carolina Preflight. They capped the season with a 14-7 victory over Oklahoma. Front (from left): Hubard, Johnson, Korczowski, Knox, Warrington, Bass, Vandeweghe, Ramsey, Fields, Holloway, Clowes, Forkovitch. Middle row: Weaver, Sazio, Chipok, Blagg, Safko, H. Knox, Poplinger, Johns, Kline, Wright, Irvin. Back: Steckroth, Ream, Schultz, Graham, Brown, Abbotts, Bucher, Longacre, Grimbowitz, Gooden, Freeman.

L. Quimby (Huducol) Hines, the little fellow with the big kick for W & M's "Iron Indians" of 1953.

Rube McCray enjoyed six successive winning seasons as coach of the William & Mary football team.

Coach Marv Levy (left) is congratulated by W & M President Dr. Davis Y. Paschall after the Indians scored a stunning 27-16 upset over Navy in 1968. It was one of the great victories in W & M history.

The Indians raise their coach, Bill Chambers, in triumph after W & M defeated West Virginia during the 1959-60 basketball season and ended the Mountaineers' 56-game basketball winning streak against Southern Conference opposition. When he played for W & M, Chambers pulled down 51 rebounds in a game against Virginia, 1953. It still stands as an NCAA major college record.

The crowd attending the William & Mary-Virginia Tech game at Richmond in 1929.

The "Iron Indians" of 1953. With one of the smallest squads in personnel ever to represent a major college, these "Iron Indians" got amazing results. They won five of 10 games and tied Navy. Front row (from left) George Parozzo, John Bednarik, Tommy Martin, Steve Milkovich, Bill Bowman, Jack Place, and Quinby Hines. Second Row: Al Grieco, Tom Hamilton, Charles Copeland, Aubrey Fitzgerald, Linwood Cox, Bob Elzey and Jerry Sazio. Third row: Chet Waksmunski, George Karschner, Shorty Herrman, Bill Marfizo, Bill Riley, and John Risjord. Fourth row: Bill Nagy, Charlie Sumner, Sam Scott, Doug Henley, and Bill Martin.

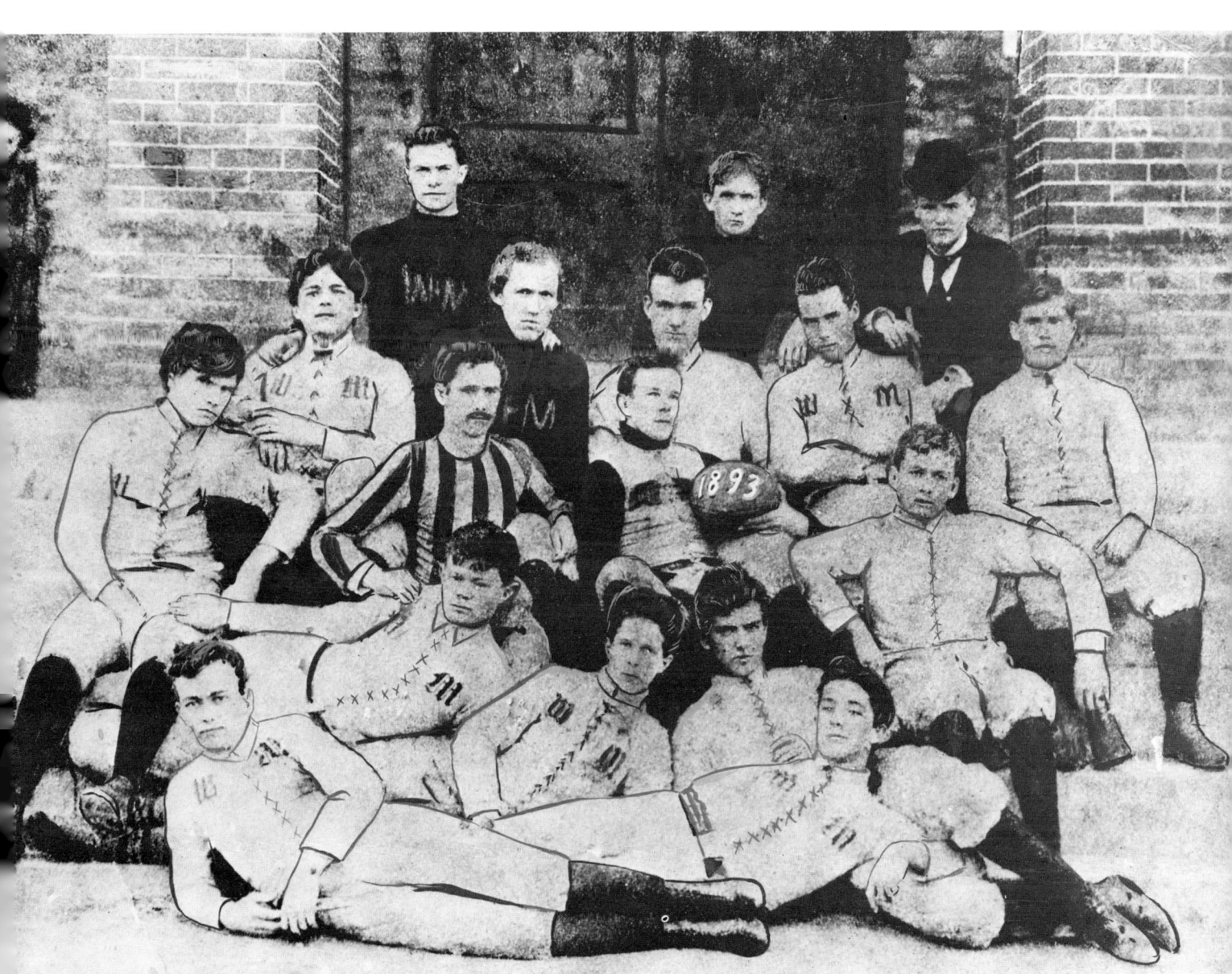
William & Mary's first football team, 1893.

RANDOLPH-MACON COLLEGE
When President Taft came to the rescue

Randolph-Macon College has been playing intercollegiate football since 1881, and through the years the students have taken the game seriously. And never in a more serious vein than when they called on the President of the United States to use his influence so a game could be played.

It happened in 1910. No team in the Virginia Eastern Intercollegiate League had a clear claim to the championship. Only Hampden-Sydney stood in the way of the Yellow Jackets and a showdown with Richmond College for the title.

Randolph-Macon defeated the Tigers, 10-3, clearing the way for the championship game with Richmond until R-MC President Dr. Blackwell put his foot down. Apparently a misunderstanding between Dr. Blackwell and the students developed after the Hampden-Sydney game.

At first, Dr. Blackwell said there would be no championship game at all. After some meetings, he relented somewhat, ruling the Jackets could play the game but not one R-MC student—not even the football manager—would be allowed to see it.

Two students, E. Barrett Prettyman and Marion N. Fisher, refused to take Dr. Blackwell's ultimatum sitting down and decided to do something to induce him to change his mind and allow the students to attend the game and cheer for their team.

So they took the issue to the highest authority in the land—the President of the United States. At the time, and conveniently enough, President William Howard Taft was visiting the Governor of Virginia in Richmond. So Prettyman and Fisher called on the President, who listened to their story. They reminded the President that he should carry out the duties of his office "to prevent injustices and rectify wrongs." In this case, it was the football situation at R-MC.

Mr. Taft said he would do what he could if arrangements could be made so his train could be stopped at Ashland. It so happened that William H. White, president of the Richmond, Fredericksburg and Potomac Railroad, was also a Randolph-Macon alumnus. When he heard the request of the R-MC students he immediately gave the order for the Presidential train to be stopped in Ashland.

Then Dr. Blackwell was advised of a "rumor" that President Taft would be stopping in Ashland. Dr. Blackwell had the report confirmed by the Governor's Mansion. The R-MC president went to Richmond and rode back to Ashland with President Taft.

On the stop at Ashland, President Taft spoke to a large crowd of students, faculty and townspeople, saying he had asked Dr. Blackwell to permit the students to attend the football game, and hoped it would all turn out fine.

It did.

Dr. Blackwell rescinded his original order. The students went to the game and cheered the Yellow Jackets to an 11-6 victory over Richmond, returning home with the championship trophy. The two students who engineered President Taft's visit...well, E. Barrett Prettyman became Chief Judge of the U.S. Court of Appeals for the District of Columbia, and Marion N. Fisher became a law partner of John W. Davis, the Democratic nominee for President of the U. S. in 1924.

The trophy the Jackets won in 1910 is placed on display about once every year in the Walter Hines Page Library, a symbol not only of a championship but

Dr. Robert Emory Blackwell, president of Randolph-Macon College, 1902-1938. U.S. President William Howard Taft changed his mind about a football game.

Gus Welch, who played with the immortal Jim Thorpe and the Carlisle Indians, served as chairman of the R-MC department of physical education from 1923 to 1929. He was recently named to the National Collegiate Football Hall of Fame.

the visit and assistance of a President of the United States who helped make it all possible.

Gus Welch, a teammate of the immortal Jim Thorpe with the famous Carlisle Indians, also became one of the most popular coaches and most resourceful athletic directors on the college scene. Welch coached football at R-MC from 1923 to 1929 and served as Director of Physical Culture.

He set standards to put the Jacket teams on a sound financial footing. He did away with the managers of each team, bought three Fords to save money on train fares, employed a full-time caretaker for the fields and opened a varsity shop on campus. The administration had said the teams could not compete unless they made enough money to cover expenses. Welch later traded the three Fords for one bus to cut down on costs. He was instrumental in the development of the R-MC athletic program, introducing boxing, track and lacrosse.

The stability of the R-MC athletic program through the years of hard knocks and successes is perhaps the reason for the longevity of the current coaching staff, headed by Hugh Stevens, who has been baseball coach since 1948 and athletic director since 1949. Head football coach Ted Keller, one of the most successful in the college division, has been on the job since 1964. Paul Webb was basketball coach 19 years before he departed for Old Dominion University in 1975.

Randolph-Macon has produced many outstanding athletes, including first team Little All-Americans in football—Arthur Oley, Jr. (1947), Jack Wilson (1951) and David B. Young (1957). But perhaps the Jackets' most sensational football player was Howard Stevens, who as a freshman from Harrisonburg in 1968 was the national leader in the college division in rushing (1,468 yards) and scoring (142 points). Afterwards he transferred to the University of Louisville, setting NCAA records in five categories, and later was drafted by the New Orleans Saints of the National Football League.

Jack Wilson, Little All-American, 1951.

David B. Young, Little All-American, 1957.

Arthur Oley, Jr., Little All-American, 1947.

Perfect Record: The 1968 Yellow Jackets, only unbeaten and untied football team in Randolph-Macon College history.

Knute Rockne Bowl Champions: The 1969 Yellow Jackets, who defeated the University of Bridgeport, 47-28, for the NCAA Division Two Eastern championship.

Dedicated in 1887 and reputed to be the first building in the South built specifically as a gymnasium, Randolph-Macon razed the landmark in 1974. One of the great moments in this gym occurred in 1919 when the R-MC defeated Richmond for the Virginia College Conference basketball championship by the unlikely score of 63-1! As evidenced by the picture, the old gym was a prime target for sports graffiti.

HOWARD STEVENS
All-Time college rushing, scoring champion

As a freshman at Randolph-Macon College in 1968, Howard Stevens of Harrisonburg won the college division rushing championship, gaining 1,468 yards in nine games, an average of 191 yards a game. And they said it could only happen in the Mason-Dixon Conference because Stevens was only 5-feet-5, 165 pounds. Then he went to the University of Louisville and became one of the great runners in major college football. In 1971-72 he gained 2,723 yards, and his 136.2 yards per game ranks him behind Ed Marinaro of Cornell and O. J. Simpson of Southern Cal among the all-time leaders.

However, combining the figures he compiled at Randolph-Macon and Louisville, Stevens is second to none. His 5,297 yards rushing and 69 touchdowns are all-time college records. He also caught 83 passes for 738 yards and eight touchdowns, 74 punt returns for 782 yards and 30 kickoff returns for 748 yards. His 418 points scored is also a collegiate record. He earned second team All-America honors as a senior and was team and conference Most Valuable Player in each of his four collegiate seasons.

Howard, originally drafted by New Orleans Saints, is now running for the Baltimore Colts, the smallest man in the National Football League.

Coached by Paul Webb, the 1974-75 R-MC basketball team is considered the best the college ever produced. The Jackets lost to Old Dominion University, 83-76, in the final game of the NCAA South Atlantic Region. They compiled a 27-3 record, the three losses by a total of nine points. Ranked among the top ten nationally during the season.

Front row (from left): Manager Mark Giragosian, Paul Jez, Eddie Webb, Paul Feeley, Jerry Ross, Fletcher Johnson, Paul Zuidema, Mike Love and Richard Hoffman, assistant coach; standing: Hal Nunnally, assistant coach, Jimmy Price, Billy Hanger, Joe Allen, Lew Welge, Paul Dreiling, Danny O'Connor, Gary Miller, Bruce Ganey and head coach Paul Webb.

Ted Keller, one of the winningest active coaches in college division football. His 1967-69 Yellow Jackets won 19 games in a row. In 1968, he produced the only unbeaten, untied team in R-MC history. His 1969 team won the Knute Rockne Bowl. Won four Mason-Dixon Conference Championships.

Paul Webb, a fixture at Randolph-Macon for 19 years before moving to Old Dominion University after 1974-75 season. His Jackets won three Mason-Dixon titles. His career record at R-MC was 315-158.

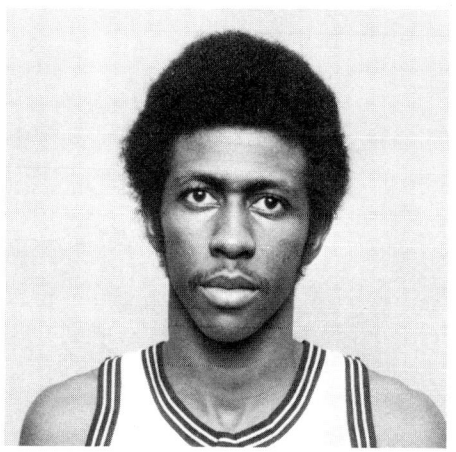

Fletcher Johnson, Randolph-Macon's all-time leading scorer with 2,216 for career. He scored a game high of 52 points against Catholic University on February 3, 1975. Graduated in 1975.

Hugh Stevens became R-MC athletic director in 1948 and the Jackets prospered under his regime. As baseball coach, he had only one losing season in 27 years.

UNIVERSITY OF RICHMOND
Spider immortals and an upset remembered

When Ed Merrick was head coach they tell a story of how he "sold" out-of-state prospects on coming to Richmond and playing football for the Spiders. Merrick would take the prospect on a walking tour of Monument Avenue, where such Virginia heroes as Robert E. Lee, Stonewall Jackson, J. E. B. Stuart and Jefferson Davis are immortalized in magnificent statues.

"See," Merrick would say, pointing to the statues with pride, "that's what we do for our boys."

Whether the story is true or not, Richmond has been able to recruit outstanding athletes through the years. Merrick himself fits into this category, an All-Southern center and captain of the Spiders, who compiled a 6-3-1 record under Coach Glenn Thistlewaite in 1939. Ed was the first Spider selected to play in the College All-Star game at Chicago. Merrick enjoyed a 15-year tenure as head coach of the Spiders and, in 1958, was voted Southern Conference Coach of the Year.

It was the season after Merrick graduated that the Spiders produced perhaps the greatest football upset in their history. In 1940, the Spiders weren't supposed to have a chance when they went against the University of North Carolina at Richmond City Stadium. Coach Ray Wolfe's Tar Heels were loaded with such stars as All-American end Paul Severin and Jim (Sweet) Lalanne, the talented triple-threat.

But the Spiders had their own combination, a triple-threat named Artful Art Jones and Dick Humbert, an end with great capabilities. Both played on the same Suffolk High School team and on this particular day they turned the tables on the Tar Heels. Jones passed for two touchdowns and kicked two extra points as he brought the Spiders from behind in the final quarter for a 14-13 victory.

The Spiders, with a line led by tackles Hal McVay, who was team captain, and Andy Fronczek, scored their first touchdown when Jones passed to Bob Erickson. Jones set up the clincher with a 35-yard run, then fired to Humbert, who made the grab in front of the goal posts while surrounded by a host of Tar Heel defenders. Jones kicked the tie-breaker to win one of the biggest shockers of the college season. Jones was the No. 1 draft pick of the Pittsburgh Steelers and Humbert was drafted by the Philadelphia Eagles. Both became NFL stars.

The Spiders enjoyed some of their most successful years in football under another Jones—Coach Frank Jones, who took the job after Richmond lost all ten games in 1965. It took Jones two years to put the Spiders on the right course, twice in the direction of the Tangerine Bowl at Orlando, Florida.

With sensational passer Buster O'Brien operating at quarterback and Walker Gillette, Richmond's consensus All-American, at end, the Spiders met Ohio University in the 1968 Tangerine Bowl.

In one of the most explosive offensive battles ever, the Spiders emerged victorious, 49-42, as O'Brien completed 38 of 58 passes for 447 yards and four touchdowns. Gillette snagged only one touchdown pass in this thriller but caught 20 passes for 242 yards.

The Spiders returned to the Tangerine Bowl in 1971, but lost this time to Toledo, 28-3.

O'Brien was named Athlete of the Year in the Southern Conference for 1968 and Gillette received the honor in 1969 after being picked on every major

Richmond's first football squad, 1892.

All-Southern center Ed Merrick was the first player from Virginia to be selected to play in the College All-Star game in Chicago. He was captain of the 1939 Spiders, who went into their final game undefeated and lost to W&M while several Richmond stars, including Art Jones, were sidelined by injuries.

All-America team. Jones bagged a big share of honors, too, in his nine years as head coach. He was voted Southern Conference Coach of the Year in 1967, 1968 and 1971.

In the so-called modern era, the Spiders have produced outstanding football stars in addition to O'Brien and Gillette. To name a few: halfback Earl Stoudt, who was conference player of the year in 1961; center Don Christman (1961), winner of the Jack Jacobs Blocking Trophy; Ray Easterling, all-conference end in 1970; and Barty Smith, the powerful fullback who set Richmond rushing records and was invited to play in practically every post-season college all-star game.

Malcolm U. (Mac) Pitt was a legend among college coaches. He's in both the Helms Foundation basketball and baseball Hall of Fame, also the American Association of College Baseball Coaches Hall of Fame. He was head coach of Richmond basketball for 19 years, bringing Richmond its only undefeated team (20-0) in 1934-35. His overall coaching record in basketball was 197-68, winning three state championships. He coached baseball 37 years, winning 16 state championships, two Southern Conference titles and tying for another.

H. Lester Hooker, Jr., succeeded Pitt as basketball coach in 1952. He went out and corralled some outstanding talent. With such stars as Ed Harrison, Walt Lysaght, Ken Daniel, Warren Mitchell and Butch Lambiotte, the Spiders under Hooker enjoyed some of their most glorious years on the court. In fact, the Spiders were 20-7 in Hooker's first season, counting South Carolina, West Virginia, Virginia Tech, North Carolina, Virginia, and William & Mary among their victims.

Richmond went on to six consecutive winning seasons, recording the largest number of victories (23) in its history in Hooker's second season. Harrison still holds the Spider record with most career points (1,843), and Daniel the school record for rebounds for season (421) and career (1,255).

In 1972-73, Aron Stewart was the first Richmond basketball player to gain national acclaim, finishing fourth among the NCAA scoring leaders with a 30.2 average. In 1973-74, he also was the nation's fourth leading scorer with a 26.5 average. Then in 1974-75, Bob McCurdy won the NCAA scoring championship, averaging 32.9 points a game.

Both Stewart and McCurdy were selected to the Helms Foundation first team All-America.

Coach Frank Jones led the Spiders to two Tangerine Bowl games, 1968 and 1971.

Dick Humbert is considered one of the greatest ends in Richmond football history. He had six outstanding seasons with the Philadelphia Eagles in the NFL.

Triple-threat Art Jones, an all-time Spider great, No. 1 draft choice of the Pittsburgh Steelers, NFL interception leader in 1941. First player to wear low-top football shoes in NFL. Picked to play with Pro All-Stars against world champion Chicago Bears in 1941.

The 1940 Richmond football team which upset the University of North Carolina.

The 1905 University of Richmond football team. Captained by H. A. Mench, the Spiders finished with a 3-4-2 record that season.

All-Southern Spider center Don Christman, winner of the Jacobs Blocking Trophy in 1961.

Hal McVay, captain of the 1940 Spiders who upset North Carolina.

Ed Merrick, Richmond's All-Southern center in 1939, and Dick Humbert, the Spiders' great end in 1940 who was NFL Rookie of the Year with the Philadelphia Eagles in 1941. Merrick coached the Spider football team from 1951 to 1965, and was voted Southern Conference Coach of the Year in 1958.

Les Hooker coached the Spiders to some of their greatest basketball successes and later became athletic director at William and Mary.

Richmond halfback Earl Stoudt, the Southern Conference Player of the Year in 1961.

Buster O'Brien passed Richmond to a spectacular 49-42 victory over Ohio University in the 1968 Tangerine Bowl.

The Spiders' Petey Jacobs scores on a layup in 1935 basketball game played in Richmond's old Millhiser Gym.

Ray Easterling, Richmond's All-Southern defensive back in 1970, was drafted by the Atlanta Falcons.

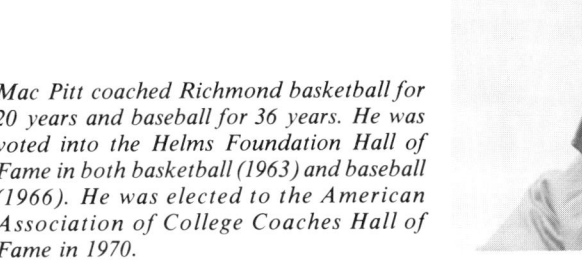

Mac Pitt coached Richmond basketball for 20 years and baseball for 36 years. He was voted into the Helms Foundation Hall of Fame in both basketball (1963) and baseball (1966). He was elected to the American Association of College Coaches Hall of Fame in 1970.

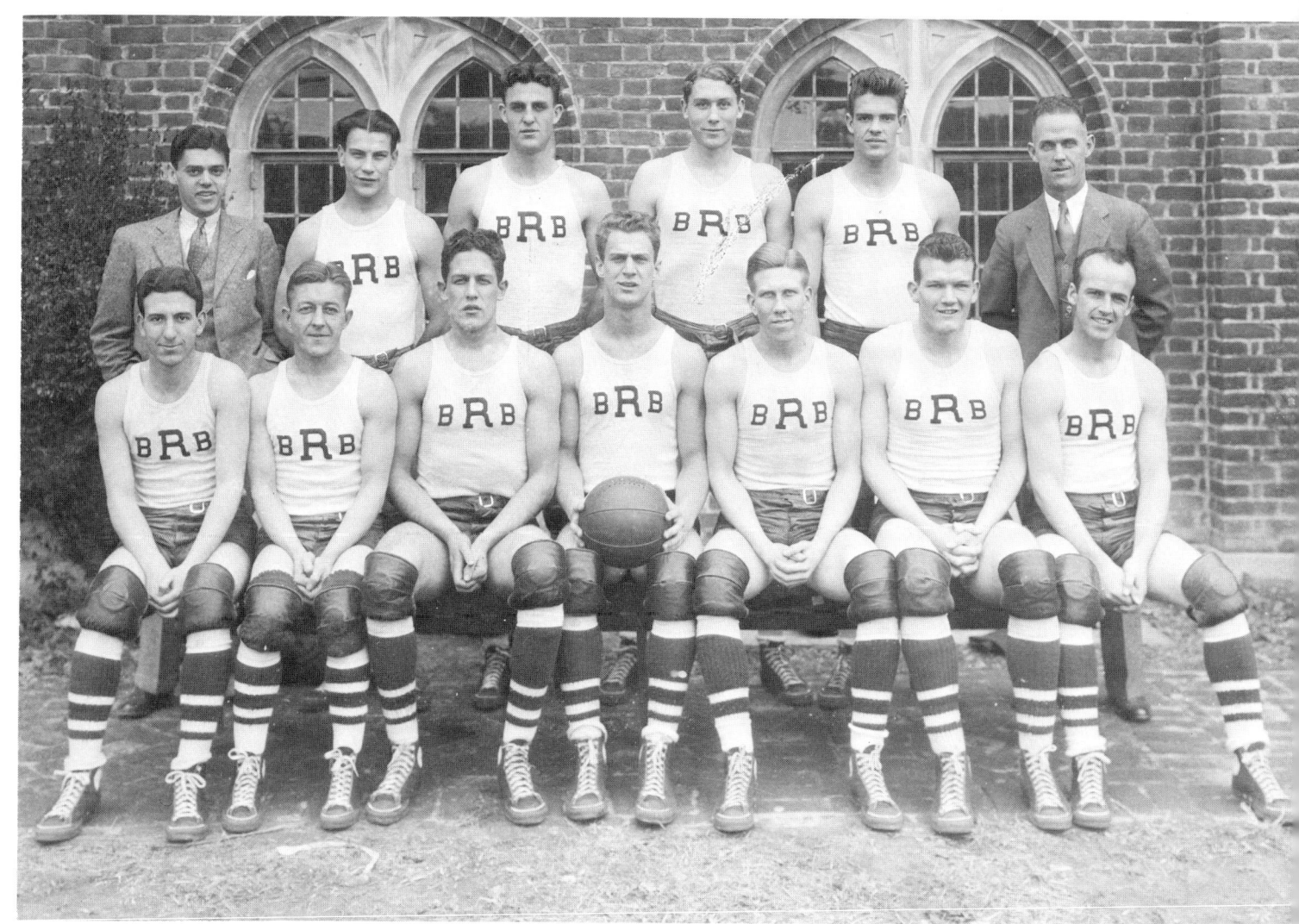

The Spiders of 1934-35, the only unbeaten basketball team in Richmond history. Captained by Roger Leverton, the Spiders won all 20 games that season to win the state championship. Coach Mac Pitt is on the right, back row.

Warren Mills, the Spiders' All-Southern in 1954 and 1955, was also Richmond team captain both seasons.

Aron Stewart scores two for the Spiders. He had a total of 41 in a double over-time, 94-93, victory over Virginia Tech in 1974. Aron was elected to the Helms Foundation All-America team in both 1973 and 1974.

Bob McCurdy, the NCAA scoring champion in 1974-75, averaging 32.9 points a game.

Ed Harrison (1953-56), Richmond's all-time leading basketball scorer with a career total of 1,843 points.

HAMPTON INSTITUTE
A great coach named Gideon Smith

Gideon Smith wasn't much of an athlete when he attended Hampton Institute in 1905. Hampton Institute was then a prep school, Gideon was a scrub on the football team but played the clarinet on the band's first team. After leaving Hampton Institute, Gideon found out he could play a mean game of tackle as well as the clarinet at Ferris Institute in Michigan. He became quite a star. Next stop was Michigan State, where he was the heart of the Spartan defense from 1913-15.

He was the first black to play a varsity sport at Michigan State and was on the first Spartan team to beat the University of Michigan. His play was so outstanding that Michigan Governor Woodbridge Ferris once wrote him a letter congratulating him on his performance.

After coaching at West Virginia State College, Virginia State College and Maryland State College, Gideon Smith returned to Hampton Institute in 1921.

There he became a legend.

Smith coached football and track at Hampton Institute for 34 years. When he retired in 1955, his Pirates had won a total of five Central Intercollegiate Athletic Association football championships and nine CIAA track titles. His teams won numerous awards in the Penn Relays.

Smith produced the first black athletes from a predominately black college to win events in the Penn Relays and National Collegiate Athletic Association (NCAA) meets.

Hampton Institute, established in 1868 as a school for freed slaves, can point to a rich heritage. Coach Gideon Smith and the athletes he produced have been a prominent part of it.

Tom Casey, one of Hampton Institute's all-time greats, is pictured with 1943 track team (second man from right, front row). Casey played football, basketball and track for the Pirates. He played professional football with the New York Yankees in the All-American Football Conference in 1948. The first time he ever touched the ball as a pro with the Yankees he returned a kickoff 97 yards for a touchdown.

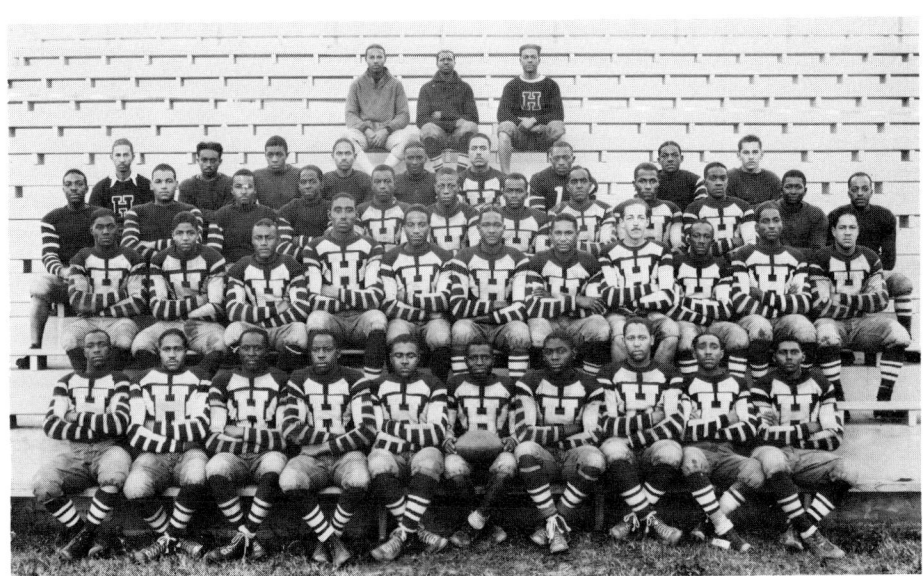

The 1932 Hampton Institute football team. Many consider the 1931 Pirates as Coach Gideon Smith's greatest, and this team is composed of practically the same players. Coach Smith is the middle man on the top row.

The Pirates' CLAA championship track team of 1935, one of Coach Gideon Smith's finest. Front (from left): Byrd, Jeffries, Hill, Paige, Captain L. Lipscombe, Penn, Kerry, Howell, Tucker. Back: Scott, trainer; Cooper, Dunmore, Smith, Grier, Sharp, Beverly, Hooker, Antoine, Paige, Chas, Sylvius Moore (present athletic director) and Coach Smith.

NORFOLK STATE COLLEGE
All it takes is speed

Bob Smith coached Norfolk State basketball four years and his Spartans were the nation's highest scoring college division team in 1969-70 with an average of 107.6 points in 26 games. His teams won two CIAA championships and were runners-up in NAIA District 29 playoff in 1973.

Coach Charles Christian kept the Spartans at top in CIAA basketball.

Although their campus athletic facilities rate about last among colleges in Virginia, the Norfolk State Spartans somehow come in first. For instance, the Spartans don't even have an adequate track of their own, practicing on the pavement or using the track at a nearby high school.

Despite these drawbacks, the Spartan runners have enjoyed spectacular success. When he was coaching track, Dick Price built Norfolk State into a power of national stature. They won six consecutive Central Intercollegiate Athletic Conference championships (1971-76). In 1972, the Spartans were runners-up in the NCAA College Division championships, won it all in 1973 and were co-champions in 1974.

Their lightning-fast 440 team, composed of Condie Pugh, Steve Riddick, Zack Rogers and William Cuffee, won 14 consecutive relay races, setting a record of 39.4 in winning the NCAA title in 1972. It was the fastest time in the nation, including the major college division.

Riddick reigned as king of the dashmen in the CIAA, tearing off the 100-yard dash in 9.3 and the 220 in 20.4. In 1972, he was the second fastest in the country. Running independently for Philadelphia Pioneers, Riddick won a berth on the 1976 U. S. Olympic team.

The Spartans have ruled the CIAA in basketball, too, under such outstanding coaches as Ernie Fears (a 152-32 record in nine years), Bob Smith (86-26 in four years) and Charles O. Christian has carried on the winning tradition. The Spartans have won seven CIAA basketball tournament championships, including three straight (1974-75-76), under Christian, the first ever to win three straight. The Spartans were the highest scoring team in the NCAA college division in 1968-69 (106.1

Richard (Pop) Pitts

Bob Dandridge

average) and in 1969-70 (107.6 points average).

The greatest NSC basketball players? That would be hard to say. The Spartans have had some great ones, but if you go by statistics, the top three would have to be Richard (Pop) Pitts, Bob Dandridge and Eugene Cunningham, all members of the 2,000-point club. In pro basketball, Dandridge has reached the top with the Milwaukee Bucks of the NBA and Cunningham was drafted by Golden State in 1976.

Now the Spartans are beginning to jell in football because Dick Price apparently has the magic touch. When an emergency arose in the football office, Price was summoned to replace Bob Ledbetter, who left to assist the New Orleans Saints. He carried over his track success to football and under his guidance, the Spartans captured the CIAA championships his first two seasons (1974-75).

Pro scouts keep an eye on the Spartans, and there is rarely a practice in which several NFL talent scouts aren't watching. In 1976, four former Norfolk State players were in the NFL—Ray Jarvis (Detroit Lions), Ron Bolton (Cleveland Browns), Leroy Jones (Los Angeles Rams) and Kenny Reaves (St. Louis Cardinals). You see, any time a team has the ambition to schedule Grambling College, a national power, the word gets around.

No story of Norfolk State would be complete without the mention of Joe Echols. The former Virginia State football star came to Norfolk State in 1955. He served as assistant basketball coach and athletic director. He introduced track, baseball, tennis, golf, swimming and riflery to the Spartans' intercollegiate program. Echols is now a professor and head of the physical education department.

Eugene Cunningham.

Ernie Fears is the coach who built Norfolk State basketball into a CIAA power. In seven years, his Spartans compiled a 108-18 record, winning the CIAA titles in 1964-65 and 1967-68 (in triple overtime, 134-132), competing in the NCAA and NAIA tournaments four seasons. In 1966, Fears' team finished fourth in the NAIA National tournament.

The Norfolk State 440 relay team, which in 1972 won the NCAA (college division) championship. Their 39.4 time was the fastest in the nation. Front to back: Condie Pugh, Steve Riddick, Zack Rogers and William Cuffee.

Coach Dick Price, builder of Norfolk State's NCAA champions in both track and football.

Steve Riddick (1971-74) was the fastest Spartan ever, running the 100 in 9.3 and 220 in 20.4. He was ranked No. 2 in the nation.

ROANOKE COLLEGE
33 years after the "Five Smart Boys," a national championship

Back in the late 1930s, Roanoke College got smart and produced a basketball team which ruled the Virginia courts for three years and gained national prominence. Roanoke College had an intercollegiate football team since 1905, but it took a basketball team called the "Five Smart Boys" to put the Salem school on the map. And the "Smarts" were the high spot of Roanoke athletic history until Charles Moir's "Magnificent Maroons" walked off with the NCAA College Division championship in 1972.

But the "Five Smart Boys" remain a legend in Roanoke College history. The team, coached by Gordon C. (Pop) White, was composed of Bob Leib, Paul Rice, Gene Studebacher, Bob Sheffield and Johnny Wagner.

And that was about it, although it was enough. These five young athletes played together for all four years in college, and in three years they were never beaten by a Virginia team, staking an undisputed claim to the state championship in 1937-38 and again in 1938-39.

In 1938, the "Five Smart Boys" were runners-up in the National Intercollegiate Basketball Tournament at Kansas City, Missouri. Lieb was named all-tournament guard, with Wagner, Sheffield and Rice winning honorable mention.

The Maroons were invited to play in the prestigious Metropolitan Writers Invitational Tournament in New York's famed Madison Square Garden in 1939. The "Five Smart Boys" lost to powerful St. John's of Brooklyn, New York, and by two points to New Mexico A&M.

In three years, the "Five Smart Boys" won 53 games and lost 11, scoring 2,792 points to 2,072 for their opponents. The team made a big hit and had supporters from Kansas City to the Carolinas to New York and Virginia. Roanoke College students became so involved with their famous team that one year they forgot the student body elections.

"This team had a certain personality and color that isn't coached," Pop White said after the "Smarts" graduated. "We did have our problems. The small squad precluded using the fast break on offense and the full-court press on defense. Too, we had to hold the score down and yet make a good game of it when playing the weaker teams."

Under Coach Buddy Hackman, the Maroons captured the state basketball championship in 1948, winning 16 of 17 games with a powerful defense that was No. 1 among the small colleges and second only to Oklahoma A&M in the major colleges. Jim Doran, Jim Redmond, Jim Ruscick, Ed Harless and Karl Kummer led the Maroons to 16 victories in 17 games.

Charlie Moir came on the scene as head coach in 1948 and the Maroons, led by Frankie Allen, who broke nearly all Roanoke College scoring records, lost in the NCAA regionals two straight years. Then, in 1972, the Maroons hit the jackpot. Sparked by Hal Johnston and Jay Piccola, Roanoke College won it all at Evansville, Indiana, defeating Missouri-St. Louis, 94-69; Eastern Michigan, 99-73, and Akron, 84-72, en route to the national championship.

Moir was voted College Division Coach of the Year, sharing honors with the University Division's UCLA's Johnny Wooden. Johnston was named first team small college All-American, and Piccola the second team. A year later, Piccola was first-team All-American.

Roanoke College dropped intercollegiate football after the 1942

Little All-America Jay Piccola (40) gets off a jump shot.

season. The Maroons compiled their best football record under Coach Pop White in 1936 when they won six, lost two and tied one. Losing to Virginia Tech, 16-7, the Maroons tied Richmond, 0-0, and beat William and Mary, 13-0. In soccer and lacrosse, the Roanoke College teams have been nationally ranked in recent years.

As for the No. 1 oddity in Roanoke College sports, back in 1915 Earle H. Tiffany pitched both games of a baseball doubleheader—and won both, pitching righthanded in the first game and lefthanded in the second game. His feat won a spot in Ripley's "Believe It or Not."

With net around his neck, Hal Johnston after Roanoke won 1972 NCAA national basketball championship.

Roanoke's "Five Smart Boys," who were practically unbeatable, winning 40 of 45 games over a two-year period, 1938-39 and played in two national tournaments under Coach Pop White. They are (l. to r.) Bob Leib, Paul Rice, Gene Studebacher, Bob Sheffield and Johnny Wagner.

Frankie Allen in a familiar drive to the basket. He broke a multitude of Roanoke records as a freshman, leading the Maroons to a 22-8 record and the NCAA regional tournament.

Charlie Moir, NCAA College Coach of the Year, 1971-72, with stars of national championship basketball team, Hal Johnston and Jay Piccola.

VIRGINIA STATE COLLEGE
A Thanksgiving to remember

On Thanksgiving Day, 1938, Morgan College invaded Virginia State boasting the longest unbeaten streak in college football history. Morgan hadn't lost in 54 consecutive games.

Coached by Harry (Big Jeff) Jefferson, the Trojans were rolling through an undefeated season and needed an upset over Morgan to wrap up the CIAA championship.

Two weeks before the Trojans had a narrow escape at Shaw. Late in the final quarter Shaw led Virginia State, 15-13, in what was developing into a stunning upset. The Trojans were back on their 13 yard-line and their situation appeared hopeless.

"We were running the single wing," halfback Joe Echols recalled, "and Coach Jefferson had us shift both left and right. Normally, in the single wing you shifted to the right. Anyway, there we were deep in our own territory and a long ways to go in a short time.

"Henry (Red) Briscoe went to our quarterback, Dick Burr, and told him to let me run the ball every time, and that he would do the blocking. Well, I ran the ball eight straight times and reached the Shaw one-yard line before they finally stopped us. But the drive put them in deep water and we blocked a punt for a 19-15 victory. I'll never forget that game."

Nor will Echols and the other Trojans ever forget the Thanksgiving Day battle with Morgan. Echols scored a touchdown on a 15-yard run and Briscoe ran over for another touchdown as the Trojans handed Morgan its first defeat in six years, 15-0. It gave Coach Jefferson his third CIAA football title in four years.

"Briscoe was one of the finest football players I've ever seen," says Echols, now a full professor and head of the physical education department at Norfolk State, and a former NFL scout. "He was a great all-around athlete."

Echols gave up his senior year of eligibility at Virginia State to play professional baseball with the Newark Eagles.

"We had no scholarships then," Echols said. "The athletes had to work their way through school. I know I did. And you were lucky to get a job."

Coach Jefferson arrived at Virginia State in 1934 after coaching Bluefield to the Negro national football championship. The Jefferson era was one of the Trojans' most successful. In 16 years as head football coach, Big Jeff's teams compiled a 75-35-15 record and won four CIAA titles.

After Big Jeff retired, Sylvester Hall took over the football job and, in 1955, the Trojans went 8-1-0 and won both the CIAA and national small-college championships. Hall's four-year record was 21-12-1.

William Lawson coached football at Virginia State for 16 years and compiled a 68-60-9 record. Then, in 1970, came the highly-successful Walt Lovett years and the Trojans won the CIAA championship in each of the three seasons Lovett coached. In addition, they also won the Virginia College Athletic Association title in 1972.

William (Pete) Bennett and John D. Marshall followed Lovett as head coach. High spot of Bennett's reign was 21-0 shellacking of Delaware State and their first Ujima Classic crown in a 5-5 season. Coach Marshall guided the Trojans to their second Ujima Classic title with a 10-9 squeaker over Morgan State. The Trojans have been trying to regain the successes of the Lovett era.

In the early 1900s, basketball was started at Virginia State when a group of

The Virginia State College football team, which won the CIAA championship in 1938, capped an undefeated season on Thanksgiving Day by snapping Morgan State's remarkable 55-game unbeaten streak, 15-0.

Front row (from left) Pankey, Robinson, Lamb, Terrell, Rose, Captain Briscoe, Ballard, Nelson, Downing, Holmes, Cook. Cook.

Second row: Land, Hall, Bennett, Brown, James Brewer, Burr, Woods, Bartee, Coleman Lewis, Joe Echols, John Brewer.

Third row: Dr. James A. Moore, athletic director; McCain, Jefferson, Bond, Cobb, Donald Harris, Travis, Taylor, Jackson, Granston.

Fourth row: Assistant Coach Verdell, James Harris, Hurst, Chandler, Kersey, Harris, Patterson, Glasker, Thompson.

Fifth row: Manager Hardy, Younge, Coleman, Rowe, Bailey, Taylor, Denny, Reid, Mitchell.

Back row: Head Coach Harry R. Jefferson, Lynch, Slade, Tull and McCain, managers.

students placed a basket supported by old metal posts in the first floor hallway of the original Virginia Hall. Tom Harvey coached pick-up teams in 1923, and during the 1925-26 seasons the Trojans had to play all their games away from home because they had no gymnasium. Many of the players were picked from the football team.

Moose Slaughter, Lawrence Cropp and Dave Brown were among the early VSC basketball standouts. VSC students and faculty, determined to have a gym, built practically by hand the old Daniel Gymnasium in 1928. Trojan basketball then started to make progress under coaches James D. Barnes and Harold Martin and such stars as Dick Bell (1928-32), Cabell (Bumble) Scott and Percy Van Pelt helped built a 52-15 record.

Jefferson was successful as a basketball coach, too, using two and three-sport stars like Red Briscoe, Doc Hurley and Ben Whaley. Then came basketball specialists Percy Smith, Elmore Rainey, Charles (Dome) Christian and Leroy (Lanky) Banks. The Trojans won the CIAA title in 1938.

In 1949, Coach Shelton M. Matthews, a fundamentalist, took over the basketball reins and under his regime, the Trojans enjoyed 11 winning seasons in 14 years. Matthews, named Outstanding Coach in the 1955-57 CIAA Basketball Tournament, was fatally injured in an automobile accident in 1963. But he left behind a legacy that VSC and the CIAA will always remember, giving leadership to stars like Leroy Banks, John Williams, Lewis Brown, Leonard George, Ronald Crosby, Gene Jud Hudgins, Johnnie Johnson, Percy Oliver, Clyde Bonds, Samuel Simmons, Harold Deane, William Lawson, Ernest Brock and Franck Stephens.

Joe Echols (right) with the late Vince Lombardi. Echols was a close friend of Lombardi's and served as his scout for the Washington Redskins. The photo was taken at the Redskins' training camp in 1969.

John Borican (1935-38) was perhaps Virginia State's greatest athlete. Outstanding in football and basketball, he gave up these sports to concentrate on track. While competing for the Trojans, Borican never failed to place in any event, and won most, in the CIAA.

It was after he graduated from Virginia State that John Borican ran his way to national and international fame as one of America's greatest track stars.

Winning the senior AAU Pentathlon championship at Lincoln Field, Jersey City, New Jersey, in 1938 was only the beginning for this dedicated athlete. At the same time he was National Junior AAU 800-meter champion.

Borican won the AAU 1,000-yard run four straight years (1939-42), breaking the existing record each time. He repeated as National Pentathlon champion in 1941, giving him the unusual distinction of holding the Decathlon and Pentathlon titles the same year.

One of Borican's greatest achievements came in the 1939 Knights of Columbus 1,000-yard run when he defeated Kansan Glenn Cunningham, America's great distance champion. His time of 2:08.8 shattered all records for the event, indoors or outdoors.

Also in 1939, the Virginia State grad set a record of 1:49.8 for the half-mile on the Dartmouth track. And in the Knights of Columbus meet in Madison Square Garden in 1941 and 1942, he won the 600 and 1,000-yard races within a hour.

John Borican was a super star.
No doubt about it.

John Borican, a Virginia State star, is on the way to victory over Olympic miler Glenn Cunningham in the Knights of Columbus 1,000-yard run in 1939.

VIRGINIA COMMONWEALTH UNIVERSITY
The Rams' answer is Noe

No longer that "small school in Richmond" when it was known as RPI in athletics, Virginia Commonwealth University has gone bigtime and making no bones about it. They're shooting for the moon. Under the influence of Coach Chuck Noe, the Golden Rams are recent additions to the NCAA Division 1 ranks, and their basketball schedule, loaded with major schools, is a tough as any played in the state.

Virginia Commonwealth came about in 1968 after a merger of the Medical College of Virginia and Richmond Professional Institute, two state-aided institutions located in the capitol city. In 1970, Noe arrived on the scene and set out to improve VCU's status in the college basketball world. Noe wasn't exactly a newcomer to the game. He had already built a fine reputation coaching at VMI, Virginia Tech and the University of South Carolina. At Virginia Tech his teams compiled a 109-51 record, and were undefeated on their home court during Noe's final four years as coach. At South Carolina, his Gamecocks received national recognition.

Noe is credited with originating the "mongoose" defense-offense. He developed these systems as a desperate means of survival when he was coaching South Carolina because his personnel wasn't as good as the opponents. Noe was very successful with it, as his record shows. His theories have been developed by many basketball coaches, and all it is, is a simple spread, amounting to a one-on-one game.

Whatever the reason, the Golden Rams have enjoyed five winning seasons under Noe, going into the 1976-77 season; and perhaps the best team was the 1973-74 edition, which produced a 17-7 record and three players (Jesse Dark, Bernard Harris and Richard Jones) who were drafted by the pros. The three are members of the Rams exclusive "Thousand Point Club."

"We want to be as good as anyone in the country," Noe says of future VCU basketball plans.

Chuck Noe, Virginia Commonwealth athletic director and head basketball coach.

Richard Jones   *Jesse Dark*   *Bernard Harris*

They led the Golden Rams to 17-7 record in 1973-74, and they're in VCU's Thousand Point Club.

EMORY & HENRY COLLEGE
The Wasps were stinging

They called Bob Miller the "Emory Express," the Wasps' first Little All-American. He won first-team honors both in 1950 and 1951. As a freshman in 1948, Miller scored nine touchdowns. And he was only a substitute. From then on, it was full steam ahead for the "Emory Express."

He was a major factor in the Wasps unbeaten campaign of 1949. The Wasps won ten straight, averaging 28.4 points a game. Then the Wasps rolled over Hanover College, 32-0, in the Burley Bowl, with Miller scoring twice.

Miller gained recognition not only in Virginia, but the East and the nation. With Miller the key, Emory & Henry lost only one game in 1950 and 1951. He was among the top four scorers in the nation his last two years. When he graduated, his famed No. 33 jersey was retired.

Bill Earp won All-America first team honors in 1956 as the Wasps' offensive center.

Then, in 1966, Sonny Wade, a 6-3, 205-pound quarterback, from Martinsville, launched a brilliant career with the E&H varsity. In 1971, he was the leading scorer among the nation's colleges and universities with 141 points. In 1968, Wade led the Wasps to nine victories in ten games and the District VI NAIA championship.

He finished his college career as second in total offense (285.8 yards per game) in the NAIA and second leading passer in NAIA (268 yards per game). He broke all E&H total offense records.

Selected to play in the North-South Shrine game at Miami, Florida, Wade was the tenth round draft choice of the Philadelphia Eagles (NFL). But he decided to play in the Canadian Football League. In 1970, he was selected as the CFL Player of the Year, and the MVP in the 1970 and 1971 Grey Cup (the Canadian championship) games.

In the early years of Emory & Henry football, the team had no nickname. Around 1920 someone dubbed them "The Jackrabbits" and later the "Wasps," and this moniker was the one that stuck.

The Board of Trustees discontinued football at E&H in 1895, and the sport was not reinstated until 1915, when they put the game on a trial basis under faculty supervision. Coach Thomas B. (Bingo) Fullerton was the man in charge, arriving at E&H in 1914. He remained coach of all sports at E&H until 1928. Fullerton Field on the E&H campus was named in his honor.

It was in the Roaring Twenties that the Wasps rolled up the greatest winning streak in Virginia college football. From 1926-29, Emory and Henry won 23 games in succession.

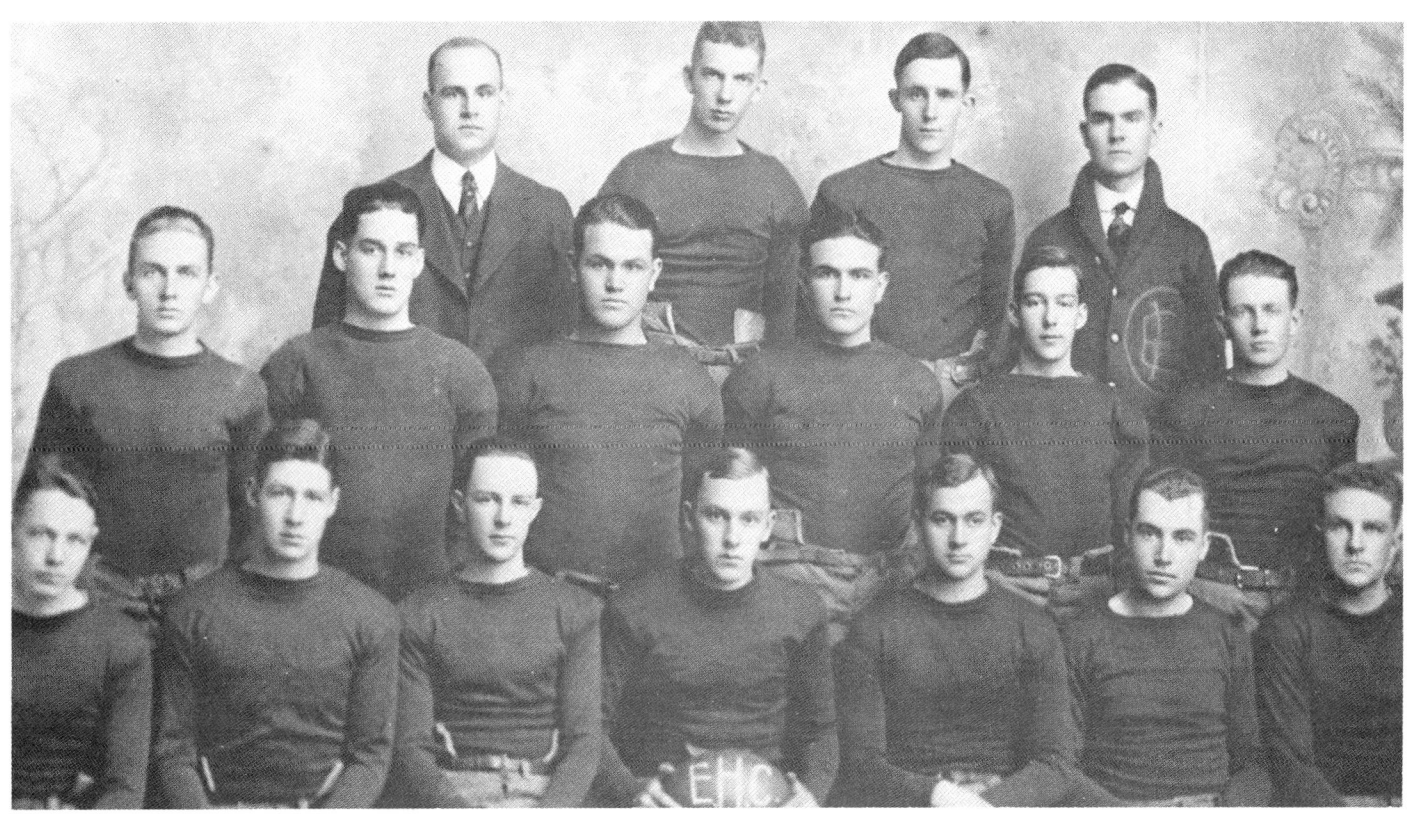

Although football at Emory & Henry was given some attention in the late 1880s, the 1915 team (pictured above) is regarded as the Wasps' first official representation on the gridiron.

FERRUM COLLEGE
The power and the glory

On a national scale, Ferrum College has won more national titles than any school in the Commonwealth.

From 1964 to 1974, this magnificent school surrounded by the Appalachian Mountains won 82 football games, lost nine and tied three, claiming the best ten-year record in the country. Over that period, Ferrum produced three national junior college football champions, a national runner-up and eight regional titles.

Over the same period in basketball, Ferrum won eight conference championships, six regional titles and were national tourney runner-up in 1972. The Panthers won 243 and lost only 49 games through this period.

Ferrum's move to prominence began in 1960 when the football team was unbeaten and ranked eighth in the nation. The Panthers reached the top in 1965, winning the first national football title ever by a Virginia college, scoring 260 points en route to ten victories and a resounding 16-0 upset over McCook College of Nebraska in the Shrine Bowl for the national championship at Savannah, Georgia.

In 1966, Ferrum again went unbeaten but lost to Kilgore of Texas, 28-7, in the national championship game. Ferrum limited Kilgore to 60 yards rushing but Kilgore went to the air in the final six minutes to break a 7-7 tie.

The 1967 Panthers averaged 42 points a game but were upset by Lees-McRae College of North Carolina in the finale. But the next season Ferrum rolled through another unbeaten campaign and topped Phoenix College of Arizona, 41-19, for the national title.

Ferrum was also undefeated in 1971 and ranked in the top ten. After an 8-2 season in 1972 and 9-1 in 1973 and being ranked in the top ten both seasons, the Panthers went unbeaten in 1974 and were awarded their third national crown via a new ranking system.

Among the outstanding players over that period were Cleo Johnson, Rock Perdoni and Lou Santospago (Georgia Tech), Ray Harris, Jim Huff, Bob Newman (Miami), Willard Arthur, Tommy England, Bob Haggerty, Dennis Wiley and Charlie Tysinger (Richmond), Wayne Stinnette and Randy Vey (Virginia Tech), Jim Hambacher (North Carolina), Ed George, John Mazalewski and Jim Schubert (Wake Forest), Ted Powell (Ohio State), Alex Hill (Virginia Tech), Dexter Pride (Minnesota), Jim Culbreath (Oklahoma), Frank Fontes and Jim Malkiewicz (Florida State), Russ Bauda and Jim Grobe (Virginia), Wade Hughes and Charlie Matthews (Clemson), Billy Evans (Maryland) Don Shannon (Duke), Cary Stockdell (U. of Arkansas), Phil Mosser, Phil Elmassian and Randy Troupe (William and Mary), Billy Joe Mantooth (West Virginia), Frank Haywood, George Gantt, and Johnny Huff (North Carolina State).

Rock Perdoni, the Yellow Jacket captain, was a consensus All-American at Georgia Tech and a finalist in the Lombardi Award as the outstanding lineman in the nation. Rock also won the Swede Nielson Sportsmanship Award.

Coach W. H. (Hank) Norton was named National Junior College Coach of the Year in 1965, 1968, and again in 1974. Norton has had six unbeaten teams at Ferrum since coming to the school in 1960.

In the professional ranks Bruce Gossett (Ferrum '62) is in the all-time top ten scorers in the NFL, with the Los Angeles Rams and San Francisco 49ers. Don Thompson (Ferrum '59) spent five years in the NFL, including stints with the Baltimore Colts, Philadelphia Eagles and St. Louis Cardinals; Billy Joe Mantooth (Ferrum '70) Philadelphia Eagles; Larry Robinson (Ferrum '70), Dallas Cowboys; Ed George (Ferrum '68), Montreal Alouettes four years, Baltimore Colts in 1975; Rock Perdoni (Ferrum '69), Hamilton Tiger Cats, Saskatchewan Rough Riders, in the Canadian Football League.

The Ferrum tennis story is as amazing as the school's success in football. From 1964-1974, the Panther netmen won nine conference titles, going unbeaten nine times. In one stretch, the tennis team won 99 of 100 matches. Coach Bud Steens was named conference Coach of the Year six times, and region Coach of the Year twice. His overall coaching record after the 1976 season: 203 wins, only seven losses. Fifteen of his 18 teams have gone undefeated in team play during his coaching career, which included hitches at Roanoke, Radford and University of Virginia before coming to Ferrum.

Among the top tennis stars produced by Coach Steens at Ferrum were Tom Bryant (U. of Mississippi), Brian Clark (Virginia Tech), Steve Gallagher (Oral Roberts U.) and Murrie Bates (Westchester State).

In track, Ferrum has turned out such performers as Bill Holloway, who became a top-ranked sprinter at East Tennessee; Ed George, outstanding in the weights, and Dennis Castello, who holds all distance records at this school.

The 1965 N.J.C.A.A. football champions. First row (l. to r.): Coach Norton, Ray Harris, Lou Santospago, Brad King, Ray Austin, Jerry Little, John Anderson, Jim McCarty, Alex Carter, Wade Crutchfield, Dennis Wiley. Second row (l. to r.): Coach Webb, Sam Baity, Pete Batte, Bob Haggerty, Frank Sorrells, Willard Arthur, Wayne Koch, Bob Newman, Temple Kessinger, E.B. Snow, Don Brown. Third row (l to r): Coach Tolley, Joel DeBoe, Bill Clear, Jim Casertano, Andy Austin, Bob Profitko, Frank Whaley, Joe Coppolla, Joe Crabtree, John Burkes. Fourth row (l. to r.): Jim Golladay, Tom England, Randy Powell, Tom Gibbs, Jim Bland, Bill Bryant, Jud Mason, Randy Cline.

Renso (Rock) Perdoni, a consensus All-American in 1970 as a defensive tackle at Georgia Tech, is a Ferrum product.

Coach Hank Norton, the man who built Ferrum's national football champions.

Ed George, who played defensive tackle at Ferrum in 1968, and made his mark in pro football. He was named to the All-Canadian Football League team playing with the Montreal Alouettes.

Bud Skeens (center), Ferrum's highly-successful tennis coach, shown with his 1973 co-captains, Steve Gallagher (left) and Brian Clark. Both all-regional and all-conference selections, Gallagher and Clark were undefeated in their two years at Ferrum.

Larry Robinson, a Ferrum All-America who became the University of Tennessee's first black basketball captain. Also played football with the Dallas Cowboys (1973).

Phil Mosser, leading rusher and voted Southern Conference's outstanding athlete in 1970 at William and Mary, was a star with Ferrum.

MADISON COLLEGE
The Dukes grow up fast

Madison College used to be where the girls were. Now it's where the boys are, too.

The rise of the Dukes in intercollegiate athletics has been phenomenal, especially when you consider the fact that the college really didn't go co-educational until 1966. That's the year the General Assembly authorized Madison to construct male dormitories. At the time there were only 222 male students in a student body of 2,510.

According to Madison historians, the first male athletic team was the basketball team of 1947, when male day students approached then-President Samuel Page Duke about forming a team. The president obliged and the team was named in his honor—The Dukes, playing junior varsity teams and male teams from other predominantly-female schools.

To give you an idea of what has happened since, in the fall of 1975 Madison had a total enrollment of 7,343, including 3,106 male students.

The growth of Madison's athletic program has been as astounding as the growth of its student body. Only a few years ago, the Dukes (the name stuck) were playing a junior varsity basketball schedule in a high school gym.

With athletic facilities ranking among the best, Madison now competes in 24 intercollegiate sports, 12 for men and an equal number for women.

While the Dukes are considered upstarts in collegiate competition, they are certainly no patsies. That's for sure. Coached by Lou Campanelli, the Dukes have made remarkable headway in basketball in a few years, having appeared in the NCAA Division II post-season tournament in 1974 and 1976, and winning the Virginia College Athletic Association championship in 1974-75.

Among the Dukes' 18 conquests in 1975-76 were VMI, which went to the final eight in the NCAA Division I National Tournament; East Tennessee State and Baltimore University.

What's more, Madison applied for NCAA Division I status, beginning with the 1976-77 session, in all sports but football. The football team will play in Division III for the time being.

The Dukes have been most surprising in football, too. To give you an idea of the progress made on the Madison gridiron, the Dukes organized their first football team in 1972. They didn't even score a point playing a junior varsity schedule.

Well, Madison and Coach Challace McMillin had more elaborate plans for the future, and started upgrading the football program with patience and startling success. Still playing junior varsity and prep schools, the Dukes were 4-5 in 1973.

Playing their first season with a full varsity schedule in 1974, the Dukes produced a 6-4 record. If the so-called football experts were surprised by the showing of the Dukes in 1974, they must have been flabbergasted in 1975 when the unbeaten Dukes won nine and tied one and captured the Virginia College Athletic Association championship.

The Dukes nailed down the VCAA title with a 12-7 victory over Randolph-Macon, a school that has been playing intercollegiate football since 1893.

Madison's unbeaten 1975 VCAA Football Champions. These unbeaten Dukes won nine and tied one and compiled a 5-0 record in the Virginia College Athletic Association in just their second full season with a full varsity schedule. Front row (from left) Head Coach Challace McMillin, Phil Culkin, Brian Grainer, Tim Phillips, Terry Daley, Jeff Adams, Leslie Branich, Henry Pike, Brian Young, Craig Hoepfl, Mike Atalla, Brent Good, Winston Bersch, Asst. Coach Jim Prince. Second Row: Asst. Coach Harry Van Arsdale, David Payne, Shane Hast, Rich Jackson, Dale Eaton, Bernard Slayton, Chip Deringer, Ron Stith, Bob Ward, Jon Brentlinger, Chris Pineda, Tom Parisi, Asst.

Coach George Nipe. Third Row: Asst. Coach Ellis Wisler, Joe Carico, Terry Hansrote, John Gatewood, Glenn Knox, Mike Marston, Dave Sensabaugh, Don Sears, Keith Pope, Eric Douglas, Tom Mitchell, Ron Borders, Asst. Coach Mike Clem, Trainer Robbie Lester. Fourth Row: Asst. Coach Brad Babcock, Jim Hardesty, Robbie Nicholson, Chip West, Jon Tuell, Bob Logan, Bob Dunn, Jim McHugh, Woody Bergeria, Mark Baird, Rich Burkhart, Joe Taylor, Manager Bob Snyder. Fifth Row: Manager Buster Blincoe, Fred Garst, Warren Coleman, Staon Jones, Dewey Windham, Ed Huff, Jeff Krauss, Greg Sears, Pat Cavanaugh, Larry Smith, Floyd Young, John Bowers, O. C. Hailey.

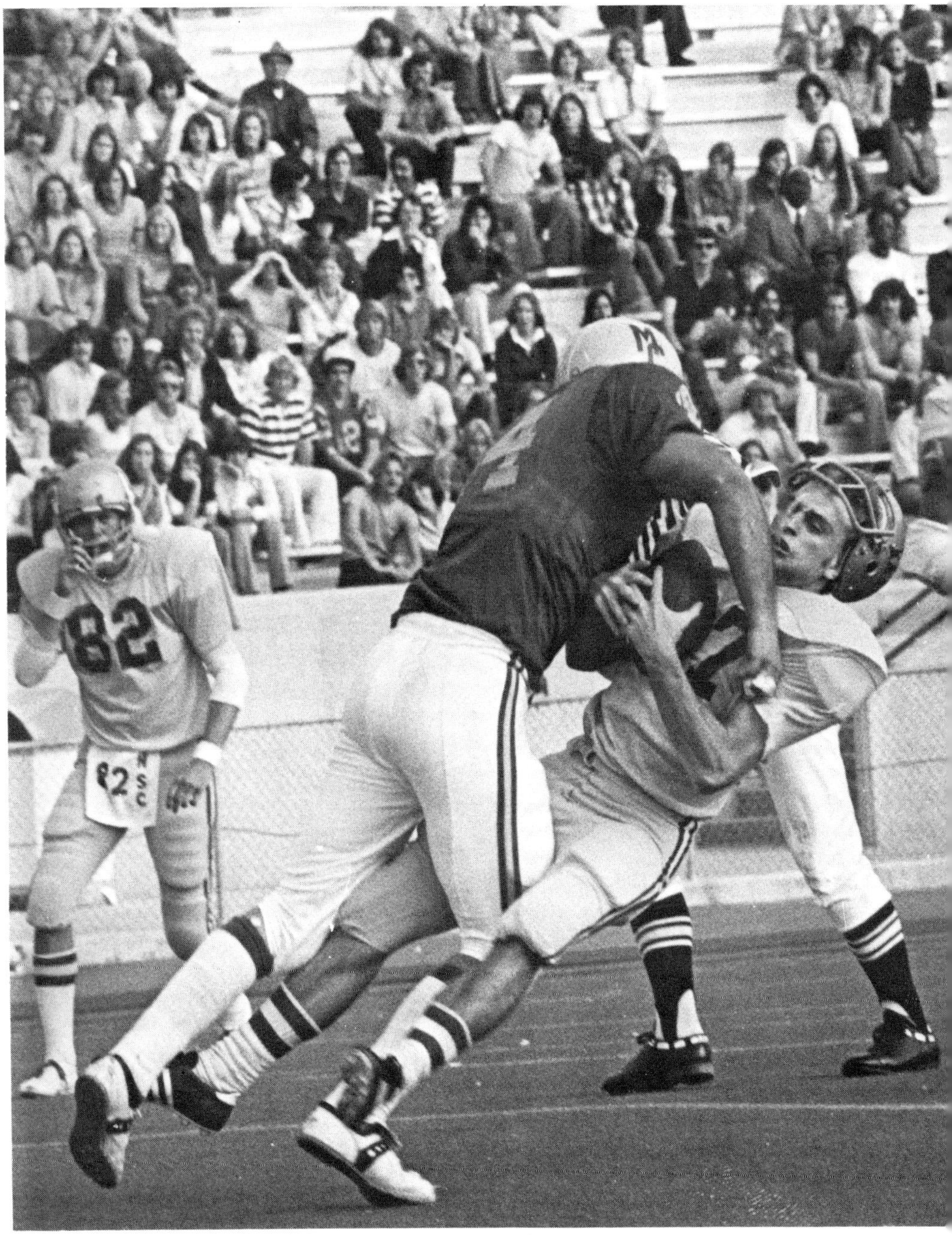

Madison linebacker Dewey Windham (dark uniform) stops a Hampden-Sydney runner during the 1975 season.

Tailback Ron Smith, Madison's leading rusher and scorer in 1975, named Virginia College Division Offensive Player of Year by Richmond Sports Club, first team All-VCAA.

Linebacker Dewey Windham, first team All-VCAA and honorable mention AP College Division All-America.

Woody Bergeria, defensive guard, First All-VCAA, honorable mention AP College Division All-America as a sophomore in 1975.

Challace McMillin, the only head football coach Madison has had, was named VCAA Football Coach of the Year and the Kodak College Division Coach of the Year for District III by the Association of Football Coaches in America in 1975 after his Dukes compiled a 9-0-1 record and won the VCAA championship.

Madison quarterback Leslie Branich (15) leading the Dukes to victory over Randolph-Macon and the 1975 VCAA championship. A four-year starter, Branich was a first team All-VCAA selection in 1974.

Sherman Dillard in action against Washington and Lee (1976).

Madison's Pat Dosh scores against Florida State. Dosh was voted Madison's Most Valuable Player for 1975-76.

Joe Pfahler drives for a basket against Roanoke College. Pfahler made 158 assists during the 1976-76 season, a Madison record.

Under Coach Lou Campanelli's direction, the Dukes captured the VCAA crown in 1974-75, and made two appearances in the NCAA Division II tournament berth in 1974 and 1976. His Dukes were 20-6 in 1974, 19-6 in 1974-75 and 18-8 in 1975-76. His record since coming to Madison in 1972 is 73-31.

Sherman Dillard, Madison's all-time scoring leader with 1,566 points, takes aim for a two-pointer. He was named to the College Division Academic All-America first team. He scored 516 points in 1975-76 to lead the Dukes in scoring for the third year in a row. The Bassett athlete was voted on the National Association of Basketball Coaches' All-America second team, and was an all-tournament selection in the 1976 NCAA Division II South Atlantic tournament.

OLD DOMINION UNIVERSITY
Monarchs crowned

The Monarchs of Old Dominion University have come a long way in basketball, their specialty, since the school was founded during the Great Depression. When it opened its doors in 1930, the school was known as Norfolk Division of William and Mary.

Tommy Scott, a former VMI star, was practically a one-man coaching staff for ten years, directing the football, basketball and track teams.

Bud Metheny, the former New York Yankees' outfielder, coached basketball 17 years, and his last eight teams enjoyed winning records. The teams were called the Braves, more or less a link with the parent William and Mary Indians in Williamsburg.

Metheny's Braves hit their stride in 1960-61, winning 16 of 20 games chiefly because of a sharpshooter named Leo Anthony, a senior who had been scorching the nets for four years. Anthony was the school's first player to gain national recognition, being selected on the third-team small college All-America in 1958-59. He left behind a bundle of records, ending his career as the third highest scorer in the state's history with 2,181, which is still an ODU record. His 31.0 points a game average in 1960-61 and most career free throws (639) also remain ODU records.

In 1961-62, with Anthony graduated, Metheny's team produced its best record yet (17-3), with Bobby Hoffman, Billy Phelps, Ray Dougan, Bill Boyce, Jim Bettis and Marion Carroll giving the Braves a balanced scoring attack.

In the fall of 1962, Norfolk Division gained its independence, changed the name to Old Dominion College, and joined the Mason-Dixon Conference. They competed in their first conference tournament, losing to Hampden-Sydney in the opening round.

The student body was growing. They were the Monarchs now. In 1969, the school became Old Dominion University.

In June of 1965, Sonny Allen was brought in from Marshall University as head coach. The idea was to build a basketball power in the NCAA College Division. Allen did just that with the fastest fast-break in the game.

The Monarchs, led by all-American Dave Twardzik, lost to Evansville in the championship game of the NCAA College Division, forerunner of Division II, in 1971.

Despite the efforts of Joel Copeland, ODU's second full-fledged All-American, the Monarchs bowed to Norfolk State, 89-76, in the finals of the 1974 South Atlantic Regional in the ODU Fieldhouse.

But the following year the Monarchs hit the jackpot at Evansville, defeating North Dakota University, 78-62, Tennessee State, 77-60, and then New Orleans, 76-74, for the national Division II championship. Wilson Washington, a 6-9 sophomore, showed the way with 21 points and 12 rebounds in the final, winning for him tournament most valuable player honors.

It turned out to be Allen's farewell at ODU. He signed to coach Southern Methodist and was replaced by Paul Webb, who enjoyed great success in 19 seasons at Randolph-Macon.

In his first season Webb carried the Monarchs back to Evansville, but they fell to Puget Sound in the semifinals. Still, Washington was voted first team Little All-America.

With 11,000 students, the ambitious Monarchs moved up to Division I status for the 1976-77 season.

Leo Anthony broke all offensive basketball records in 1957-61, when ODU was known as Norfolk Division of W & M. His career scoring (2,181 points), game average (31.0) and most free throws (639) are still ODU records.

Bud Metheney, the ex-Yankee, is dean of the ODU coaching staff. Beginning in 1948, he served as basketball coach, athletic director and baseball coach. In baseball, the NCAA Coach of the Year in 1965, and Region Coach of the Year in 1963-64-65. He is in the William & Mary Hall of Fame.

Coach Sonny Allen....the Monarchs blasted their way to the very top with the "Allen Fast-Break."

Dave Twardzik

We're No. 1! Old Dominion cheerleader Craig Davis perches on the shoulders of Wilson Washington as each flashes No. 1 sign after the Monarchs had captured the NCAA college division championship at Evansville, Indiana, in 1975.

Old Dominion University's 1975 NCAA Division II National Championship Squad. Front row—head manager Carroll Hudson, Jr., Joe Caruthers, assistant coach Ed Hall, head coach Sonny Allen (standing), assistant coach Charlie Woollum, Windell Morrison, and assistant manager Mike Wrigley. Back row (also l-r)—Rich Tackaberry, Joey O'Brien, Leon Hylton, Curtis Cole, Tom Street, Jay Rountree, Wilson Washington, Jeff Fuhrmann, Dave Moyer, Gray Eubank, and team captain Oliver Purnell.

Joel Copeland

Wilson Washington

BRIDGEWATER COLLEGE
Where the Eagles nest

Bridgewater College, located in the heart of the Shenandoah Valley, was the first college in Virginia to play basketball on an intercollegiate basis. Rich in athletic tradition, the Eagles produced a number of outstanding athletes, the foremost being Bob Richards, the Olympic pole vault champion, among its alumni.

On several occasions in the early years, it appeared Bridgewater would have no intercollegiate athletics at all. A baseball team was started in 1898, football the following year. In 1903, Bridgewater's football team won three, tied one and lost one. Then objections came from the church constituency and influenced by those objections, the Trustees discontinued football the following year. In the meantime, basketball was introduced as a varsity sport.

In 1909, the Trustees ordered the discontinuance of all intercollegiate athletics, and it wasn't until 1917, when the students petitioned for the return of athletics, that the Trustees formerly sanctioned an intercollegiate athletic program.

And the Eagles have been flying ever since as bona fide amateurs. Only students in good academic standing can compete. The college does not subsidize athletes, and it hires physical education teachers rather than professional coaches, to coach the teams.

Most successful of the Bridgewater coaches has been Dr. Harry G. M. Jopson, known by one and all as just plain Doc Jopson. Doc didn't have the pleasure of coaching Bob Richards.

Richards became a two-time Olympic Gold Medal winner (see The Olympians section) in the pole vault. In his three years at Bridgewater, he also made his mark in basketball and, in a game against Lynchburg, scored 61 points in a 93-33 victory.

Coming to Bridgewater College in 1936, Doc Jopson reactivated spring track as an intercollegiate sport after a six-year lapse at Bridgewater. By 1939 he produced his first unbeaten track squad. His record since then can rank with the best in the country. His track and cross-country teams have had 26 undefeated seasons and about 27 championships.

A dedicated coach of the first order, he's also a naturalist, conservationist, teacher, herpetologist, geologist. His greatest star was distance runner Merle Crouse.

Among the outstanding athletes produced at Bridgewater:

Ray Bussard ('54), a great competitor in field events, National AAU All-Around champion in 1952, swim coach at the University of Tennessee, and was named Coach of the Year in 1972 in the Southeastern Conference.

Jim Upperman ('68), the Eagles' all-time basketball scorer with 2,237 points in a four-year career, is now assistant principal and athletic director at Montevideo High School in Penn Laird.

Emery Ervin (Kit) May ('25), pitched for Philadelphia Athletics under the immortal Connie Mack; played for the Memphis Chicks in Southern League, 1927-32, pitching them to pennant in 1930.

Marshall Flora ('71), voted co-captain of the Virginia All-Small College football team, also All-Mason Dixon Conference and third team All-America running back. He was second in NCAA college division individual rushing yardage. Career total of 3,474 yards on 772 carries. In his senior year, he averaged 170.2 yards a game, scoring 12 touchdowns and total of 26 for career.

Chris Sizemore ('75) career total of 3,394 yards as tailback.

D. C. DeWitt ('76), Kodak College Division III All-American, finished as the nation's leading receiver in Division III, catching 64 passes for 836 yards, which amounted to 45 per cent of the Eagles' offense.

Jim Reedy ('61), second highest Bridgewater all-time basketball scorer, now chairman of the Bridgewater Athletic Department.

And Merle Crouse, who paced the Eagles to their most successful years in track. Crouse broke all kinds of records in cross-country and distance runs in track. He won wide attention, competing in the National AAU championships and the Penn Relays. While running for Bridgewater in the late 1940s and early 1950s. Crouse led the Eagles to no less than nine championships. Bridgewater had built a track dynasty. Coach Doc Jopson and Crouse made an unbeatable combination. Jopson Field is named in Doc's honor.

Doc Jopson, the highly-successful Bridgewater coach, roots his man to victory.

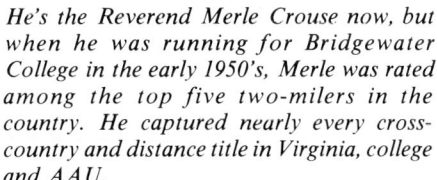

He's the Reverend Merle Crouse now, but when he was running for Bridgewater College in the early 1950's, Merle was rated among the top five two-milers in the country. He captured nearly every cross-country and distance title in Virginia, college and AAU.

LYNCHBURG COLLEGE
The Hornets nest

"College endowments may increase, a state may spend millions, but while students spend half their time smoking, swearing, football playing and general sporting, another part being coached or crammed to meet any examination of which they live in fear, they have no time for real study, reflection or idealizing; not time for hearing the silent voice."

These words summed up Lynchburg College President Dr. Josephus Hopwood's philosophy toward athletics in 1904. Dr. Hopwood hadn't changed his mind four years later when he wrote:

"An institution of learning is not merely a place to have a good time, to compete on the field of athletics, or even to prepare for money-making propositions."

In 1911, the attitude of the administration toward athletics took on a different tune.

"All healthy sports are encouraged," said the college catalogue. "The greater part of our work is done in the open air. To give proper emphasis to this department of college life, is the desire of the Faculty and Board of Trustees."

While pointing out that sports are beneficial and desirable as part of college life, football was explicitly prohibited and deemed improper.

Until 1919 Lynchburg College was known as Virginia Christian College. The first baseball team was organized in 1907, basketball in 1910. It wasn't until 1917 that intercollegiate football was introduced at Lynchburg College when Dr. J. T. T. Hundley was president of the school. By 1920, the LC athletic teams acquired the name of "Hornets."

The Hornets were in the Eastern Virginia Athletic Conference with William & Mary, Randolph-Macon, Hampden-Sydney and Richmond. Following the 1931 season, Lynchburg abandoned its football program. President Hundley cited rising costs and inability to compete (5-20 record over the last three years) as the reasons. It was in the height of the Great Depression. The overall football record was 41-62-9.

The decision to abandon football was a momentous step for Lynchburg College. Hard hit by the depression, a feeling existed that the rising influence of athletics was not becoming to the school.

But the Hornets excelled in other sports. Dedicating Memorial Gym in 1923, the Hornets routed Virginia Tech, 43-16. Victories were also scored over William & Mary and Richmond.

Lynchburg basketball reached its greatest heights in 1964-67 when a fantastic shooter named Wayne Profitt twice blazed his way to Little All-America honors. The little playmaker with the uncanny shooting touch became one of the most prolific scorers in Virginia collegiate basketball history.

While boosting the sagging Hornet basketball fortunes, Profitt broke nearly every Lynchburg offensive record, finishing with a career scoring average of 32.3. He scored 482 free throws, 680 field goals and 1,842 points. He had a streak of 23 consecutive free throw attempts, and scored 68 points in a game against UNC-Charlotte.

Profitt returned as head coach of the Hornets in 1970 and has become one of the winningest basketball coaches in Virginia. Going into the 1976-77 season, Profitt's Hornets had compiled a 113-52 record and three Dixie Conference championships. Under Profitt, the Hornets posted 22-win seasons in 1974-75 and 1975-76.

Soccer is Lynchburg's most successful venture on the sports scene. The Hornets

Still a winner... Wayne Profitt, coach of the Lynchburg Eagles.

have prospered under Bill Shellenberger, the winningest active college soccer coach in the country with 227 victories, 91 defeats and 23 ties. He ranks third on the all-time list of winners behind Glenn Warner of Navy and the late Pete Leaness of Temple. Warner retired in 1976 with 51 years. Leaness had 249 victories. Shellenberger threatens to take the No. 1 spot, becoming the first soccer coach to reach 300 wins.

Shellenberger sold small colleges, unable to field football teams, on the virtues of soccer as an inexpensive sport. He sold it to Lynchburg College in 1954, and operated on a $600 budget.

The result has been six state titles, four Mason-Dixon Conference championships, and eight Dixie Conference crowns. The Hornets have engaged in NCAA regionals four times and the NAIA area playoffs three times.

Shellenberger has produced 51 All-Southern players and four All-Americans—Mutt Werner, now coach at Randolph-Macon; Glenn Taylor, Rusty Taylor and Eric Wagner.

In baseball, the Hornets have thrived under Coach Gerry Thomas. Led by sophomore righthanded pitcher Rick Pillow (7-0 and 0.50 earned run average), the Hornets ranked third nationally in Division 3 in 1976. The Hornets won 30 of 37 games, and four players—Randy Thomas, son of the coach; David Owen, Donnie Vaden and Steve Goff signed pro contracts.

For four consecutive seasons (73-76), the Hornets won at least 20 games per season, playing in the NCAA South Atlantic Regionals in 1975-76.

Other Lynchburg baseball players who signed pro contracts include pitcher Keith Scruggs (1971), catcher Stu Friedman (1971) and in the 1960s pitcher Kenny Holt, catcher Lawson (Slick) Andrews and infielder Bill Booker.

Although surrounded by two Hampden-Sydney players, Little All-American Wayne Profitt (right) manages to get off a pass. The Lynchburg College ace was named to the Little All-America team two years.

The High Schools
A proud collection of records

A coach of a major college once remarked that if he could recruit the best high school football players produced in Virginia every year his team would always be ranked among the national powers. It was a compliment to the high school program in Virginia, the gifted young athletes as well as dedicated coaching through the years.

Running the show is the Virginia High School League, which has kept scholastic athletics at a high level under the leadership of the principals, and executive secretary William C. Pacc and his staff at Charlottesville.

Actually, the league originated in 1913 as a debating society, a student activity of the Washington and Jefferson Societies at the University of Virginia. Debating was sponsored in 20 schools. Soon baseball, basketball, track and then football were added.

Now there are nearly 400 schools competing in the VHSL.

Back in the early 1920s, Jefferson Senior, then Roanoke High, produced the first football dynasty among major high schools in Virginia. After losing a playoff for the state title to Coach Norman LaMotte's Maury Commodores of Norfolk in 1921, the Magicians walked off with the next three crowns, 1922-23-24. And on each occasion, the Magicians defeated Woodrow Wilson of Portsmouth in a playoff.

You can say the powerful Magicians, or rather a tackle named Earl Fitzpatrick, got a kick out of their work. After defeating Wilson, 8-0, in 1922, the Roanoke school won the next two playoffs with the Easterners by identical 3-0 scores. Fitzpatrick was pulled from the line each time to kick the winning goal.

In the 1922 playoff game with Wilson, Albert Barnes scored the touchdown and Jefferson collected a safety for the other two points on a muddy field at Portsmouth. The Wilson team included Dick Esleeck, a fullback who later gained fame as a high school coach. In the 1923 championship game at Roanoke's Maher Field, Jefferson Senior didn't make a substitution as Fitzpatrick's field goal was the deciding factor. Fitzpatrick duplicated his feat in 1924 at Portsmouth.

Three of the Roanoke stars became rival football captains the same year in college—Fitzpatrick at Washington & Lee, Albert Barnes at VMI and Albert Bailey at Virginia Tech. Barnes, regarded as one of the best halfbacks in VMI history, was killed in an automobile accident shortly after his graduation from VMI. Bailey went with General Motors and is now retired.

Fitzpatrick spent 20 years in the Virginia House of Delegates, including three terms as State Senator.

Ironically, it was a field goal that put Wilson into the playoffs in 1923—and made history. Playing arch-rival Maury in Norfolk, Maxie Leitman kicked his way into immortality with a 55-yard field goal for a 3-0 victory. And this was no ordinary kick. It was a dropkick!

This amazing dropkick has become a legend in Virginia high school sports history. The story goes that Maxie was supposed to punt but dropkicked instead, the ball clearing the crossbar with much to spare. Not before or since has anyone dropkicked a football that far in Virginia, high school or college.

While sweeping to successive state championships in 1926-27, Woodrow Wilson established one of the greatest defensive records of all time in the VHSL. The Presidents, coached by Lester E. Kibler, kept their goal line uncrossed for 18 consecutive games

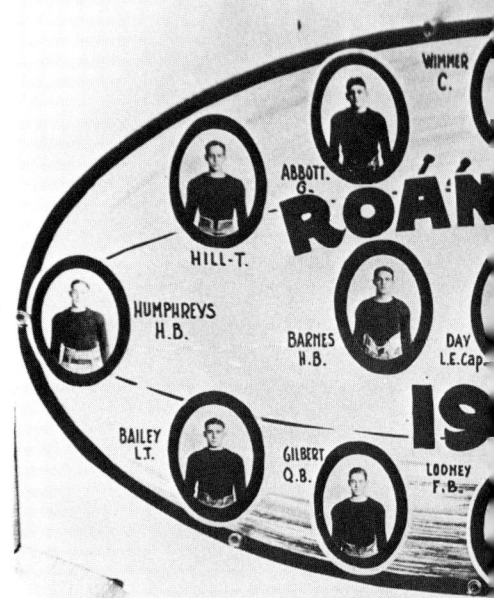

The Magicians who brought home their third straight state championship.

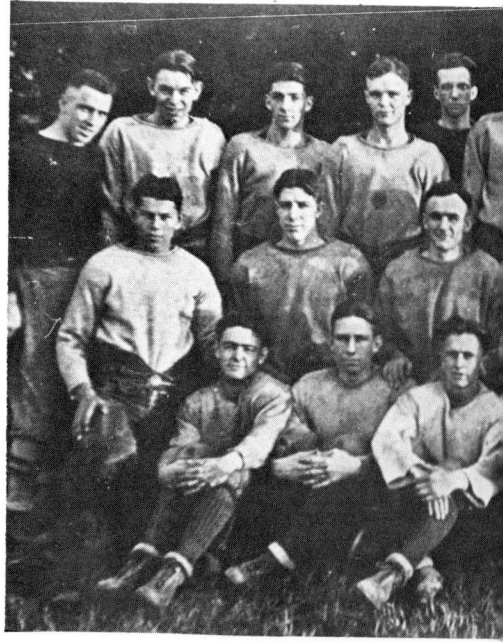

Maury's State football champions of 1921.

until Jefferson Senior scored on them in 1927. Not only was this team powerful on defense, but had a fine attack with Al Casey, the "Galloping Ghost," and Cocky Rose.

Although Wilson won the game, 26-7, Portsmouth's fickle fans blamed the coach for permitting the Magicians to score and end the streak, claiming he had his second stringers in the game at the time. It was an indication that pressure was on high school coaches as it was in the colleges, and it was to remain so through the years. Kibler, however, remained on the job for 13 years and bowed out with a fine record, including a hand in developing Clarence "Ace" Parker.

In 1941-42, John Marshall of Richmond, coached by Dick Esleeck, was two games away from matching Wilson's unscored-on streak. After holding 16 opponents scoreless, the Justices finally yielded a touchdown to Maury.

Esleeck, a star fullback at Wilson in 1922, is the only coach in VHSL history to produce a state championship football team at three different high schools—Hampton (1936), Johnson Marshall (1940-41) and Wilson (1947).

There have been many other outstanding high school coaches in Virginia —Hunk Hurt (Jefferson Senior), Dave Miller (John Marshall) Dick Fletcher (Maury), Bill Story (Granby of Norfolk), Suey Eason (Hampton), Vince Bradford (E. C. Glass of Lynchburg), Bill Merner (Hopewell), Chester Fritz (Hermitage of Richmond), Merrill Gainer (Patrick Henry of Roanoke), Pete Sachon (Wilson, Norview, Princess Anne), Charles McClurg (Norview), Larry Weldon (Cradock), Billy O'Brien (Great Bridge), Ralph Gahagan (Wilson), Jerry Sazio (Maury), Mike Smith (Hampton), Tommy Theodose (Charlottesville), Bobby Tyler (Petersburg) and Johnny Palmer (Hampton and E. C. Glass).

Among the most successful coaches in the 1930s were Dick Fletcher, who produced two Maury championship teams (1932, 1935), and Roland Day, whose Petersburg teams were always top contenders, winning the 1937 Virginia championship with one of the most powerful teams ever. Petersburg produced many stars, including Marvin Bass and Eric Tipton, who became a Duke great and a major league baseball player. Tipton was elected to the National College Football Hall of Fame.

Coach Roland Day's great football teams of the thirties gained a national reputation by playing intersectional games. In 1933, the unbeaten Crimson Wave won 11 straight games and in a post-season attraction, defeated a Jacksonville high school all-star team, 6-0, at Jacksonville, Florida, in a game that was the forerunner of the Gator Bowl. Other intersectional opponents played by the Crimson Wave included Baldwin, N. Y., and Miami, Florida, Senior High. The 1937 unbeaten state championship team is considered Petersburg's greatest.

"We were almost forced to schedule intersectional opponents," says Coach Day. "There weren't enough state high schools in our classification to play. At one time there were only three schools in what we called Class A high schools in our area—Petersburg, Hopewell and John Marshall. Now schools don't have to leave the area to fill a schedule."

Other than Petersburg, Portsmouth's Wilson High enjoyed a diet of intersectional opposition during the thirties, meeting such high school powers as Ashland, Kentucky, Roosevelt High of

Earl Fitzpatrick, whose field goals won the state championship for Roanoke in playoffs with Woodrow Wilson of Portsmouth by the scores of 3-0 in 1923 and 1924.

Wilson's unbeaten and unscored-on Presidents of 1926.

Eric Tipton carrying ball for Petersburg High School in 1934. He became an outstanding back at Duke University, 1936-38. He was named to the College Football Hall of Fame.

Maxie Leitman of Wilson, a 55-yard dropkick.

New York, Chaney of Youngstown, Ohio, featuring Frank Sinkwich, who won the Heisman Trophy at the University of Georgia, and Tech High of Atlanta.

Granby High of Norfolk opened its doors in 1939 and six years later ruled football. This dynasty was started in 1944 by Bill Story, who in later years made a good run for the Governor of Virginia. The Comets rolled through three successive unbeaten seasons (1944-45-46), with Story coaching two state championship teams before moving on to Davidson College as head coach. In 1946, with Snookie Tarrall coaching, Granby ran its winning streak to a record 32 games, including a 6-0 victory over Clifton, New Jersey, in the first Oyster Bowl game. Lynn, Massachusetts, ended Granby's streak in the Shrine game at Miami, Florida, on Christmas night, 1946.

In the late 1940s, Hampton and Hopewell dueled for state football supremacy. Hopewell became the first school since Jefferson Senior to capture three consecutive state championships (sharing one with Hampton). The Blue Devils broke Granby's record streak with an undefeated, untied march of 35 straight. Ironically, it was Granby that ended the Hopewell streak.

But the longest unbeaten football streak in VHSL history was compiled by Lane High of Charlottesville.

In 1951, Mickey Riggs of Cradock set a Group AAA scoring record for one season with 176 points. It was tied 20 years later by Robert (Ton) Davis of Woodrow Wilson.

But no high school player in Virginia has scored more points than Johnny McFall of Group A Clintwood. He scored an incredible 309 points in 1975 and a record 608 career points (1972-75).

From 1955 to 1961, the Pilots of Norfolk's Norview were the untouchables in football. In five of the seven years, the Pilots went unbeaten, won seven consecutive Eastern District championships, but could annex only two clear claims to the Group AAA championship. Their overall record in this stretch was 64-3-3, two of the losses coming in one season. Pete Sachon, who

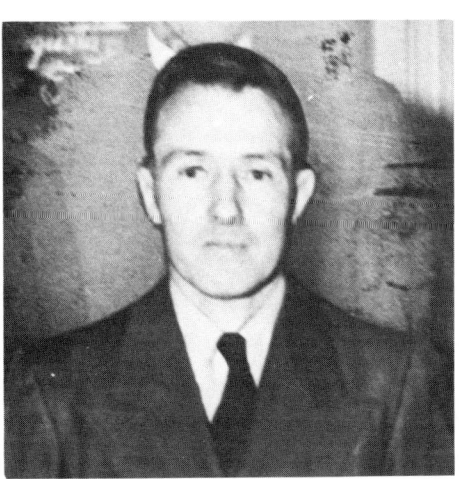

Lester E. Kibler coached the Wilson Presidents to three successive unbeaten seasons (1926-27-28) in VHSL competition. His 1926-27 teams won state championships, establishing a defensive record in holding 18 straight opponents scoreless.

The 1937 Petersburg High School Crimson Wave, unbeaten and untied, undisputed champions of Virginia. Coach Roland Day, who produced many outstanding teams at Petersburg, says the 1937 edition was perhaps his greatest. Among the players who went on to stardom in college were Captain Aubrey Gill (No. 83) at Duke, Marvin Bass (No. 70) at W & M, Jimmy Matthews (No. 76) at VMI, Harry Hartman (No. 81) at W & M, Gene Kidd (No. 80) at W & M, Alton Belcher (No. 88) at Virginia Tech and Robert Gill (No. 87) at Richmond.

Highly-successful coach at Hampton High School, J. M. (Suey) Eason, developed state championship elevens in 1942, 1948, and 1950. His winning record ranks him among the best in the VHSL.

They played together for Roanoke's state championship football teams in 1922-23-24. They graduated together and then each went to separate colleges and became stars. In their senior year, each was elected captain of his college team for 1928. From left: Ab Barnes (VMI), Bill Bailey (VPI) and Earl Fitzpatrick (W & L).

Coach Dick Esleeck, who produced state championship football teams at three different high schools—Hampton, John Marshall and Woodrow Wilson.

The 1945 Granby state champions, who rolled up 440 points in bowling over ten opponents, for a staggering 40 points a game average. Coached by Bill Story the Comets started their football dynasty in 1944, winning three successive state titles with unbeaten records. The boy standing at the left on the second row is Team Manager Lefty Driesell, who is now head basketball coach at the University of Maryland.

coached Wilson to a state title in 1954, was at the helm in 1955-56 and compiled a 20-0-0 record, and Charles McClurg the next five.

The coach with the golden touch was Newport News' Julie Conn. Newport News High School no longer exists— only Conn's records. Conn coached 44 years before retiring in 1970. His Typhoon track teams captured 27 state titles and nearly 40 district championships. In basketball, his teams won 321 of 389 games, including three successive state titles.

Billy Martin of Granby is regarded as the father of wrestling in Virginia high schools. His record may never be equaled. Hailed from coast to coast as one of the top wrestling coaches in the country, Martin's Granby teams won 259 dual meets, lost nine and tied four in 24 seasons. From the time the VHSL instituted a state tournament in 1949 to his retirement as head coach after the 1969-70 season, Granby lost only one title—the year the Norfolk city schools were closed in 1959 due to integration. From 1959 through 1970, Granby wrestlers won 105 individual titles. Martin's "Granby Roll" has become famous in college wrestling as well as high schools.

Not only is Martin in the Wrestling Hall of Fame, but two of his Granby proteges, Gray Simons (Lock Haven State) and Edward Eichelberger (Lehigh University), who became champions in college wrestling, have been elected to the shrine.

In basketball, Maury of Norfolk ruled the state for three consecutive years, winning the championship in 1924-25, 1925-26, 1926-27, before Woodrow Wilson ended the Commodores' reign in 1927-28. In three seasons, Coach Waverly Jones' Commodores swept to 64 victories while losing four, all to opposition outside the VHSL. Two of the losses were by one point, another by two.

It was an era of low-scoring basketball, but the 1925 Commodores totaled 1,037 points in 26 games, a record production then. Many experts regarded the 1927 Maury team, which competed in the National High School Tournament at Chicago, as the best.

Frank Darden played on all three championship teams. But Leigh Williams, who became one of Washington & Lee's immortals, once said the 1925 Maury team was the greatest he ever played on.

The Commodores shut out Suffolk, 38-0, on one game and in another trampled Eastern Virginia rival Hampton, 92-9. The Maury streak wasn't matched until 28 years later when Julie Conn's Newport News Typhoon rolled to three consecutive state championships, 1955-56, 1956-57, 1957-58. In later years, after Conn stepped down, Lefty Driesell coached Newport News to 59 consecutive victories.

Frankie Peralta of Portsmouth Catholic was the all-time Virginia scholastic scorer with 2,567 career points, 1963-64 through 1966-67.

Moses Malone, the Petersburg sensation who turned pro in the American Basketball Association following his high school career, holds the record for one season (896) in 1973-74.

The VHSL career record was set in 1975-76 by Steve Marsee of Pennington, who scored a total of 2,449.

Fred James of Churchland, then a Group AA school, holds the one-game record of 83 points, set February 19, 1954, against Poquoson.

But wait! In a game against Mary N. Smith at Accomac on February 22, 1961, Johnny Morris of Portsmouth's Norcom scored 127 points in a 139-33 victory. Morris netted 57 field goals and 13 free throws.

"Never saw anything like it," remarked coach Bob Smith, later to become head coach at Norfolk State. Norcom was then a member of the Virginia Interscholastic Association, the black schools' counterpart to the VHSL. Soon after the public schools were integrated, the VIA dissolved after a long and fine record and the schools were admitted to the VHSL.

Armstrong and Maggie Walker of Richmond, Booker T. Washington of Norfolk, Norcom, and Huntington of Newport News were among the VIA powers. Coach Thaddeus S. Madden of Huntington had one of the winning-

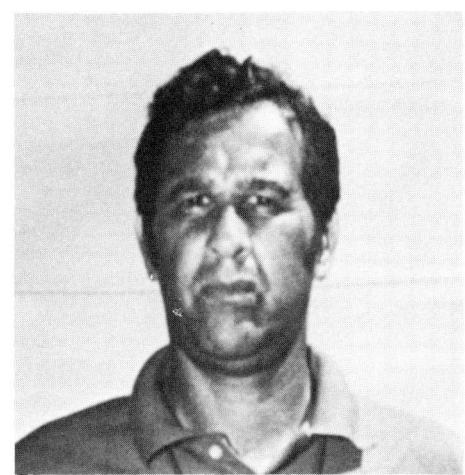
Thaddeus S. Madden coached Huntington High of Newport News to 26 state track titles in Virginia Interscholastic Association (VIA), winning 102 meets and losing only six from 1943-70. His overall coaching record for basketball was 112-13 at Huntington. Moved to Warwick High as head football coach.

Julie Conn of Newport News, shown in 1951 photograph, was the winningest coach in basketball and track in the history of the Virginia High School League. One of the most colorful, too. His Typhoon track teams captured 27 state championships and nearly 40 district titles. Conn's basketball teams, drilled in fundamentals to well-nigh perfection, also ruled the state for many years, winning 321 of 389 games. His Typhoon won three successive state basketball titles. Conn retired in 1970 after 40 years of coaching at Newport News.

est records. Madden's team won 26 VIA state titles, 1943-1970. His basketball teams compiled a 112-13 record and his track teams won 102 meets while losing only six.

In the State Catholic League, Benedictine of Richmond has been the big winner in basketball. The Cadets have won 18 of the 31 championships, including the last six straight (1971-76), in the State Catholic High School Basketball Tournament conducted by the Knights of Columbus. Warren Rutledge, coaching at Benedictine 19 years, has won 12 titles.

The 1972-73 Benedictine team is considered by many to be the Cadets' best, compiling a 31-3 record and mopping up in the tournament. The team featured center Mark Crow, who went on to Duke, and guard John Kuester, who went to the University of North Carolina.

Ronnie Valentine of the 1976 Norfolk Catholic team set three-game tourney record of 106, including 42 in a 75-74 triple-overtime loss to Benedictine in the championship game.

Bobby Stewart of Lynchburg's Holy Cross holds the tourney record for points (115 in four games) and field goals (46 in four games) as he led the Gaels to the 1953 championship.

Coach Pete Sachon produced successive state championship football teams at Woodrow Wilson (1954) and Norview (1955).

They started the Norview football monopoly. The Norview Pilots, who won the 1955 state football championship powering their way to ten consecutive victories. The Pilots also went 10-0 in 1956. Front row (from left): B. Hehl, B. White, W. Dodge, B. Tugwell, S. Wood, D. Dean, L. Bridges, A. Whittier, F. Seehorn, B. Stanley, W. McCoy, W. French, T. Jones, J. Calder. Second row: D. Dodge, B. White, G. Hermann, J. Sereno, R. Tolston, J. Phillips, J. Long, R. Garrett, H. J. Rust, C. Barnett, J. Watkins, J. Riddick, G. Vesprille, B. Bryant, E. Russell, R. Polk, B. Barr. Back row: M. Crowling, manager; B. Ballentine, manager; J. White, J. Busby, C. Stevens, D. Hudson, W. Woolard, M. Tomlinson, R. Rusbult, C. Lancaster, B. Tugwell, C. Coverdale, J. Wells, W. Rumpf, manager; D. Herron, manager; B. Stevens, manager.

Roland Day, who coached many of the finest football teams in the state at Petersburg High School, developing many stars who became outstanding in college.

The Longest Winning Streak

Lane's streak was hanging in the balance.

After two consecutive unbeaten seasons, the Black Knights found themselves trailing Hopewell, 14-13, in the final period of the 1965 game. Hopewell had a first and goal at the one-yard line. In a remarkable defensive stand Lane held for four downs and then drove 99 yards for the winning touchdown.

Lane went on to compile the longest unbeaten streak (53 games) in the history of Virginia high school football. At the time it was the longest unbeaten streak in the nation.

After an opening game loss to Thomas Jefferson of Richmond in 1962, the Knights won their remaining games that season. They were 10-0-0 in 1963 annexing the State AAA championship, 9-0-1 in 1964 (tied by Patrick Henry of Roanoke, 6-6), 9-0-1 in 1965 (again tied by Patrick Henry, 0-0), and 10-0-0 in 1966.

Winning its first four games in 1967, Lane saw its remarkable streak broken at 53 by Douglas Freeman, 27-14, in a game played at Richmond. Douglas Freeman went on to win a share of the state crown.

Tommy Theodose, the "Golden Greek," coached the streaking Black Knights. He's still coaching—and winning—at what became Charlottesville High School. In 1975, his team went 10-0, losing to E. C. Glass of Lynchburg in the state playoffs. In 17 years of coaching, Theodose compiled a 125-40-5 record, putting him on the all-time list among the winningest Virginia high school coaches.

Theodose developed three straight first-team all-state quarterbacks: Gene Arnette in 1963, David Trice in 1965 and Mike Cubbage in 1967. Arnette led the University of Virginia to a 7-3 season in 1968, the Cavaliers' only winner since 1952. Trice played at Duke and Cubbage went to Virginia and then to the Texas Rangers and Minnesota Twins in the American League.

Theodose gives credit to his assistants for the Knight's streak. For 16 years Joe Bingler was Theodose's No. 1 assistant before moving over to Albermarle. Ralph Harrison was assistant coach with the 1963 state champions. Harrison has coached eight winning teams at Albermarle, including 10-0 elevens in 1966, 1968 and 1969.

The Black Knights of Lane protected their remarkable unbeaten streak with this magnificent goal line stand against Hopewell in 1965. Hopewell, leading 14-13 in the fourth quarter, had four cracks at the Lane line from the half-yard line. Hopewell's star fullback, Butch Altman was repulsed four times. Lane then took over and marched 99½ yards for the winning touchdown.

The Golden Greek, Tommy Theodose, who coached Lane to the longest unbeaten streak in Virginia football history.

Lane's unbeaten (10-0-0) state champions of 1963.

Gene Arnette (11) carries ball against Prince George in the final game in 1963. The Knights won to wrap up the state championship.

Lefty Driesell, a star on Granby High's state championship basketball team in 1946, enjoyed great success as coach at Newport News High School. Then he moved to Davidson College, where he built the Wildcats into a national basketball power. The next stop was the University of Maryland, where he is regarded as one of the top basketball coaches in the country. In 1975-76, he ranked seventh among the winningest active major college coaches.

Johnny Morris of Portsmouth's Norcom High scored a record 127 points in a single basketball game in 1961.

Frank Peralta, of Portsmouth Catholic, had 2,567 career points.

Moses Malone, who scored a record 896 points in 1973-74 at Petersburg, was the first high school basketball player to step directly into pro basketball. The Utah Stars of the American Basketball Association signed Malone to a contract worth a reported $3 million. When the Stars folded, Malone signed with the Spirits of St. Louis, also of the ABA. Although fresh out of high school, he has more than held his own with the pro stars.

Coach Billy Martin of Granby, who pioneered wrestling in Virginia high schools. He compiled one of the greatest winning records of all time, and his "Granby Roll" has become famous in college wrestling as well as the high schools. Elected to Wrestling Hall of Fame.

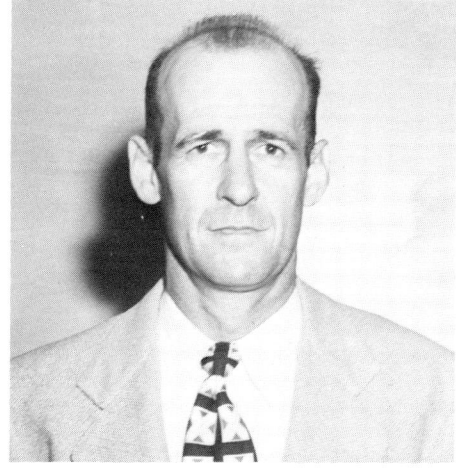

Charles McClurg coached Norview to three straight unbeaten football seasons. His four-year record was 42-1-3.

Washington-Lee High School Crew

In a sport not recognized by the Virginia High School League, Washington-Lee's crew has achieved remarkable success, both in the United States and abroad.

George Washington High of Alexandria had the first crews in northern Virginia, in 1947-48, and then Charlie Butt organized and coached the first W-L crew in 1949. Butt notes that one of the great moments in W-L sports history came in 1949 when the baseball team won the state championship and the crew captured the national scholastic rowing championship at Detroit—on the same day!

The W-L crew twice won the Princess Elizabeth Challenge Cup, 1964 and 1969, in the ancient and famed Henley Royal Regatta, which has been raced on the Thames River, west of London, since 1837.

It cost approximately 12,000 dollars to send the W-L crew to England. Funds were raised through donations from interested citizens, business and parents.

"The first crew in 1949 had a lot of natural ability," Butt said in explaining the instant success of this sport at W-L. "The boys were strong and very competitive. The crew lost its first race, but went on to win the rest in 1949, including the national championship. Major factors in the success in following years were tradition, a good program, and a large turnout of kids for tryouts. One year 120 came out.

"Two amateur boat clubs in the Washington area—Potomac Boat Club and Dominion Boat Club sponsored high school crews and helped provide the school with equipment. This support was a big factor in the success of this sport."

Since they started the sport, W-L oarsmen, in addition to Henley, have won the American Schoolboy Regatta 12 times, Stotesbury Regatta 14 times, and the Northern Virginia Regatta 17 times. The Stotesbury Regatta is raced on the Schuylkill River in Philadelphia.

Among the outstanding W-L crew members were Peter Sparhawk and P. A. (Tony) Johnson. Sparhawk is now head crew coach at Princeton University and Johnson the head coach at Yale.

The prestigious Princess Elizabeth Challenge Cup won by W-L High School.

Victory on the Thames. The 1964 W-L crew defeating Groton School of Massachusetts in the finale of the Henley Regatta.

And they did it again in 1969. The W-L crew crossing the finish line ahead of Emanuel School of England to win the Henley Regatta for the second time.

Extra Innings
Fox Hill and Ron Peterson

Ron Peterson, a pitching wizard for Fox Hill for 10 years, was the first from Virginia to be named to the Amateur Softball Association of America All-America team. In all the Hampton resident, who led Fox Hill to four national tournaments, pitched 400 victories in a 16-year career.

Softball has been a popular sport in Virginia since the early 1930s, highly-competitive especially among the well-organized men's adult leagues, where teams aim for the state and national honors through a series of tournaments.

Fox Hill of Hampton probably has been the most successful of these teams, and the best pitcher was Ronald E. Peterson. The Fox Hill team was organized in 1946, winning its first Virginia State softball championship in 1955, and its first Central Atlantic Regional Tournament in 1965. The Central Atlantic Region consists of state and metropolitan champions from Maryland, Pennsylvania, District of Columbia, Virginia, Delaware, Metro Philadelphia, Metro Richmond and Metro Norfolk.

Fox Hill won nine state championships and four Central Atlantic Region titles, and made its leap into the nationals after Peterson joined the team in 1964. A year later, in 1965, Ron pitched the Peninsula team to the National Tournament at Clearwater, Florida. Although he pitched successive shutout victories over St. Thomas of Ontario, Canada, 3-0, and Lakewood, California, 2-0, the 6-4 righthander finally bowed to Clearwater, Florida, 1-0, and Chattanooga, Tennessee, 3-0. Fox Hill came out of the tourney as the sixth best team in the nation.

Peterson led Fox Hill to the National Tournament again in 1967, 1969 and 1973. Ron pitched the championship game in all four Fox Hill Regional successes. Most valuable honors piled up for the big pitcher at state and regional level. He won his first 19 games he pitched for Fox Hill, a record tied by Bill Covington in 1972.

Peterson reached his greatest heights in the 1969 National Softball Tournament at Springfield, Missouri. He pitched a one-hit, 3-1 victory over the defending champion Clearwater, Florida, Bombers, and then shut out Oxnard, California, the 1968 national runner-up in eight innings, 1-0. After losing a 3-2 thriller in 16 innings to the Armed Forces, Peterson came back and pitched a perfect game against Mesa, Arizona, striking out 14 in a 6-0 victory. Peterson lost to Aurora, Illinois, by 1-0 as Fox Hill finished fifth in the nation.

It was no wonder that Peterson was selected on the Amateur Softball Association All-America team for 1969. After the 1973 season, Peterson retired. In ten years, he pitched 249 victories for the Fox Hill team. Overall including the years he pitched at Canton, North Carolina, and Greensboro, North Carolina, his victory total reached 400.

Jack Hull managed Fox Hill's National Tournament teams in 1965, 1969 and 1973. Rudy Forrest managed the team that went to the nationals in 1967.

The 1965 Fox Hill softball team, the first of four to compete in the National Tournament. Front row (from left): Don Winegrad, Jesse Kensey, George Weikel, Charlie Mayer, Keith Goodson, Joey Lawrence and Bud Porter. Back: Phil Routten, business manager, Randy Dale, Manager Jack Hull, Ron Peterson, Herb Weaver, Ronnie Weber, Don Brandt, Jim Dugan, and Coach Rudy Forrest. Bob Atterholt was absent when photo was taken in front of Philadelphia Phillies' Spring training headquarters in Clearwater, Florida, where tournament was played.

In 1959, this scrawny, bunt-happy group from Phoebus Fuller-Urick American Legion Post 48 in Hampton scrambled all the way to the Legion World Series finals in Hastings, Nebraska, before losing to Detroit. Standing, left to right: Manager Tommy Gear, George Weikle, Hartwell "Hardrock" Routten, Bobby Ball, George Jones, Glen Wilson, Post Commander Jim Parker. Middle row: Hugh Boyd, Brink Miller, Russell Anderson, David Walton, Coach Bill Ball. Seated: Tommy Arnold, Robert Sleigher, Joe DeAtkine, Jackie Drause. Batboys: Tommy Gear, Jr., Jimmy Parker, Jr.

The little league from Tuckahoe in 1968 had 13 tournament victories, and played in the Little World Series at Williamsport, Pennsylvania. Tuckahoe lost to Wakayama, Japan, 1-0, in the final game. The coach was Harry Humphrey and the manager Wes Voltz. The 1976 Tuckahoe team reached the semifinals of the Little League World Series.

A Champion on Water

Henry Lauterbach was elected to the American Power Association Honor Squadron in 1974, the highest possible honor in power boat racing. It put the Portsmouth racer-builder in some high class company that includes famed power boat racers like Gar Wood, Sir Malcolm Campbell, Don Campbell and Guy Lombardo.

In 1954 and 1956, Lauterbach was elected to the Gulf Hall of Fame.

Competing in the highly competitive 135, 225, and 266 cu. in. classes, Lauterbach personally won five United States high point awards, two national championships and set one world competitive record. He won about eight championships in limited inboard hydroplane racing.

He won the Miami International Grand Prix in 1956 and 1958.

Regarded as one of the outstanding powerboat builders in the country, Lauterbach now leaves the racing to his son, Larry, who is following his dad's footsteps in setting records.

Henry Lauterbach (left) makes a final check with son, Larry, before a big race.

DICK SHEA
A Nation's hero

A hero, according to Webster's Dictionary, is a man of extraordinary courage, one who performs great deeds.

Dick Shea was a hero in every sense of the imagination.

Portsmouth-born, Churchland High and Virginia Tech educated, and West Point trained, Dick Shea was the U.S. Military Academy's greatest distance runner of all time. He won nine championship races and set five Academy track records. He won the national cross-country championship and was ranked among the country's top runners in the mile and two-mile.

The young track star also included the two-mile title in the Penn Relays and a new record in the Heptagonal indoor meet at Boston among his conquests. In one race, Shea defeated Horace Ashenfelter, who won a gold medal in the 1952 Olympics at Helsinki.

Shea became interested in track during an overseas assignment in Berlin as an enlisted man in World War II.

Twice named to the coaches' All-America track team, the Virginian graduated from West Point with high honors, receiving the award as the cadet contributing most to athletics during the Academy career.

Shea was invited to become a member of the U.S. Olympic track team but rejected the invitation in order to go right into the Army as a second lieutenant.

Shea, 28, was killed while leading an assault on Pork Chop Hill in Korea on July 8, 1953.

On May 16, 1955, Lieutenant Richard T. Shea, Jr., was posthumously awarded the Congressional Medal of Honor, the nation's highest military award. Army Secretary Robert T. Stevens made the award to his widow, Mrs. Joyce Shea, in impressive ceremonies at Ft. Myer.

Shea was cited for his "conspicuous gallantry and indomitable courage above and beyond the call of duty in action against the enemy near Sokkogae, Korea."

The U.S. Military Academy didn't forget this hero, naming its track field close to the Hudson River in his memory.

Dick Shea

Handball

In 1976, Dr. Claude Benham won the U.S. Handball Association Masters championship for men 40 years of age and older. At the same time, Fred DeNuccio captured the Golden Masters (50 and older). Both are from Chesapeake and both have collected an impressive stock of championship handball trophies.

Dr. Benham, an all-state quarterback at Norview High School and then All-Ivy League at Columbia University under Lou Little, was the Southeastern handball champion, 1965-72; runnerup in the USHA National Invitation, 1969, and nine times Virginia State open champion.

DeNuccio, a chief in the Navy serving as Reserve Recruiter at Little Creek, is a former AAU lightweight boxing champion. After the age of 37, from 1958-1976, he has won over 100 handball tournaments. In 1965, he became the only player in Virginia to win three tournaments in one weekend—the AAU singles and doubles at Richmond, and the Southeastern Master doubles. His other titles include the Art Linkletter Open singles, All-South Masters Open, Old Dominion Open singles, and twice winner of the Open Masters in Pittsburgh. He is also a Navy squash champion.

Dr. Claude Benham on the court.

Fred DeNuccio

Dr. Claude Benham

Surfing

Robert (Bob) Holland of Virginia Beach is the only surfer to win the coveted United States Surfing Championships on all three continental coasts. Holland won the Senior Men's division (over 35 years old) in Huntington Beach, California, in 1967. In 1974, Holland became the first to win on both east and west coasts by taking first place at Cape Hatteras, North Carolina. He completed his domination of the Senior Men's by winning the championships in Corpus Christi, Texas, on the gulf seaboard.

Holland admits to surfing "about 35 years." He grew up on the shore where his father was a harbor pilot. His father, Captain Bob Holland, was among the original surfers in the east. Captain Bob began surfing in Virginia Beach during the early 1920s. At 73 years old, Captain Bob is still an active enthusiast. Like his father, Holland is a harbor pilot in Virginia Beach.

Holland's three children also have won honors in the sport. Bobby, 24, has placed in several regional and local events. John, 23, participated in the United States Surfing Championships in Huntington as a Junior Men's entry. Honey, 19, has won the women's division of the East Coast Surfing Championships second regional contests.

The East Coast Surfing Championships (ECSC) is annually held at the south end of Virginia Beach during the last weekend of August. Holland, at the request of the Virginia Beach Jaycees, helped organize the ECSC in 1963. Holland's clout got big names from the west coast and Hawaii to enter the event, and at one time the ECSC was the largest contest on the east coast. It is still the oldest regularly-scheduled surfing event on the seaboard.

Holland is a member of the Eastern Surfing Association's Hall of Fame, having served as head of the organization.

Robert Holland

Walking and Running

Todd Scully, a pig farmer in rural Bedford County, is shown warming up for the 1976 Olympic Games at Montreal in this photo by Steve Harriman. A Lynchburg College graduate, Scully became the United States' top hope in 20,000-meter walk in the Olympics after winning the walk in the Olympic trials at Eugene, Oregon, on June 19, 1976. He has been racewalker since 1955. Scully is 5-9, weighs 125 pounds. He is a former track coach at Liberty High School in Bedford County, having received his bachelor's degree in chemistry at Lynchburg in 1970 and his master's in education there in 1974.

Jack Fultz of Arlington cools off en route to victory in the 26-mile, 385-yard Boston Marathon on April 19, 1976. The Georgetown University senior outdistanced 1,897 participants in capturing the 80th edition of the gruelling race. Born in Franklin, Pennsylvania, and now calling Virginia his home, Fultz holds the Georgetown records in the six-mile run and marathon, placed fourth in the 1972 National AAU marathon championships when he was a member of the U.S. Military cross-country team.

Fishing

Claude Rogers of Virginia Beach has won numerous angling awards. Tops among them was the 1960 "World Series of Sport Fishing," held at several places in Florida and climaxed by a fish-off at famed Lake Okeechobee. Long a pioneering angler, Rogers now is the sport fishing promotion specialist for the Virginia Department of Conservation and Economic Development. Within that capacity, he is director of the highly successful Virginia Salt Water Fishing Tournament.

Coliseums of Virginia

Norfolk's Scope

Hampton Coliseum

Richmond Coliseum

Roanoke Civic Center

Salem-Roanoke Valley Civic Center

The Great Seal of Virginia

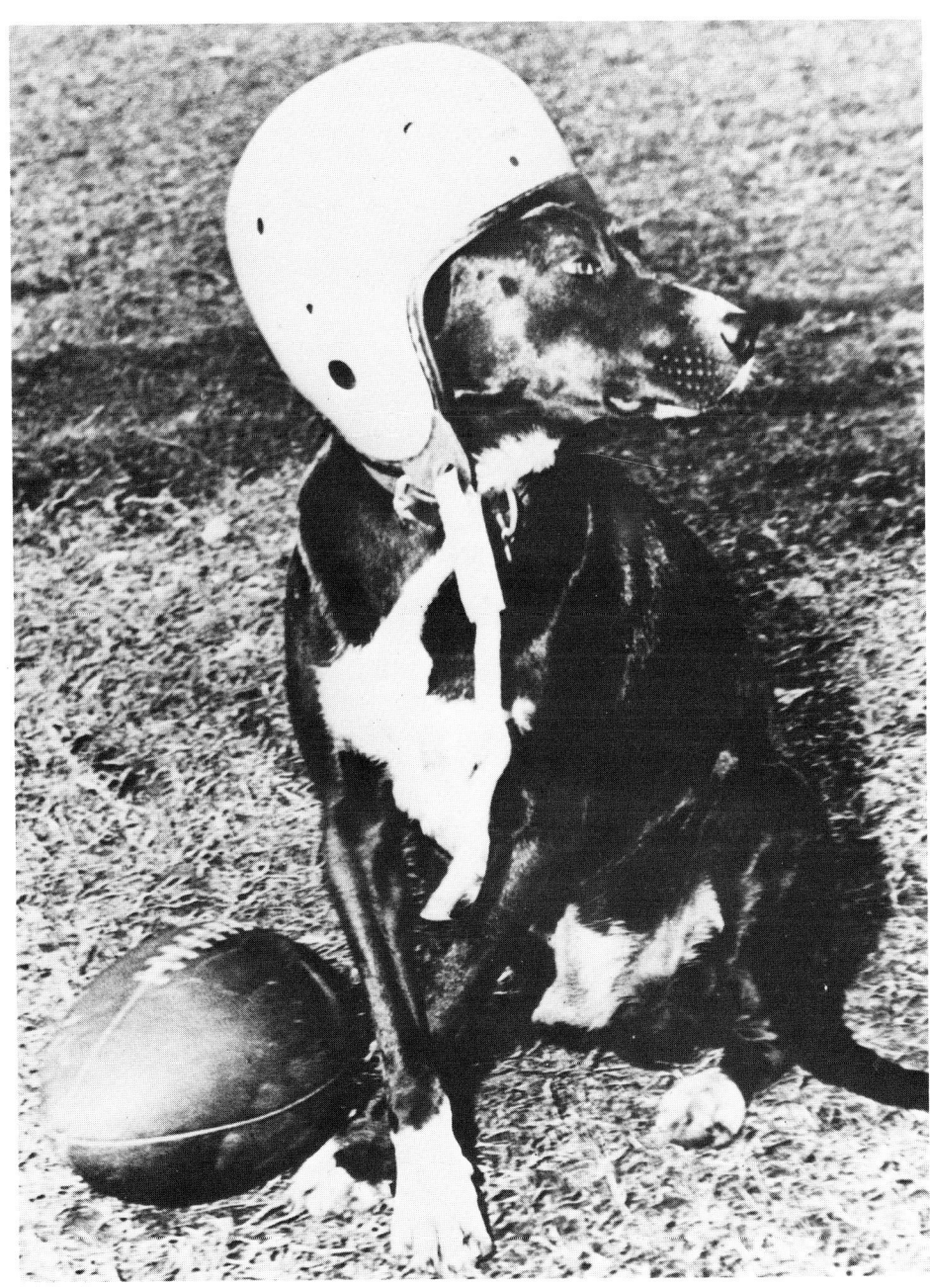

Seal was the undisputed king of the dogs that roamed the campus of the University of Virginia during the late nineteen-forties. A mascot and friend of the student body and football team, Seal was present on the Saturday afternoon in 1949 when the University of Virginia upset powerful Pennsylvania, 26-14. When victory was assured Seal crossed the field, and to the delight of the University of Virginia fans, did an unkind thing to a megaphone of a Penn cheerleader, thus earning himself a place among the great and the near great of sports in Virginia.

Statistical Index

All-Time Roster Virginia College Players in Pro Football

Anderson, Roger (Virginia Union)—Tackle—1964-65, 1967-68, New York Giants; 1966, Atlanta Falcons.

Baker, John (Norfolk State)—End—1970, New York Giants (NFC).

Baldwin, George (Virginia)—End—1925, Cleveland Bulldogs; 1926, Brooklyn Dodgers (AFL).

Barber, Benjamin (VMI)—Tackle—1925, Buffalo Bisons.

Barefoot, Kenneth (Virginia Tech)—End—1968, Washington Redskins.

Barrett, John (Washington & Lee)—Back—1919, 1922-23, Hammond Pros; 1920, Chicago Tigers.

Biscaha, Joseph (Richmond)—End—1959, New York Giants; 1960, Boston Patriots (AFL).

Bolton, Ronald (Norfolk State)—Back, Kicker—1972-74, New England Patriots (AFC).

Bowling, Andrew (Virginia Tech)—LB—1967, Atlanta Falcons.

Bowman, Williams (William & Mary)—Back—1954-56, Detroit Lions; 1957, Pittsburgh Steelers.

Boyda, Michael (Washington & Lee)—Back—1949, New York Bulldogs; 1949, Punting Leader.

Braxton, Hezekiah (Virginia Union)—Back—1962, San Diego Chargers (AFL); 1963, Buffalo Bills (AFL).

Breen, Joseph Eugene (Virginia Tech)—LB—1964, Green Bay Packers; 1965-66, Pittsburgh Steelers; 1967-68, Los Angeles Rams.

Brooks, Lawrence (Virginia State)—Tackle—1972-74, Los Angeles Rams (NFC).

Brown, Thomas (William & Mary)—End—1942, Pittsburgh Steelers.

Cambal, Dennis (William & Mary)—Back, End—1973, New York Jets (AFC).

Cameron, Edmond (Washington & Lee)—Guard—1926, Detroit Panthers.

Carrington, Edward (Virginia)—End—1969, Houston Oilers (AFL).

Carroccio, Russell (Virginia)—Guard—1954-55, New York Giants; 1955, Philadelphia Eagles.

Cavalli, Carmen (Richmond)—End—1960, Oakland Raiders (AFL).

Chipley, William (Washington & Lee)—End—1947-48, Boston Yanks; 1949, New York Bulldogs.

Christensen, Erik (Richmond)—End—1956, Washington Redskins.

Churchman, Charles (Virginia)—Back—1925, Columbus Tigers.

Cloud, Jack (William & Mary)—Back—1950-51, Green Bay Packers; 1952-53, Washington Redskins.

Clowes, John (William & Mary)—Tackle—1948, Brooklyn Dodgers (AAFC); 1949, Chicago Hornets (AAFC); 1950-51, New York Yanks; 1951, Detroit Lions.

Coolbaugh, Robert (Richmond)—End—1961, Oakland Raiders (AFL).

Creekmur, Louis (William & Mary)—Guard—1950-59, Detroit Lions.

Crow, John David (William & Mary)—Tackle—1960, Boston Patriots (AFL).

Cuozzo, Gary (Virginia)—Q. Back—1963-66, Baltimore Colts; 1967, New Orleans Saints; 1968-69, Minnesota Vikings; 1970-71, Minnesota Vikings (NFC); 1972, St. Louis Cardinals (NFC).

Dale, Carroll (Virginia Tech)—End—1960-64, Los Angeles Rams; 1965-69, Green Bay Packers (NFC); 1970-72, Green Bay Packers (NFC); 1973, Minnesota Vikings (NFC).

Darragh, Dan (William & Mary)—Q. Back—1968-69, Buffalo Bills (AFL); 1970, Buffalo Bills (AFC).

Davis, Harrison (Virginia)—End—1974, San Diego Chargers (AFC).

Davis, Robert (Virginia)—Q. Back—1967-69, Houston Oilers (AFL); 1970-72, New York Jets (AFC); 1973, New Orleans Saints (NFC).

Davis, Ronald (Virginia State)—Tackle—1973, St. Louis Cardinals (NFC).

Diehl, John (Virginia)—Tackle—1961-64, Baltimore Colts; 1965, Dallas Cowboys; 1965, Oakland Raiders (AFL).

Douglas, Otis (William & Mary)—Tackle—1946-49, Philadelphia Eagles.

Dudley, Bill (Virginia)—Back—1942, 1945-46, Pittsburgh Steelers; 1947-49, Detroit Lions; 1950-53, Washington Redskins; 1942, 1946 Rushing Leader; 1946 Interception Leader; 1966 Hall of Fame.

Easterling, Charles Ray (Richmond)—Back—1972-74, Atlanta Falcons (NFC).

Elliott, Carlton (Virginia)—End—1951-54, Green Bay Packers.

Emelianchik, Peter (Richmond)—End—1967, Philadelphia Eagles.

Ferguson, Eugene (Norfolk State)—Tackle—1969, San Francisco Chargers (AFL); 1970, San Diego Chargers (AFC); 1971-72, Houston Oilers (AFC).

Forkovitch, Nicholas (William & Mary)—Back—1948, Brooklyn Dodgers (AAFC).

Fowler, Wayne (Richmond)—Tackle—1970, Buffalo Bills (AFC).

Fronczek, Andrew (Richmond)—Tackle—1941, Brooklyn Dodgers.

Gassert, Ronald (Virginia)—Tackle—1962, Green Bay Packers.

Gillette, Jim (Virginia)—Back—1940, 1944-45, Cleveland Rams; 1946, Boston Yanks; 1947, Washington Redskins, Greenbay Packers; 1948, Detroit Lions.

Gillette, Walker (Richmond)—End—1970-71, San Diego Chargers; 1972-73, St. Louis Cardinals; 1974-75, New York Giants.

Gossett, Daniel Bruce (Richmond)—Kicker—1964-69, Los Angeles Rams; 1970-74, San Francisco 49ers (NFL); 1966 Scoring Leader; 1966 Field Goal Leader.

Graham, David (Virginia)—Tackle—1963-66, 1968-69, Philadelphia Eagles.

Graham, S. Lyle (Richmond)—Center—1941, Philadelphia Eagles.

Grimes, George (Virginia)—Back—1948, Detroit Lions.

Gunderman, Robert (Virginia)—Back—1957, Pittsburgh Steelers.

Hardy, Isham (William & Mary)—Guard—1923, Akron Pros.

Harvey, James "Waddy" (Virginia Tech)—Tackle—1969, Buffalo Bills (AFL); 1970, Buffalo Bills (AFC).

Henning, Daniel (William & Mary)—Q. Back—1966, San Diego Chargers (AFL).

Hilton, John (Richmond)—End—1965-69, Pittsburgh Steelers; 1970, Green Bay Packers (NFC); 1971, Minnesota Vikings (NFC); 1972-73, Detroit Lions (NFC).

Horner, Sam (VMI)—Back—1960-61, Washington Redskins; 1962, New York Giants.

Humbert, Richard (Richmond)—End—1941, 1945-49, Philadelphia Eagles.

Johnson, Cornelius (Virginia Union)—Guard—1968-69, Baltimore Colts; 1970-73, Baltimore Colts (AFC).

Johnson, Frank (Washington & Lee)—Tackle—1919, Massillon Tigers; 1919-21, Akron Pros; 1920, Hammond Pros.

Johnson, Harvey (William & Mary)—Back—1946-49, New York Yankees (AAFC); 1951, New York Yanks.

Jones, Arthur (Richmond)—Back—1941, 1945, Pittsburgh Steelers; 1941 Interception Leader (Tied with Marshall Goldberg).

Jordan, Henry (Virginia)—Tackle—1957-58, Cleveland Browns; 1959-69, Green Bay Packers.

Knight, David (William & Mary)—End—1973-74, New York Jets (AFC).

Kowalkowski, Robert (Virginia)—Guard—1966-69, Detroit Lions; 1970-74, Detroit Lions (NFC).

Kreamcheck, John (William & Mary)—Guard—1953-55, Chicago Bears.

Lamberti, Pasqualie (Richmond)—LB 1961, New York Titans (AFL); 1961, Denver Broncos (AFL).

Lesabem, James (Virginia)—Back—1952-54, Chicago Bears; 1954, Baltimore Colts.

Lewis, Herman (Virginia Union)—End—1968, Denver Broncos (AFL).

Lusk, Robert (William & Mary)—Center—1956, Detroit Lions.

Mallory, Irvin (Virginia Union)—Back—1971, New England Patriots (AFC).

Maskas, John (Virginia Tech)—Guard—1947, 1949, Buffalo Bills (A-AFC).

Mason, Samuel (VMI)—Back—1922, Minneapolis Marines; 1925, Milwaukee Badgers.

Matsu, Arthur (William & Mary)—Back—1928, Dayton Triangles.

Mikula, Thomas (William & Mary)—Back—1948, Brooklyn Dodgers (A-AFC).

Miles, Leo (Virginia State)—Back—1953, New York Giants.

Miles, Mark (Washington & Lee)—Tackle—1919, Cleveland Indians; 1920, Cleveland Panthers; 1920, Akron Pros.

Miller, Robert (Virginia)—Tackle—1952-58, Detroit Lions.

Miller, Thomas (Hampden-Sidney)—End—1943, Pittsburgh Steelers—Philadelphia Eagles; 1944, Philadelphia Eagles; 1945, Washington Redskins; 1946, Green Bay Packers.

Milling, Albert (Richmond)—Guard—1942, Philadelphia Eagles.

Miodeuszewski, Edward (William & Mary)—Back—1953, Baltimore Colts.

Mitchell, James Halcot (Virginia State)—Tackle, End—1970, Detroit Lions (NFC).

Moore, Alexander (Norfolk State)—Back—1968, Denver Broncos (NFL).

Muha, Joseph (VMI)—Back—1946-50, Philadelphia Eagles; 1948 Punting Leader.

Myles, Henry (Hampden-Sidney)—End—1930, Newark Tornados.

Negri, Warren (Virginia Tech)—Guard—1940, Boston Bears (AFL); 1941, New York Americans (AFL).

Nutter, Madison "Buzz" (Virginia Tech)—Center—1954-60, 1965, Baltimore Colts; 1961-64, Pittsburgh Steelers.

Oakes, Donald (Virginia Tech)—Tackle—1961-62, Philadelphia Eagles; 1963-68, Boston Patriots (AFL).

Papit, John (Virginia)—Back—1951-53, Washington Redskins; 1953, Green Bay Packers.

Parker, Donald (Virginia)—Guard—1967, San Francisco 49ers.

Preas, George (Virginia Tech)—Tackle—1955-65, Baltimore Colts.

Pritchard, Abisha "Bosh" (VMI)—Back—1942, Cleveland Rams; 1942, 1946-49, 1951, Philadelphia Eagles; 1951, New York Giants.

Quayle, Frank (Virginia)—Back—1969, Denver Broncos (AFL).

Ragunas, Vincent (VMI)—Back—1949, Pittsburgh Steelers.

Ramsey, Gerrard (William & Mary)—Guard—1946-51, Chicago Cardinals.

Ramsey, Knox (William & Mary)—Guard—1948-49, Los Angeles Dons (A-AFC); 1950-51, Chicago Cardinals; 1952, Philadelphia Eagles; 1952-53, Washington Redskins.

Randle, Ulmo "Sonny" (Virginia)—End—1959, Chicago Cardinals; 1960-66, St. Louis Cardinals; 1967-68, San Francisco 49ers; 1968, Dallas Cowboys.

Reaves, Kenneth (Norfolk State)—Back—1966-69, Atlanta Falcons; 1970-73, Atlanta Falcons (NFC); 1974, New Orleans Saints (NFC); 1974, St. Louis Cardinals (NFC).

Reutt, Raymond (VMI)—End—1943, Philadelphia Eagles—Pittsburgh Steelers.

Richards, James (Virginia Tech)—Back—1968-69, New York Jets (AFL).

Rowley, Robert (Virginia)—LB—1963, Pittsburgh Steelers; 1964, New York Jets (AFL).

Ryczek, Daniel (Virginia)—Center—1973-74, Washington Redskins (NFC).

Ryczek, Paul (Virginia)—Center—1974, Atlanta Falcons (NFC).

Sazio, Ralph (William & Mary)—Tackle—1948, Brooklyn Dodgers (A-AFC).

Schroeder, Engene (Virginia)—End—1951-52, 1954-57, Chicago Bears.

Schweickert, Robert (Virginia Tech)—Q. Back—1965-67, New York Jets (AFL).

Selfridge, Andrew (Virginia)—LB—1972, Buffalo Bills (AFC), 1974, New York Giants (NFC).

Soleau, Robert (William & Mary)—LB—1964, Pittsburgh Steelers.

Stevens, Howard (Randolph-Macon)—Back—1973-74, New Orleans Saints; 1975, Baltimore Colts.

Strock, Donald (Virginia Tech)—Q. Back—1974-75, Miami Dolphins (AFC).

Sullivan, David (Virginia)—End—1973-74, Cleveland Browns (AFC).

Sumner, Charles (William & Mary)—Back—1955, 1958-60, Chicago Bears; 1961-62, Minnesota Twins.

Sweetland, Fred (Washington & Lee)—Back—1919, Cleveland Indians; 1920, Cleveland Panthers; 1920, Akron Pros.

Thomason, Robert (VMI)—Q. Back—1949, Los Angeles Rams; 1951, Green Bay Packers; 1950-53, Cleveland Browns.

Thompson, Tommy (William & Mary)—Center—1949 Cleveland Browns (A-AFC); 1950-53, Cleveland Browns.

Vandeweghe, Alfred (William & Mary)—End—1946, Buffalo Bisons (A-AFC).

Van Horne, Charles (Washington & Lee)—Back—1927, Buffalo Bisons; 1929, Orange Tornados.

Walker, William (VMI)—Guard—1944-45, Boston Yanks.

Warrington, Caleb (William & Mary and Auburn)—Center—1946-48, Brooklyn Dodgers (A-AFC).

Whaley, Benjamin (Virginia State)—Guard—1949, Los Angeles Rams (A-AFC).

Worden, Stuart (Hampden-Sydney)—Guard—1930, 1932-34, Brooklyn Dodgers.

Virginia High School Group AAA Football Champions

1920	Newport News
1921	Maury, Norfolk
1922	Jefferson Senior, Roanoke
1923	Jefferson Senior, Roanoke
1924	Jefferson Senior, Roanoke
1925	Newport News
1926	Woodrow Wilson, Portsmouth
1927	Woodrow Wilson, Portsmouth
1928	Jefferson Senior, Roanoke
1929	Maury, Norfolk & Newport News (tie)
1930	E. C. Glass, Lynchburg
1931	Newport News
1932	Maury, Norfolk
1933	E. C. Glass, Lynchburg
1934	Lane, Charlottesville
1935	Maury, Norfolk
1936	Hampton
1937	Petersburg
1938	E. C. Glass, Lynchburg
1939	Maury, Norfolk
1940	John Marshall, Richmond
1941	John Marshall, Richmond
1942	Hampton
1943	Thomas Jefferson, Richmond
1944	George Washington, Danville and Granby, Norfolk (tie)
1945	Petersburg, Granby, Norfolk
1946	Granby, Norfolk
1947	Woodrow Wilson, Portsmouth
1948	Hampton
1949	Hopewell
1950	Hopewell & Hampton
1951	Hopewell
1952	Thomas Jefferson, Richmond
1953	Granby, Norfolk
1954	Woodrow Wilson, Portsmouth
1955	Norview, Norfolk
1956	Washington & Lee, Arlington
1957	Jefferson Senior, Roanoke
1958	Hermitage, Richmond
1959	Norview, Norfolk
1960	Washington & Lee, Arlington
1961	Highland Springs, Richmond
1962	Graham, Bluefield
1963	Lane, Charlottesville
1964	Andrew Lewis, Salem
1965	Annandale
1966	Granby, Norfolk
1967	Princess Anne, Douglas Freeman, Annandale
1968	George Washington, Danville
1969	Hampton
1970	James Wood
1971	T. C. Williams
1972	Annandale
1973	Patrick Henry, Roanoke
1974	Bethel
1975	Hampton

Virginia High School Group AAA Basketball Champions

1914-15	Charlottesville
1915-16	Salem
1916-17	Salem
1917-18	Salem
1918-19	None Declared
1919-20	John Marshall
1920-21	Maury
1921-22	Jefferson, Roanoke
1922-23	Maury
1923-24	Lane
1924-25	Maury
1925-26	Maury
1926-27	Maury
1927-28	Woodrow Wilson
1928-29	Maury
1929-30	Jefferson, Roanoke
1930-31	Newport News
1931-32	John Marshall
1932-33	George Washington, Danville
1933-34	Jefferson, Roanoke
1934-35	Jefferson, Roanoke
1935-36	John Marshall
1936-37	John Marshall
1937-38	Newport News
1938-39	Hampton
1939-40	E. C. Glass
1940-41	Jefferson, Roanoke
1941-42	Newport News
1942-43	Newport News
1943-44	Thomas Jefferson
1944-45	George Washington, Alexandria
1945-46	Thomas Jefferson
1946-47	Granby
1947-48	John Marshall
1948-49	E. C. Glass
1949-50	Granby
1950-51	Newport News
1951-52	Newport News
1952-53	E. C. Glass
1953-54	John Marshall
1954-55	Jefferson, Roanoke
1955-56	Newport News
1956-57	Newport News
1957-58	Newport News
1958-59	E. C. Glass
1959-60	Highland Springs
1960-61	Wakefield, Arlington
1961-62	Washington-Lee, Arlington
1962-63	Washington-Lee, Arlington
1963-64	Newport News
1964-65	Woodrow Wilson
1965-66	Washington-Lee, Arlington
1966-67	E. C. Glass
1967-68	Andrew Lewis, Salem
1968-69	Hampton
1969-70	Jefferson, Roanoke
1970-71	Maggie Walker, Richmond
1971-72	Hopewell
1972-73	Petersburg
1973-74	Petersburg
1974-75	Thomas Jefferson
1975-76	Maggie Walker, Richmond

Virginians Who Played Major League Baseball

Name and Birth Date	City of Birth	Teams and Years Played	Position
Alley, Gene July 10,	Richmond	PITTS 1963-68	SS
Archer, Jim May 25, 1932	Max Meadows	P, KCA 1961-62	P
Atwell, Toby March 8, 1924	Leesburg	CHI-N, PT	C
Baker, Floyd October 8, 1875	Luray	ST, LA, CHI-A, WAS A	3B, SS
Baldwin, Billy	Tazewell	DETA-A 1975	GF
Boehling, Joe March 20, 1891	Richmond	WASH, CLEV	P
Booker, Buddy May 28, 1942	Lynchburg	CLEV, CHI-N 1966-68	C
Brodie, Steve September 11, 1868	Warrenton	BOS-N, STL-N, PITT, BALT, NY 1890-1902	OF
Brown, George March 12, 1876	Richmond	PHL-N, NY-N, BOST-N, PHI 1901-1912	OF
Buchanan, Jim January 12, 1925	Smyth County	ST, LA 1905	P
Bucher, Jim March 11, 1911	Manassas	BEK, ST-N, BOST-A—1934-45	2B, 3B
Bumbry, Al April 21, 1947	Fredricksburg	BAL-A 1972-1975	OF
Caldwell, Charles 1901	Bristol	NY-A 1925	P
Campbell, Soup 1915	Sparta	CLEVE 1940-41	OF
Chittum, Nels March 1933	Harrisburg	STL-N, BOST-A—1958-60	P
Churn, Chuck February 1, 1930	Bridgetown	PITT, CLE, LA—1957-59	P
Clarkson, Bill September 28, 1898	Portsmouth	NY-N, BOS 1927-29	P
Clay, Kenny April 6, 1954	Lynchburg	NY-A 1975	P
Clyde, Thomas August 17, 1923	Wachapreague	PHIL-A 1943	P
Coates, James Alton August 4, 1932	Farahan	NY-A, CAL-A 1956-67	P
Comer, Wayne February 3, 1944	Shenandoah	DET-A 1967-68	OF, C
Connelley, Bill June 29, 1925	Alberta	PHIL-A, NY-N—1945-53	P
Corcoran, Art		B /, PHIL-A 1915	3B ?
Craft, Maurice 'Molly' November 28, 1895	Portsmouth	WASH-A 1916-1919	P, OF
Creger, Bernie March 21, 1927	Wytheville	STL-N 1947	SS
Cress, Walker March 6, 1917	Ben Hur	Cin-N 1948-49	P
Crockett, Davey October 5, 1875	Lammoor	DET-A 1901	1B
Crump, Art November 29, 1901	Norfolk	NY-N 1924	OF
Cubbage, Mike July 21, 1950	Charlottesville	TEX-A, MINN 1974-1975-6	2B, 3B
Cullop, Nick September 12, 1887	Chishowie	CLE-A, KC-F, NY-A, STL-A 1913-1921	P
Dailey, Bill May 13, 1935	Arlington	CLEV-A, MINN-A—1961-1964	P
Davis, Bud December 7, 1889	Merrypoint	PHIL-A 1915	P
Dear, Buddy December 1, 1905	Norfolk	WASH-A 1927	2B
Dietrick, Bill April 30, 1902	Hanover	PHIL-N 1927-28	SS, OF
Diggs, Reese September 22, 1915	Mathews	WASH-A 1934	P
Durham, Joe July 31, 1931	Newport News	Balt-A, STL-N 1954, 57, 59 IN SERV 55	OF
East, Carl August 27, 1893	Marietta	STL-A, WASH-A—1915 & 1924	P, OF
Ferguson, Charlie April 17, 1863	Charlottesville	PHIL-N 1884-87	P, OF
Foiles, Hank June 10, 1929	Richmond	CLE-A, PIT-N, BALT-A, CIN-N, LA 1953-1964	C
Ford, E. L. 1884	Richmond	RICH-A 1884	SS, 1 B
Foster, Beddy 1887		NY-N 1896	?
Franklin, Jay March 16, 1953	Arlington	San Diego 1975	P
Fultz, Dave May 29, 1875	Staunton	PHIL-N, PHIL-A, NY-A 1898-1905	OF, 2B, SS, 3B
Gaines, N. December 23, 1897	Alexandria	WASH-A 1921	
Glenn, Ed September 19, 1860	Richmond	RICH-AA, PIT-AA, BOS-N, KC-AA 1884-1888	OF, 3B
Goodson, Ed January 25, 1948	Pulaski	S.F.-N 1970-71-75	SS, 1B, 3B
Grubb, John August 4, 1948	Richmond	S.D.-N 1972-1975	1B, OF, 2B, 3B
Hamner, Garvin March 18, 1924	Richmond	PHIL-N 1945	2B, SS, 3B
Hamner, Granny April 26, 1927	Richmond	PHIL-N, KC-A 1944-1962	SS, 2B, 3B, P
Haney, Larry November 19, 1942	Charlottesville	BALT-A, OAK-A—1966-1968, 1969-1973	C
Hard, Tom May 27, 1913	Danville	BOS-A 1954-1956	P

Name and Birth Date	City of Birth	Teams and Years Played	Position
Harman, Bill January 2, 1919	Bridgewater	PHIL-N 1941, IN SERVICE 1942	CP
Harris, Earl October 15, 1931	Abingdon	NY-N, DET-A 1955-1960	1B
Heflin, Randy September 11, 1918	Fredricksburg	BOS-A 1945-1946	P
Henry, Jim June 26, 1910	Danville	BOS-A, PHIL-N—1936-1939	P
Hepler, Bill September 25, 1945	Covington	NY-N 1966	P
Hernstein, John May 31, 1938	Hampton	PHIL-N 1962-1966	OF, 1B
Hicks, Joe April 7, 1933	Ivy	CHI-A, WASH-A, NY-N—1959-1963	OF
Hillman, Dave September 14, 1927	Dungannon	CHI-N, BOS-A 1955-1962	P
Hodges, Ron June 22, 1949	Rocky Mount	NY-N 1973-1975	C, 3B, OF
Holland, Mul January 6, 1903	Franklin	CIN-N, NY-N, STL-N—1926-1929	P
Hooker, Cy 1880	Richmond	CIN-N 1902-1903	P
Hopkins, Sis January 3, 1883	Phoebus	STL-N 1907	OF
Horton, Willie October 18, 1942	Arno	DET-A 1964-1975	OF, 3B
Huffman, Ben July 18, 1914	Rileyville	STL-A 1937	C
Hulvey, Hank July 18, 1897	Mt. Sidney	PHIL-A 1923	P
Humphreys, Bob August 18, 1935	Covington	DET-A, STL-N, CHI-N, WAS-A—1962 1968	P
Humphreys, John June 25, 1915	Clifton Forge	CLE-A, CHI-A, PHI-N—1938-1946	P
Hundley, Randy June 1, 1942 1964-1975	Martinsville	SF-N, CHI-N, MIN-A, SF-N	C, 3B, OF
Hush, Herb February 13, 1911	Woolwine	BOS-A 1940-1941	P
Jim Hutto	Norfolk	PHIL-N 1972-75	C
Jacobs, Bucky March 21, 1913	Altavista	WAS-A 1937-1940	P
Jefferson, Jesse March 3, 1950	Midlothian	BAL-A 1973-1975	P
Kahn, Owen June 5, 1905	Richmond	BOS-N 1930	
Kay, Bill February 14, 1878	New Castle	WAS-A 1907	OF
Kennedy, Bill December 22, 1918 SERVICE	Alexandria	WAS-A—1942, 1946, & 1947, 1943-45	P
Kennedy, Monte May 11, 1922	Amelia	NY-N 1946-1953	P
Lawson, Bob August 23, 1876	Brookneal	BOS-N, BAL-A 1901-1902	P
Lee, Wyatt August 12, 1879	Lynch's Station	WAS-A, PIT-N—1901-1904	P, OF
Lemon, Tim March 23, 1928	Covington	CLE-A, WAS-A, MINN-A—1950-1963	OF, 1B
Leonhard, Dave January 22, 1942	Arlington	BAL-A 1967-1968	P
Mabe, Bob October 8, 1929	Danville	STL-N, CIN-N, BAL-A—1958-1960	P
Mallory, Jim September 1, 1918	Lawrenceville	WAS-A, NY-N, STL-N—1940 & 1945, 1942-44 IN SERVICE	OF
Marshall, Willard February 8, 1921	Richmond	NY-N, BOS-N, CIN-N, CHI-N—1942-1955	OF
Martin, J. C. December 13, 1936	Axton	CHI-A, NY-N 1959-1968	3B, 1B, C
Mattox, Cloy November 21, 1902	Leesville	PHIL-A 1929	C
Mattox, Jim December 17, 1896	Leesville	PITT-N 1922-1923	C
May, Jerry December 14, 1943	Parnassals	PITT-N 1964-1968	C
McKenna, Kit August 19, 1915	Lynchburg	BKN-N, BAL-N—1898-1899	P, OF
McQuillen, Glenn April 19, 1915	Strasburg	STL-A 1938-1947	OF
McQuillen, George March 29, 1909	Arlington	CIN-N, STL-A, PHIL-A, NY-A—1936-1948	1B
Meadows, Rufus August 19, 1907	Hopewell	CIN-N 1926	P
Menefee, Jocko	Augusta County	PITT-N, LOA-N, NY-N, CHI-N—1892-1903	P
Miller, Tom July 5, 1897	Powahatan Ct. House	BOS-N 1918-1919	?
Minnick, Don April 14, 1931	Lynchburg	WAS-A 1957	P
Montague, Jr., Johnny September 12, 1947	Newport News	MONT-N 1973-1975	P
Morgan, Vern April 8, 1928	Emporia	CHI-N 1954-1955	3B
Bill, Moran 'Bugs'	Portsmouth	CHI-A—1974	P
Nash, Billy June 24, 1865	Richmond	RIC-AA, BOS-N, BOS-P, PHI-N—1884-1898	3B, 2B SS, OF,
Neff, Doug October 8, 1891	Harrisonburg	WAS-A 1914-1915	SS, 3B 2B
Parker, Ace May 17, 1912	Portsmouth	PHI-A	SS, 2B OF, 3B

228

Name and Birth Date	City of Birth	Teams and Years Played	Position
Perkowski, Harry September 6, 1922	Dante	CIN-N, CHI-N 1947-1955	P
Peters, Rusty December 14, 1914	Roanoke	PHI-A, CLE-A, STL-A— 1936-1947	SS, 3B, 2B, 1B, OF
Phillipe, Deacon May 23, 1872	Rural Retreat	LOU-N, PIT,N 1899-1911	P, OF
Pick, Charlie April 12, 1888	Rustburg	WAS-A, PHIL-A, CHI-N, BOS-N—1914-1920	OF, 2B, 3B, 1B
Pickrell, Clarence March 28, 1911	Gretna	PHI-N, BOS-N 1933-1934	P
Porterfield, Bob August 10, 1923	Newport	NY-A, WAS-A, BOS-A—1948-1959	P
Post, Sam November 17, 1896	Richmond	BKN-N 1922	2B
Powell, Jim 1859	Richmond	RICH-A 1884	1B
Proctor, Red October 27, 1900	Williamsburg	CHI-A 1923	P
Quarles, Bill 1869	Petersburg	WAS-AA, BOS-N—1889-1993	P
Richter, Al February 7, 1927	Norfolk	BOS-A 1951-1953	SS
Riddleberger, Denny	Clifton Forge	WASH-A, 1970-1971, CLEVE-A—1972	P
Rixey, Eppa May 3, 1891	Culpeper	PHI-N, CIN-N 1912-1933	P
Roach, Mel	Richmond	MIL-N, PHI-N 1953-1962	1B, 2B, SS, 3B OF
Robertson, Dave September 25, 1889	Portsmouth	NY-N, CHI-N, PIT-N—1912-1922	OF
Rogers, Buck November 5, 1912	Spring Garden	WAS-A 1935	P
Russell, Harvey January 10, 1887	Marshall	BAL-F 1914-1915	C, OF, SS
Sands, Charlie December 17, 1947	Newport News	PITT-N, CAL-A—1971-1975	C, 1B
Sands, Charlie December 17, 1947	Newport News	NY-A 1967	C
Sanford, Jack June 23, 1917	Chatham	WAS-A—1940-1941 & 1946/42-45 SERV.	1B
Saunders, Ben February 16, 1865	Carpathen	PHI-N, PHI-P, PHI-AAG, LOA-N—1888-1892	P, OF, 3B, 1B
Scarce, Mac April 8, 1949	Danville	PHI-N 1972-1975	P
Chuck, Scrivener	Alexandria	DET-A—1975	SS
Shaner, Wally May 24, 1900 1923-1929	Lynchburg	CLE-A, BOS-A, LIN-N	OF, 3B, 1B

Name and Birth Date	City of Birth	Teams and Years Played	Position
Shifflett, Garland March 28, 1935	Elkton	WAS-A, Min-A 1957 & 1964	P
Smith, Mike November 16, 1904	Norfolk	NY-N 1926	OF
Smith, Vinnie December 7, 1915	Richmond	PITT-N—1941 & 1946/42-45 SERVICE	C
Spicer, Bob April 11, 1925	Richmond	KC-A 1955-1956	P
Spratt, Jack July 10, 1888	Broadford	BOS-N 1911-1912	SS, 2B 3B, OF
Stallard, Tracy August 31, 1937	Coeburn	BOS-A, NY-N, STL-N—1960-1966	P
Steiner, Ben July 28, 1921	Alexandria	BOS-A, DET-A 1945-1947	2B, 3B
Sullivan, Jim April 5, 1894	Minekun	PHI-A, CLE-A 1921-1923	P
Sullivan, Russ February 19, 1923	Fredricksburg	DET-A 1951-1953	OF
Tate, Pop December 22, 1861	Richmond	BOS-N, BAL-AA, D-D-AA 1885-1890	C, OF, 1B
Thomas, Roy June 22, 1953	Quantico	PHI-N 1975	P
Thomas, Lefty October 4, 1903	Abingdon	WAS-A 1925-1926	P
Thomas, Bud September 9, 1910	Faber	WAS-A, PHI-A, DET-A—1932-1941	P
Tipton, Eric April 20, 1915	Petersburg	PHIL-A, CIN-A—1939-1945	OF
Toms, Tommy	Charlottesville	SAN. F—1975	P
Tucker, Ollie January 27, 1902	Radiant	WAS-A, CLE-A—1927-1928	OF
Umbach, Arnie December 6, 1942	Williamsburg	MIL-N, ATL-N—1964-1966	P
Vaughan, Porter May 11, 1919	Stevensville	PHIL-A 1940-46/42-45 IN SERV.	P
Waldbauer, Doc February 22, 1898	Richmond	WAS-A 1917	P
Watson, Johnny January 16, 1908	Tazewell	DET-A 1930	SS
Whitby, Bill July 29, 1943	Crewe	MIN-A 1964	P
Willett March 7, 1884	Norfolk	DET-A, STL-F 1906-1915	P
Williams, Eoody August 22, 1912	Pamplin	BKN-N, CLA-N—1938-1945	2B, SS, 3B
Williams, Don September 14, 1931	Floyd	PIT-N, KC-A 1958-1962	P
Wingsfield, Ted August 7, 1899	Bedford	WAS-A, BOS-A—1923-1927	P
Woodall, Larry July 26, 1894	Staunton	DET-A 1920-1929	C
Yowell, Carl	Madison	CLE-A	
Yowell, Carl December 20, 1902	Madison	CLE-A 1924-1925	P

Virginia PGA State Open Champions

Year	Champion	Location
1924	Elmer Loving	Charlottesville
1925	Pat Petranck	Petersburg
1926	Pat Petranck	Petersburg
1927	Jimmy Thomson	Richmond
1928	Charles Isaacs	Richmond
1929	Roland Hancock	Lynchburg
1930	Harry Thomson	Richmond
1931	Walter Clement	Roanoke
1932	Chandler Harper	Portsmouth
1933	Bobby Cruickshank	Richmond
1934	Bobby Cruickshank	Richmond
1935	Bobby Cruickshank	Richmond
1936	Bobby Cruickshank	Richmond
1937	Bobby Cruickshank	Richmond
	(over Errie Ball in playoff)	
1938	Chandler Harper	Portsmouth
1939	Bobby Cruickshank	Richmond
1940	Chandler Harper	Portsmouth
1941	Chandler Harper	Portsmouth
1942-45	No tournament	
1946	Sam Snead	Hot Springs
	(over Harper in playoff)	
1947	George Payton	Hampton
1948	John O'Donnell	Norfolk
1949	Jack Isaacs	Langley Field
1950	Jack Isaacs	Langley Field
1951	John O'Donnell	Norfolk
1952	Chandler Harper	Portsmouth
1953	John O'Donnell	Norfolk
1954	John O'Donnell	Norfolk
1955	John O'Donnell	Norfolk
1956	Jack Isaacs	Langley Field
1957	Tom Strange (A)	Norfolk
	(over Shorty Oatman in playoff)	
1958	Jack Isaacs	Langley Field
1959	Al Smith	Danville
1960	Chandler Harper	Portsmouth
1961	Jack Isaacs	Langley Field
	(over Claude King in playoff)	
1962	Mac Main	Danville
1963	Tom Strange	Virginia Beach
1964	Tom Strange	Virginia Beach
1965	Bobby Mitchell	Danville
1966		Virginia Beach
	(over Herb Hooper in playoff)	
1967	Chandler Harper	Portsmouth
	(over Herb Hooper in playoff)	
1968	Chandler Harper	Portsmouth
1969	Chandler Harper	Portsmouth
1970	Chandler Harper	Portsmouth
1971	Claude King	Norfolk
1972	Nelson Long, Jr. (A)	Hot Springs
1973	Herb Hooper	Richmond
1974	John Bruce (A)	Danville
	(over Mac Main in playoff)	
1975	John Bruce (A)	Danville
1976	John Bruce (A)	Danville

Virginia State Women's Amateur Golf Champions

Year	Champion	Location
1922	Mrs. J. W. Zimmerman	Lexington
1923	Miss Margaret Lucado	Lynchburg
1924	Miss Margaret Lucado	Lynchburg
1925	Mrs. Wyatt	Hampton
1926	Mrs. Jean S. Jones	Richmond
1927	Miss Louise Branch	Richmond
1928	Mrs. J. G. Spitz	Richmond
1929	Mrs. Jean S. Jones	Richmond
1930	Mrs. J. T. Priddy	Richmond
1931	Mrs. H. C. Kerstern	Richmond
1932	Mrs. D. H. Clark	Virginia Beach
1933	Mrs. K. W. Rodwell	Virginia Beach
1934	Miss Lily Harper	Portsmouth
1935	Miss Lily Harper	Portsmouth
1936	Miss Lily Harper	Portsmouth
1937	Miss Lily Harper	Portsmouth
1938	Miss Lillian Lee Wood	Richmond
1939	Mrs. Carl Martin	Portsmouth
1940	Mrs. Carl Martin	Portsmouth
1941	Mrs. Carl Martin	Portsmouth
1942-45	No Tournament	
1946	Mrs. J. W. Reynolds	Richmond
1947	Mrs. J. W. Reynolds	Richmond
1948	Mrs. J. W. Reynolds	Richmond
1949	Miss Sydney Elliott	Charlottesville
1950	Mrs. J. B. Cralle, III	Richmond
1951	Mrs. William Pollard	Charlottesville
1952	Miss Sydney Elliott	Charlottesville
1953	Miss Sydney Elliott	Charlottesville
1954	Mrs. A. H. Allen	Arlington
1955	Mrs. A. H. Allen	Arlington
1956	Mrs. A. H. Allen	Arlington
1957	Miss Mary Patton Janssen	Charlottesville
1958	Miss Mary Patton Janssen	Charlottesville
1959	Miss Mary Patton Janssen	Charlottesville
1960	Miss Mary Patton Janssen	Charlottesville
1961	Miss Mary Patton Janssen	Charlottesville
1962	Miss Mary Patton Janssen	Charlottesville
1963	Miss Robbye King	Arlington
1964	Mrs. William B. Pollard	Charlottesville
1965	Mrs. Robert W. Hughes	Richmond
1966	Miss Robbye King	Arlington
1967	Mrs. Robert W. Hughes	Richmond
1968	Mrs. Mary Alice Canney	Centreville
1969	Mrs. Robbye King Youel	Charlottesville
1970	Mrs. Robbye King Youel	Charlottesville
1971	Mrs. Robbye King Youel	Charlottesville
1972	Mrs. Robbye King Youel	Charlottesville
1973	Mrs. Pamela Clark	Arlington
1974	Mrs. Candy S. Robertson	Martinsville
1975	Mrs. Nancey Hollenbeck	Arlington
1976	Mrs. Kay Schieselbein	Mt. Vernon

VSGA State Amateur Champions

Year	Champion	Location
1911	William Palmer, Jr.	Richmond
1912	James McMenamim	Hampton
1913	James McMenamim	Hampton
1914	William H. Palmer, Jr.	Richmond
1915	Matthew Paxton, Jr.	Lexington
1916	Matthew Paxton, Jr.	Lexington
1917	J. Pope Seals	Richmond
1918	S. M. Newton	Richmond
1919	J. S. Barron	Norfolk
1920	J. S. Barron	Norfolk
1921	H. H. Hume	Norfolk
1922	S. M. Newton	Richmond
1923	H. Crim Peck	Lexington
1924	Paul Jamison	Roanoke
1925	Maj. E. J. Naiden	Hampton
1926	J. T. E. Crump	Richmond
1927	Charles Mackall	Charlottesville
1928	William Howell	Richmond
1929	Pat Dillion	Virginia Beach
1930	Chandler Harper	Portsmouth
1931	William Howell	Richmond
1932	William Howell	Richmond
1933	Chandler Harper	Portsmouth
1934	Chandler Harper	Portsmouth
1935	William Howell	Richmond
1936	Robert Reigel	Richmond
1937	Dick Payne	Norfolk
1938	James O. Watts	Lynchburg
1939	Wynsol Spencer	Newport News
1940	Sam Bates	Norfolk
1941	Walter Cushman	Charlottesville
1942	Jack Hamilton	Newport News
1943-45	No tourney held during war	
1946	Ed Gravely	Richmond
1947	Jack Hamilton	Newport News
1948	Wynsol Spencer	Newport News
1949	Jack Hamilton	Newport News
1950	Dick Payne	Virginia Beach
1951	Connie Sellers	Roanoke
1952	George Gosey	Lynchburg
1953	Wynsol Spencer	Newport News
1954	George Fulton	Roanoke
1955	Wynsol Spencer	Newport News
1956	Wayne Jackson	Newport News
1957	Robert Wallace	Norfolk
1958	Jimmy Flippen	Danville
1959	Wynsol Spencer	Newport News
1960	Ned Baber	Richmond
1961	Bobby Loy	Norfolk
1962	Vinny Giles	Lynchburg
1963	Nelson Broach	Richmond
1964	Vinny Giles	Lynchburg
1965	Wayne Jackson	Newport News
1966	Vinny Giles	Lynchburg
1967	Sam Wallace	Williamsburg
1968	Vinny Giles	Lynchburg
1969	Vinny Giles	Richmond
1970	Lanny Wadkins	Richmond
1971	Vinny Giles	Richmond
1972	Bobby Wadkins	Richmond
1973	Carl Peterson	Virginia Beach
1974	Curtis Strange	Virginia Beach
1975	Curtis Strange	Virginia Beach
1976	Skeeter Heath	Hampton

Virginia High School Track Champions

1917	Roanoke
1918	Episcopal High
1919	Episcopal High
1920	Lynchburg
1921	Jefferson, Roanoke
1922	Jefferson, Roanoke
1923	Jefferson, Roanoke
1924	No championship
1925	John Marshall
1926	Maury, Norfolk
1927	Wilson, Portsmouth
1928	John Marshall
1929	John Marshall
1930	Maury
1931	Maury
1932	John Marshall
1933	Newport News
1934	Newport News
1935	Newport News
1936	Maury
1937	Maury
1938	Newport News
1939	Newport News
1940	Newport News
1941	Newport News
1942	Newport News
1943	No state contest
1944	Maury
1945	No contest
1946	Newport News
1947	Newport News
1948	John Marshall
1949	Newport, Newport News
1950	John Marshall
1951	Washington-Lee, Arlington
1952	Newport News
1953	Newport News
1954	George Washington, Alexandria
1955	Washington-Lee, Arlington
1956	Thomas Jefferson, Richmond
1957	Thomas Jefferson, Richmond
1958	Washington-Lee, Arlington
1959	Andrew-Lewis, Salem
1960	Newport News
1961	Hampton
1962	Norview
1963	Newport News
1964	Newport News
1965	Newport News
1966	Washington-Lee, Arlington
1967	Newport News
1968	Newport News
1969	Newport News
1970	Douglas Freeman, Richmond
1971	Denbigh
1972	Menchville
1973	Thomas Edison
1974	Homer Ferguson
1975	Homer Ferguson and Albermarle
1976	Charlottesville

Virginia Catholic High School AAA Basketball Champions

YEAR	CHAMPION	RUNNER-UP	COACH
1946	St. Paul's	St. Andrews	Nick Didio
1947	Benedictine	St. Vincent	Father Daniel Baran
1948	Holy Trinity	Benedictine	Ed Derringe
1949	Holy Trinity	Benedictine	Ed Derringe
1950	Benedictine	St. Paul's	Ed Koffenberger
1951	Norfolk Catholic	Cathedral	Art Spoltare
1952	Cathedral	Benedictine	Willie King
1953	Holy Cross	Benedictine	Father Henry Hammond
1954	Benedictine	Cathedral	Ed Koffenberger
1955	Benedictine	Norfolk Catholic	Marion Smith
1956	Benedictine	Norfolk Catholic	Marion Smith
1957	Benedictine	Norfolk Catholic	Marion Smith
1958	Norfolk Catholic	St. Patrick's	Bob Williams
1959	Benedictine	Norfolk Catholic	Warren Rutledge
1960	Norfolk Catholic	Benedictine	Tom Hourihan
1961	Benedictine	Bishop O'Connell	Warren Rutledge
1962	Bishop O'Connel	Benedictine	Bob Rusevlyan
1963	Bishop O'Connell	St. Emma	Bob Rusevlyan
1964	Benedictine	Bishop O'Connell	Warren Rutledge
1965	Benedictine	Bishop O'Connell	Warren Rutledge
1966	Portsmouth Catholic	Bishop O'Connell	Bernie Brennan
1967	Benedictine	Roanoke Catholic	Warren Rutledge
1968	Benedictine	Norfolk Catholic	Warren Rutledge
1969	Bishop Ireton	Norfolk Catholic	Tom O'Keefe
1970	Holy Cross	Benedictine	John Laneve
1971	Benedictine	Norfolk Catholic	Warren Rutledge
1972	Benedictine	Bishop O'Connell	Warren Rutledge
1973	Benedictine	Bishop Ireton	Warren Rutledge
1974	Benedictine	Norfolk Catholic	Warren Rutledge
1975	Benedictine	Bishop O'Connell	Warren Rutledge
1976	Benedictine	Norfolk Catholic	Warren Rutledge

Acknowledgements

Special thanks to Jerry Reed of *The Virginian-Pilot* for his careful editing of a major portion of this book and his contribution of several photographs.

The authors are equally grateful for the generous assistance of the following individuals and organizations:

Pat Quigley, Philadelphia Eagles
Milwaukee Bucks (NBA)
Pittsburgh Steelers (NFL)
Georgetown University
Charlie Butt and John C. Youngblood, Washington & Lee High School
Michael D. McOsker, Randolph-Macon College
Benny Gibson and Hank Norton, Ferrum College
Connie Madsen, Professional Golf Association
Barney Cooke, University of Virginia
Rich Murray, Madison College
United States Military Academy
Jim Hughes, Emory & Henry College
Mike Ballweg, Hampton Institute
Cal Jacox, Norfolk State
Jim Nolting and Oscar D. Robinson, Virginia State College
Steve Harriman, *The Virginian-Pilot*
Fred D. Hilton, Madison College
Harold Massie, Lynchburg College
Patricia M. Churchman, Bridgewater College
Earle Hellen, *Newport News Times-Herald*
Nick Bocella, University of Richmond
Earl McIntyre, Virginia Commonwealth University
Jack Levinson, Boxing
Roland C. Day
Floyd Adkins
Tom Shupe, Virginia Military Institute
Charlie Boswell, Roanoke College
Robert McClannana, Marshall Hawkins (Gold Cup photos)
Mrs. Mildred Van Dyke
Bob Hutchinson, *The Virginian-Pilot*
Sean Brickell
R. B. (Dick) Keeley

Stock cars—Ray Melton, Sam Elliott, Johnny Tadlock, Monk Tadlock, Pepper Martin, Charlie Whittemore, L. Shields Parsons, Paul Sawyer, Mike Poston, Bill Peants.
Chandler Harper, Bide-a-Wee Golf Course
Bob Moskowitz, *Newport News Daily Press*
Jim Russell, Purdue University
Dan McGill, University of Georgia
University of Tennessee
Ned West, Georgia Tech,
Cincinnati Reds
Baltimore Colts (NFL)
Specs Garbee, Lynchburg, Carolina Baseball League
Charlie Boswell and Bill Dorsey, Roanoke College
Bob Sheeran, Ed Derringe, and Barry Fratkin, William & Mary College
San Diego Chargers (NFL)
Bill Bain, *Richmond Times-Dispatch*
Wendell Weisend, Virginia Tech
Ruth Meredith, Virginia Gold Cup
R. G. (Bob) Ainsworth
Gary Cramer, *The Daily Progress,* Charlottesville
Ralph Thompson, and John M. Atkins, Jr., Lane High photos
Mike Litwin, *The Virginian-Pilot*
Eddie Abourjilie and David Kazzie, handball
John Hughes, Washington & Lee University
Earl A. Fitzpatrick, Roanoke
Dick Burrell, Hampden-Sydney College
Joe M. Law, Old Dominion University
Ronald E. Peterson
William C. Pace, Virginia High School League
Art Jones
Jim Van Valkenburg, NCAA
Marshall Johnson, The Associated Press
Oliver Jackson Sanos, Jr.
Mrs. Barbara Jean Schlegal